Move Toward The Gunfire

A Cardiac Surgeon's Journey

Through the Valley

of the Shadow of Death

Michael K. Pasque, MD

The people walking in darkness have seen a great light; on those living in the land of the shadow of death a light has dawned.

Isaiah 9:2

INTRODUCTION

Warrior

. . . for waging war you need guidance . . .
Proverbs 24:6

I am a heart surgeon. My hands touch the human heart almost every day. I sew new blood vessels on the heart to improve its blood supply. I repair and replace its valves. I implant machines that pump blood when the heart is so injured that it can no longer do its job.

Sometimes I even remove and replace it with someone else's donated heart.

I am a heart surgeon, and I go to war every day of my life.

So do you. The warfare in which I battle every day is not unique to heart surgeons. It is common to all human experience. Most of us are embroiled in it nearly every day of our lives. This warfare is important to God, for it involves our daily interactions with the people around us. It is referred to on nearly every page of the Holy Bible.

So although I share my story from the context of my profession, cardiac surgery, this book is really about a topic dear to God's heart—our interpersonal relationships with the people He brings into our daily lives. Jesus made it obvious how important these relationships are to Him. They were practically all He talked about during His time on earth. He is relational, and since we are made in His image, we too are relational. By His purposeful and precise design, we are relational warriors and the interpersonal interactions He orchestrates into our daily lives are the battlefields upon which we are called to be warriors of God.

The only thing that separates me from most of the warriors of this world is the fact that on one pivotal day I decided to surrender the dominion of my heart to its Creator and rightful King. I accepted the forgiveness of my sins that is found exclusively in the blood that Jesus shed on the cross of Calvary. I was, at that moment, made righteous by what Jesus did—and in the same moment I abandoned all I had tried so hard to do to make myself worthy of my purpose. Now, in spite of my status in the medical profession, despite the fact that I literally hold life in my hands nearly every day, I bring nothing before the throne of God save the amazing grace of Christ—and that is enough. Absolutely nothing else is needed.

Before the day of my redemption, I had long labored at changing my life. I wanted desperately to do what I knew I ought to do. But despite my best efforts, I was unable to bring about any significant change. In fact, until that day, the only discernable change had been for the worse.

But the day I accepted God's gracious invitation to trust in His Son brought the beginning of true change. The change has been stunning. And it is still under way. I am being forever changed, moment-by-moment, day-by-day. Oh, I still mess things up. But I am God's and He is working in me. By His grace, I am being made into the likeness of Jesus Christ, just as His Word promises He will do for anyone who trusts in Him.

I no longer strive to make myself worthy. And I no longer strive and labor to make God love me. Why? Because now I know that He simply cannot love me any more than He already does.

Some of you may have a problem with the fact that a medical professional, who's prideful past makes him so unworthy to write about such sacred truths, is writing about them. I share your concern. For sure, my past is that of a worldly warrior. I have literally committed every sin described in the Bible. Every humbling word of warning in God's Word pertains to me, for I have seen and lived in the depths of a sinful depravity that only a hardened warrior of this world could tolerate.

But here's my promise to you: My story is also full of good news. The good news is of God's endless mercy for even the lowliest of low. Ours is a God who is infinite in His holiness, righteousness and justice, but at the same time unequaled in His compassion, mercy and love. It is from such total emptiness—and simultaneous fullness—that I share my story.

You may not understand my perspective of the predicaments in which I have found myself, because you and I may view the world through very different lenses. Even though we all fight our battles, mine are probably different from yours. Because of my background, my perspective is probably different too. I learned early to rely upon aggression. I know some people have never sought or relied upon open, worldly warfare in their daily lives. I wish I were one of them, but I am not. I grew up a warrior and my frame of reference and mentality is simply not the same as that of a non-warrior.

Friends of mine who graduated from seminary have been fighting a different fight altogether. The majority grew up in godly homes with godly parents who taught them to love at an early age. Not me. It was medical school for me and I had been a rough-and-tumble, scrappy warrior from my childhood. Like many such warriors, I turned to Christ only after my apprenticeship to the world's ways of battle—only after I found myself sitting bewildered in my failed attempts to live the way God wants His people to live. Truth is, my godly friends couldn't write this book if they wanted to. To their credit, they have for the most part avoided the mud of this world's battlefields. My life, on the other hand, has made me an expert on this mess, a fact of which I am not particularly proud.

With that introduction, you may be wondering, *Then why share your story at all? If it's a problem mainly for you and your band of worldly misfits, then who cares?* The answer is easy: I am not alone. I am not even close to being alone. There are a lot of us warriors out there. You probably know us quite well, for you have certainly encountered us.

You may even be a worldly warrior yourself. When challenged, when confronted with a relational battle in our day-to-day interactions, we pick up weapons. Not swords or guns, but modern-day social weapons with nice, politically correct names such as *forethought, discernment, righteous indignation, righteous anger, justice, preparation, looking out for our families, godly stewardship,* and *planning ahead.*

In reality, however, our nice weapons deserve different, more accurate names: *scheming, conspiring, plotting, judgment, discrimination, intolerance, anger, greed, jealousy,* and *hatred.* Right now—all around me—I see warriors wielding such weapons. Our society breeds them. The world is enamored with them. We honor them. We write books and make movies about them and give them *reality* TV shows. They are our heroes.

So I share my story for everyone: the neophyte warriors just discovering their battlefields, and the veteran warriors who may have conquered all they sought to conquer only to realize that what they've been fighting for is, to quote Solomon, "meaningless." I write for those who wonder, as I came to wonder, why the victories aren't sweet for long—why the wins don't satisfy their hearts like the world has promised.

Most of my stories, unfortunately, describe the little *trips to the woodshed* to which I have been subjected during my career. I am certainly not telling you these stories because I am some sort of famous heart surgeon or great Christian warrior. My Savior had to drag me kicking and screaming to an applicable knowledge of His plan. He had to drag me into one of the most treacherous battlefields in the world, the cardiothoracic surgical operating room—the Valley of the Shadow of Death. And then, most difficult of all, God used the very special setting of that battlefield to teach me about faith. He wanted to show me that He would stand back-to-back with me in the throes of battle if I would just place my trust in Him. It is only the grace of the cross of Christ that enables palpable faith in the sovereignty and love of God. And it is precisely this faith founded in the knowledge of God's attributes that provides the only source of the strength to turn toward those things in life that we do not want to face.

The world and our self-centric nature tell us that moving toward the gunfire is a very bad idea. Alternatively, Jesus promises that obedience in following His commands is a raging battle from which we will learn that He can be trusted in any fight. He promises to always be there with us, back-to-back in the fury of battle, if we can just believe and trust. Our firsthand experience of His faithfulness allows us, in those earliest moments of the relational ambush, to mirror the response of those special warfare operators who reflexively move toward the gunfire.

In this dark valley, a Light has been slowly winning over the darkness. A dawn is coming and there has been, by the grace and power of the cross of Christ, a progression of light in this valley into which I go to war every day.

A new day is coming.

CHAPTER ONE

Into the Valley

Mrs. Marjorie Filander's* day had started like any other.

She had always been the picture of perfect health. She had developed some high blood pressure as she had gotten older, but had avoided any serious illness. In fact, the birth of her four children were the only times she had been hospitalized in all of her seventy-four years.

This was about to change.

Approximately thirty minutes after finishing her supper on a wintery Saturday evening, she suddenly doubled over the dinner table and clutched her chest in agony. Her husband rushed from the living room to her side, past the framed pictures of their four children and thirteen grandchildren, just in time for her to violently vomit her dinner all over him. He would later tell me that he had never seen anything like it, that he knew immediately something was very wrong.

"I'm getting the car," he told Marjorie, squeezing her shoulder. "We're getting you to the emergency room."

But after the initial intense moments, Marjorie's chest pain let up to just a dull ache. "I should be fine," she gasped, exhausted, and turned from the mess on the table. She stayed in her chair, her elbows on her knees, and stared blankly at the floor.

A minute later, another wave of agony ripped through her—a searing, *tearing* pain that shot from her chest into her neck and shoulder and down her back. "It feels like someone's unzipping a giant zipper inside and tearing me in half!" she shrieked. Sweat poured from her forehead.

She vomited a second time. Yes, something was very wrong. "Okay," Marjorie conceded, pawing with the backs of her hands at the sweat and tears streaming down her face. "Get my sweater and take me to the hospital."

Names of patients, medical personnel, and facilities in this book have been changed to respect privacy.

One look at Mrs. Filander and the emergency room personnel wasted no time moving her to the acute care room of the ER suite. The veteran triage nurse placed the EKG electrodes herself. Although Marjorie was initially able to tell them her story, she became progressively somnolent as they proceeded through a rapid work-up of her medical condition.

Dr. Kenneth Stillman, the first physician to see her, would not leave her bedside. The young doctor knew she was in trouble. He could barely feel a pulse and her systolic blood pressure was only 70 mmHg—nearly 50 points lower than normal. He noticed that the skin of her upper torso had a reddish-blue tint to it—*like venous stasis of the chest, neck, and face,* he wrote in his assessment note.

"Get a stat portable chest x-ray and EKG," he ordered the team assisting him, as he started an intravenous line. The IV line in place, Stillman stepped over to the wall phone and called the CAT scan suite in radiology. "We need an emergency scan," he told the radiologist. "I'll wheel her over myself in a few minutes."

Marjorie Filander underwent an emergency CAT scan of her chest and abdomen, referred to as *triple rule-out*. In one quick nine-second scan, the three most-dangerous causes of chest pain can be *ruled in* or *ruled out*. She had no coronary artery disease and had not thrown a blood clot to her lung; two of the three most-common causes of chest pain could be ruled out.

But the scan was positive for the third common cause of chest pain. Just as Dr. Stillman had suspected, Mrs. Filander had an acute aortic dissection.

Acute aortic dissections are deadly cardiovascular emergencies. They occur when blood vessel tissue abnormalities combine with high blood pressure to result in the literal shredding of the tubular walls of the largest, high-pressure, blood-carrying *pipe* in the body, the aorta. In many ways, the aorta resembles a common garden hose. It is of similar size and shape and, like most garden hoses, its flexible wall is made up of multiple layers. Understanding the layered structure of the aortic wall is critical to understanding how an aortic dissection occurs— and how it kills.

An aortic dissection happens when the pressurized blood that normally travels inside the confines of the inner lining of the wall of the aorta (the *intima*) creates a tear in this innermost layer. This tear allows the powerful, pressurized bloodstream to burrow into, separate, and travel *inside* the layers of the aortic wall. Powered by the blood pressure, which is usually elevated, the abnormal stream of blood that has escaped the inner lining of the aorta can tear down the full length of the aorta between the inner and outer layers of its wall.

The most dangerous type of aortic dissection involves the *ascending* aorta, the section of this large blood vessel that rises directly from the left ventricle of the heart and serves as the initial passageway for all of the blood pumped from the heart to the body. Coursing behind the breastbone toward the neck, the ascending aorta becomes the aortic arch where it branches to the head, neck, and arms and then turns to arch down the back to the rest of the body. When the dissection involves the ascending aorta, it places the patient in the highest-risk group and usually means a trip to the cardiac surgical operating room for very high-risk surgery.

Most patients, like Marjorie Filander, describe the pain of an aortic dissection as the worst they have ever experienced in their life. Just like Mrs. Filander, they feel like something is being violently torn apart inside. And they are correct: The agony is from the violent inner destruction that is attempting to kill them. It often feels precisely like what is actually occurring—a tearing, shearing, extremely painful *unzipping* of the biggest blood vessel in their body. They are in serious trouble, and they know it.

Most patients die soon after the dissection of their ascending aorta. Sometimes, as the blood tears apart the layers of the aortic wall, the final outermost layer of this wall becomes so thin that it can no longer hold the pressurized blood. The shredded blood vessel ruptures and the patient bleeds massively into his or her chest or abdominal cavity. It doesn't take long—this is a huge pipe that normally recirculates the patient's entire blood volume every minute or two. Death ensues almost immediately.

Sometimes the tearing of the ascending aortic wall, which usually starts near the heart, not only progresses away from the heart but also toward it. In this case, it is quite common for the layers of the aorta to thin out and rupture into the sack that contains the heart, the *pericardium*. Since the pericardium surrounds the heart, blood in the pericardium compresses the heart, restricting the heart's ability to fill with the blood that is returning from the body. This condition is called *pericardial tamponade*.

Since pericardial tamponade restricts the returning blood from entering the heart, the blood gets backed up, leading to high venous pressures. This is precisely what caused the reddish-purple discoloration of Mrs. Filander's upper body noted by Dr. Stillman.

Another (and most dangerous) result of this restriction of the inflow to the heart is a reduction in its forward output of blood. This reduction in cardiac output puts the patient into a *low-output state*, where the blood-pumping output of the heart drops to levels too low to meet the nutritive demands of the body's organs. In such cases, the blood pressure can fall to dangerously low levels and each of the body's organs is soon compromised—sometimes irreparably—because of the inadequate blood flow. If nothing is done quickly, multi-organ failure ensues. The post-operative danger of multi-organ failure can ruin a perfect surgical procedure and remains one of the most common causes of death after a "successful" surgical repair of aortic dissection.

If all of this is not bad enough, aortic dissection can also cut off the blood supply to any of the aorta's many vital branches. If the arterial blood supply to the heart is cut off, the patient has a heart attack. If a branch to the brain is compromised, a stroke occurs. If the branches to the intestines are compromised, then various segments of the intestines can die—a particularly deadly occurrence. If the branches to the kidneys are occluded, kidney failure sets in.

Aortic dissection can kill in so many different ways.

Mrs. Filander's low blood pressure (70/40), new murmur of aortic valvular regurgitation, cold clammy skin, somnolence, and reddish-purple face told Dr. Stillman that the aortic dissection found on her emergency CAT scan was about to kill her. Immediately he paged the hospital's on-call cardiac surgeon, who quickly assessed the situation and determined that his hospital did not have the necessary resources to handle such a complex cardiac surgical emergency.

"Let's put her on the chopper and get her over to University Hospital, stat," he instructed. "I'll call their cardiac team and brief them."

While all this was happening, I was enjoying a soon-to-be-interrupted night's sleep at home. The phone call jolted me from my pillow. I am much too accustomed to such middle-of-the-night calls, so it took me only a moment to shake sleep from my brain and sit on the edge of my bed as Dr. Stillman described the patient's situation. Once I'd heard what I needed to know, I responded as I knew I must:

"Get her here as fast as you can."

"We're putting her on the chopper now," Stillman said, and we hung up.

From all the indicators Stillman relayed to me, I knew the patient could die at any moment and that *time* was our enemy. Her life hung in the balance. From previous experience, I knew the situation could quickly turn very desperate.

I punched in the number for the operating room at our hospital and told them to get set up as quickly as possible. I rose from the bed, pulled on my clothes, grabbed my wallet and keys, and fast-walked to my car.

I was headed back into the Valley of the Shadow of Death.

I knew I was in for a fight.

CHAPTER TWO

When Hell Breaks Loose

W hen I first laid eyes on Mrs. Filander, I was glad I had instructed my team to expedite her transfer straight to our Intensive Care Unit. Her face and neck were a dark purplish tint. As Dr. Stillman had told me on the phone, she was indeed showing signs of severe pericardial tamponade and cardiogenic shock.

From all the signs, blood was seeping through the thinned-out wall of her dissected ascending aorta into the sac surrounding her heart. This was compressing her heart, preventing it from filling normally with blood returning from the body. This caused the blood to back up in the venous system and engorge all of her veins—thus the purplish discoloration of her skin.

All cardiac surgeons worth their stuff know this sign. It's like a neon billboard across the patient's forehead saying, *Help! Hurry! I am about to die!*

The ICU (Intensive Care Unit) nurse pumped the blood pressure cuff and listened carefully. "BP 70 over 40," she called out over the hiss of the deflating cuff.

We both glanced at the EKG monitor. The nurse put into words what both of us were thinking: "Her heart rate is 130—can't get much faster!"

I acknowledged her comment with a nod. We both knew what the fast heart rate meant. Mrs. Filander's heart was trying to compensate for its low filling by speeding up. And her problem was now my problem. We had to move immediately.

"Get her blood drawn and sent as quickly as you can. Tell them we need six units of blood typed and crossed, stat."

"Already done," she responded.

I looked at her, wondering if she knew how much I loved working with nurses who took things as seriously as I did. I told her what she already knew: "No time to lose. Let's get her into the OR."

Mrs. Filander's internal organs were dying from the low output produced by the cardiac tamponade. Her kidneys were failing. Her liver was failing. She had been drowsy at the other hospital, but upon arrival here she was nearly unresponsive. Like her other organs, Mrs. Filander's brain was not receiving enough blood flow to function normally. If things did not change soon, her brain would also begin to die.

As we scrubbed for surgery, the anesthesia team moved quickly to place intravenous, pulmonary arterial, and radial arterial lines that would monitor blood pressure in the patient's various arteries and veins. These lines would also give us ready access to infuse medications vital to a successful operation. As soon as these lines were in place, an OR nurse splashed the disinfectant solutions on Mrs. Filander's skin from her chin to her toes. Another placed sterile drapes over her to cover everything but the two surgical fields.

Often in cardiogenic shock, one of the first organs to die is the heart itself. The blood pressure stays so low for so long that the blood flow to the heart's muscle (the *myocardium*) is so compromised that the heart muscle itself begins to fail. At that point we would be pumping on the chest and slashing through the skin to try to get the patient on the cardiopulmonary bypass machine.

This thought was on the minds of everyone in Mrs. Filander's operating room. We were moving as quickly as possible to try to prevent that deadly occurrence.

We had divided into two teams. One team began opening the chest while the other made an incision over the femoral artery in the patient's right leg. The goal of the chest team was to get the chest open safely but quickly and try to gain time by relieving the cardiac tamponade. The other team's goal was to place the cardiopulmonary bypass arterial tube (*cannula*) in the femoral artery to support the patient's vital-organ function on full cardiopulmonary bypass. (In normal heart surgical procedures, this arterial cannula is most commonly placed in the ascending aorta. But this option is not available for a patient with aortic dissection, since the layers of the ascending aorta have been torn apart.)

"Heparin," I called, as soon as we could see the femoral artery.

Heparin is an anticoagulant. Our anesthesiologist gave the heparin IV to inhibit the blood's ability to coagulate and help keep it from forming a clot in the reservoir of the heart-lung machine or from forming clots that could move to such vital organs as the brain. Quickly, the leg team placed the perfusion cannula from the cardiopulmonary bypass machine into the femoral artery. This gave us access to the patient's circulatory system by which we could reinfuse the oxygenated blood that would be drained from the right atrium immediately after access was gained by the chest team.

Meanwhile, I made the chest incision and split the sternum. We inserted the stainless steel retractor to hold it open.

"Severe tamponade," I confirmed. "The pericardial sac is bulging with blood."

Cautiously, I made a small hole in the pericardial sac surrounding the heart.

No matter how many times I make that first tiny cut into the pericardium in a patient with acute tamponade, the ferocity of the blood exiting under pressure always takes my breath away. And I am not alone. Every time it happens, I hear gasps from those on the OR team whose eyes are fixed on the operative field. There is just something about a stream of blood exiting at Mach 1 from the pericardium—often shooting off the operating table—that brings back too many memories of massive hemorrhage in the cardiac surgical operating room.

We were lucky with Mrs. Filander. Despite the blood in her pericardium being under high pressure and splattering against the operative drapes, it stopped almost immediately. There was no active bleeding. Enough blood had collected in the sac to cause compression of the heart—probably during the early stages of the dissection—but the bleeding had since stopped. Swiftly, I opened the rest of the pericardium and tacked its edges up to the sternal retractor with sutures to give us full exposure and access to the heart and major vessels.

As expected, Mrs. Filander's systolic blood pressure, which had been hovering in the 70-90 range with the help of our drug infusions, had shot above 150 with the relief of the tamponade. Once the blood around her heart was removed, there was no more compression to prevent the heart from filling. Blood that had been backed up for hours now rushed into the heart, almost tripling the cardiac output. Our anesthesiologist, an experienced veteran, had expected this surge in blood pressure and rapidly administered the appropriate drug to lower the BP back into the 95-110 range. The last thing we needed was for Mrs. Filander's shredded aorta to remain exposed to a systolic blood pressure over 150.

Quickly, I placed the venous cannula that would drain the blood from the heart's right atrium to the cardiopulmonary bypass machine. As soon as the cannula was connected to the heart-lung machine circuit, I gave the command that was familiar and reassuring to all:

"Put us on bypass."

We had made it to the safety net provided by the heart-lung machine without a cardiac arrest—so far, so good.

It is interesting that operating-room vernacular has evolved so that the command to place the patient on the heart-lung machine is for "us" to go on bypass. It is really only the patient who is going on the bypass machine, but this little quirk of speech reveals much. The bypass machine most certainly saves lives. It certainly stabilized the situation with Marjorie Filander. Nonetheless, it has its own set of dangerous complications—all of which increase with the amount of time the patient is on the machine. Indeed, countless studies have shown that the longer a patient is on the machine, the higher the chance of an adverse outcome. Every member of the operative team knows that an invisible clock starts ticking when the patient goes on the heart-lung machine, that it is time to kick into ultra-efficient mode.

The "us" signifies that we are all on the clock. In a way, we are all *on* the machine.

I knew at that point that we were at the end of the low-output state that Mrs. Filander's vital organs had been subjected to for several hours. And I knew from experience that there is always damage. As we worked, I prayed silently that the damage would not be irreparable. I prayed that the awesome and expansive capacity for recovery of these vital organs—as sure a demonstration of God's grace as I've seen in His creation—was such that all of her organs would just return to their normal function. It is brutal for patients when the kidneys fail. Dialysis complicates everything. Everybody can tolerate a little liver failure, but utter liver failure is a death knell. In a similar fashion, death of the intestines (*gangrene*) or brain (*stroke*) is catastrophic. I silently asked God to spare our patient all of these complications.

And then I did what I had to do—I rejected them all. I had to treat Marjorie Filander as if all of the severe insults to her body were in fact fully reversible. Despite the specter of possible organ failure, I pushed forward with all the enthusiasm and tenacity I could muster. Nonetheless, in the back of my mind lingered the nagging thought that an elderly patient like Mrs. Filander can only take so much.

Mrs. Filander was facing a complex and dangerous operation and I faced a formidable foe. The sound of the gunfire echoing down the valley resonated in my ears. My next move had been established as reflex by countless similar battles.

I moved toward the gunfire.

CHAPTER THREE

The Extraordinary Battlefield

We all experience battle. Our battles may be with finances, health, job, friends, boss, or family. They may be small skirmishes or all-out war. But make no mistake, at any given moment, we're all in a fight—it is the very essence of our fallen world.

Cardiac surgeons share these same everyday battles, but they also willingly engage in a battle that few others experience. At any hour of the day or night, they scrub, mask, gown, glove, and then willingly stride onto an unusual battlefield—the cardiac surgical operating room.

As soon as they walk into that extraordinary room, they become its supreme commander. And they are at war. They evaluate the enemy and choose the order of battle. They command the attention and allegiance of an elite fighting force that has gathered on behalf of a patient whose life is threatened by cardiovascular disease. Every team member is a highly trained specialist who performs a vital role. But all answer to one commander, the cardiac surgeon. All recognize that this is a sacred battle between life and death, and that every decision, every action can have life-altering or even life-ending consequences. But no matter the outcome, the buck stops with the cardiac surgeon who will make the decisions that lose or carry the day. Ultimately, it is he or she alone who is held accountable.

The Valley of the Shadow of Death is not your everyday battlefield.

Battle, by its very definition, produces fear, anxiety, anger, and even depression. These emotions spill over into our homes, our workplaces, and our relationships. The same is true for cardiac surgeons, except that the stress of their daily jobs can be extraordinary in so many ways. The only good news is that the stress experienced by cardiac surgeons is not new to them. During their cardiac surgical training, they bathe in this extraordinary stress every day for years. Much like the U.S. Army Special Forces or Navy SEALs, every cardiac surgeon has been selected, tested, vetted, and pushed to extremes in their preparation to lead a cardiac surgical operating room.

Most non-medical people believe that, in general, cardiac surgeons are pretty civil people. After all, we're some of the most educated people in the world. Our education and training can extend an additional decade or more beyond medical school. And cardiac surgeons who work at academic medical centers are *professors* at their affiliated universities, at the top of the food chain in the most prominent educational institutions in the world. Moreover, cardiac surgeons make decent money and, for the most part, circulate in higher social circles. Some cardiac surgeons have become politicians, like Dr. William Frist. Some have even become television personalities, like Dr. Mehmet Oz.

One could easily be led to believe that cardiac surgeons comprise a civilized lot.

But like most settings populated by those who have risen to the top of their fields, underneath the cardiac surgical façade of privilege, accomplishment, and wealth lies a generally stressed-out, overworked, and relationally dysfunctional group of individuals. With some notable exceptions, most cardiac surgical groups—from university medical centers to private practice hospitals across the country—are notorious for being arenas of animosity and relational villainy.

Why?

We begin with a famously difficult medical subspecialty. After all, there are few medical subspecialties with death rates as high as the surgical subspecialty of cardiac surgery. Obviously, cardiac surgical outcomes have improved since the wild early days. But let there be no question, this is perilous territory. The surgical case mix for any surgical subspecialty includes a percentage of high-risk cases, but in the world of cardiac surgery high-risk cases are routine and simply cannot be avoided. For most heart surgeons, one of every twenty patients is not going to survive to leave the hospital following cardiac surgery. Every cardiac surgeon well knows that even so-called "routine" cardiac surgical cases (in which the predicted risk of death would be less than 1 percent) in fact tiptoe along the steep walls of the Valley of the Shadow of Death.

Bottom line: There is danger every time we go into the operating room, no matter how *benign* the case. Ask any heart surgeon. Every one of them can describe in vivid detail many personal examples of so-called *low-risk* cardiac cases during which the wheels came off the cart and *routine* cases quickly became anything but routine. Suffice it to say that given the high-risk stakes of each day of a cardiac surgeon's life, this profession supplies a boiling caldron in which to cook human relationships.

Into the caldron we then throw an enticingly complex group of individuals. It takes a very unique type of person to become a cardiac surgeon. Fascination with the amazing physiology and pathophysiology of the cardiovascular system is helpful, but not enough. Most physicians have their first contact with the world of cardiac surgery in medical school. Cardiac surgery, the subspecialty of *death and dying*, usually has a profound impact on young medical students.

They are either absolutely appalled at the possibility of a career in the Valley of the Shadow of Death or they are strangely and seductively tantalized by its Siren call.

Few exhibit a middle-of-the-road response to their first exposure to cardiac surgery.

In fact, most young, budding physicians—men and women alike—turn in abject horror and run from the world of cardiac surgery as if from the devil himself. They are the normal ones. Faced with the reality of intense training, outrageous hours, and the threat of death looming like a specter every day for the rest of their medical career, they flee as fast as they can from their horrifying first encounter. They are more than happy to pursue a customary medical education and professional life in more civilized medical specialties.

But those few who succumb to the mystical allure of heart surgery mysteriously choose to take another fateful step down this darkest of all subspecialty paths. For some, it is simply a venture toward that precipice where life itself hangs in the balance, for heart surgeons go there every day. Who else do you know who, in the course of a normal workday, stops and restarts the heart of another human being? A heart surgeon does this every day. To some this is alluring; to others it is horrifying.

Once these adventurous young physicians stand on that precipitous overhang and mischievously wiggle their toes over its crumbling, unstable edge, they—from that moment on—are mysteriously and irresistibly drawn to it. They can't help themselves. Maybe it is the thrill. Maybe it is because it makes them unique. Maybe it is just a fascination with death or the misguided belief that it can be mastered. Whatever the reason, they love to peer over that tantalizing edge at what lies beyond.

Others take the first step into the world of heart surgery for the same reasons I did.

I have always been a bit of an *over-compensator*. From my very first day of medical school, I demonstrated an over-response to the very normal med-student fear of *being found out*. Once medical students grasp the importance of the education they are receiving, they fear the moment when they will not know what they should know—and when they will be directly responsible for the end of a human life. They fear that a human being will be unnecessarily deprived of life because they didn't pay attention during their medical training. And I would not give a plugged nickel for a med student who has never felt this fear. It is what pushes us and makes rosy-cheeked medical students into thoughtful, focused, driven physicians.

Certainly, a healthy fear of being found a *poser* is not uncommon to any number of professions. But in the practice of medicine, the stakes are higher than other vocations. Every medical student must, in some way, deal with this very real fear of not knowing what to do in that critical moment when a patient's life hangs in the balance and every eye in the room is looking at him or her.

This was my worst nightmare.

When I was a young med-pup, I came to believe that the worst thing that could ever happen to me as a physician would be having a patient suffer or die because I didn't know what to do in the critical moment.

And this is what drove me to excel. Every time I perceived a lack of knowledge on my part in any area of medicine in which critical and timely decisions must be made, I immediately over-compensated. Instead of running away, I turned right into the fray. I ran toward the blood. I ran toward the panic. I ran toward the trauma. Whenever I saw any of my fellow students running away from something—both figuratively and literally—their trail became a guiding beacon to me. I knew exactly which direction to go. I moved toward the gunfire. Every time.

I loved the *code-blue* call that echoed down the hospital hallways. I ran to every cardiac arrest. The intermittent and unpredictable ferocity of the emergency room drew me like a magnet. I would practically sprint to the trauma unit where blood and vomit routinely splattered against the white and green ceramic tile walls. I loved the critically ill ICU patients. There were lives to be saved in these settings and I knew I was born to get right in the middle of all that. I loved the fight for a patient's life— especially when the odds were against us. The thought of jumping into furious, fast, and frenzied life-fights—where fast thinking and even faster reactions carried the day— absolutely lit me up. I was young and tireless, and running hard into the middle of the fight seemed so very right.

To many of my classmates, this all looked like a really bad idea. To me it looked like a win-win. Because of the personal attributes God had given me, I viewed this from an unusual perspective: Whether we won or lost the fight for the patient's life, in the long run I was going to win. Even if God did not reward our efforts on the patient's behalf with immediate resolution of the problem, I figured the fight nonetheless always had a purpose. I knew that I was learning important lessons from every battle. Sometimes there was more to learn from the losses than from the victories. Later in life, I would realize that God had instilled in me the promise of Hebrews 12:1, NIV: *No discipline seems pleasant at the time, but painful. Later on, however, it produces a harvest of righteousness and peace for those who have been trained by it.*

I knew that future patients would benefit from the tough lessons I was learning when things didn't go our way. In my eyes, to approach this any other way was to dishonor the very real contribution of every one of these patients to my future efforts as a cardiac surgeon. Either way, to me the furious fight for human life was precisely what I had been born to do.

So when the really sick patients who were scheduled for big and dangerous surgery were admitted to the surgical service, I asked my fellow medical students to let these patients be assigned to me. As third-year medical students, we all had to do the diagnostic work-ups—including a history and physical examination and initial lab tests—on patients admitted to the surgical service. We made rounds on them in the hospital and participated in the diagnostic and therapeutic decisions made on their behalf.

Ideally, each medical student would have a mixture of not so sick, sick, and really sick patients. Not me. I always had a pile of really sick patients. I had to work my tail off because really sick patients generate a lot more work, but I loved it. I seemed to have endless energy then. My fellow med students would just roll their eyes when they were next in line and I would ask to take the really sick patients, but they rarely turned me down.

As you might expect, there countless very descriptive medical adjectives for the psychopathology I demonstrated in my over-compensation as a medical student. Not to make any excuses, but you have to understand that I really believed I was doing more than just training for a future job. To me, this was a holy and righteous crusade. This wasn't about a job or money or security or career. This was about a war against death itself. This was about stepping courageously into the fight on behalf of those who could not fight for themselves. This was not just healthy versus sick—it was right versus wrong, good versus evil, life versus death. Ours was a noble cause and a righteous fight. How I loved it.

And I still do.

As weird as all of this may seem, I really do not think I am an unusual cardiac surgeon. I believe the vast majority of heart surgeons, men and women of similar disposition, had the exact same experience as medical students. This unique disposition and experience is then combined with the fact that surgery—and cardiac surgery in particular—is an incredibly unforgiving environment when it comes to intellectual error. In the world of heart surgery, major errors in thought, major holes in your medical knowledge database, and errors of sloth all too often result in death. And they almost universally result in dismissal from any of the major university surgical training programs. The subspecialty training process actively searches for and readily picks up on hints that suggest a dangerous player. In any competitive program—and heart surgeons are most commonly trained at the larger and very competitive university-based medical centers—the dangerous young surgeons are actively searched out, identified, and directed into less precarious medical environments and careers.

As if that weren't enough, this tiny margin for error funnels into an incredibly competitive selection process. When I entered my surgical internship at a major, internationally known university medical center, thirty-two interns were competing for only six general surgical chief resident positions to be awarded to the *winners* six short years later. My fellow interns hailed from every big-name medical school in the country. They were survivors and hungry and more than just competent competitors—they loved a good fight, just as I did.

Following my successful scaling of that pyramid and subsequent general surgical chief residency, I faced even steeper competition in obtaining a two-year subspecialty residency (sometimes referred to as a *fellowship*) in cardiothoracic surgery. Once again, things just seemed to work out well on my behalf as I was blessed with a superb cardiothoracic surgical training opportunity. As big a blessing as it was, that cardiothoracic surgical fellowship became the two most brutal years of my entire education. I have never worked harder and slept less. At the program in which I trained, the majority of my rotations required me to be on call every night. It was not uncommon for me to have sleepless night after sleepless night.

To state that my cardiac surgical fellowship beat me up would be an understatement. But for the most part, I absolutely loved it. I was doing precisely what I wanted to be doing, taking on more and more responsibility for the conduct of cardiac surgical procedures.

It was during this fellowship that one of the great truths of cardiac surgery became palpably real to me: There are very few cardiac surgical *emergencies* that are *not* long, arduous, and stressful—and carried out in horribly ill patients. If the long, elective schedule of cases didn't clobber me enough, I was relentlessly pounded by the emergencies—which always seemed to occur at the most inopportune times. The stress during this fellowship was so intense for such a prolonged period that I simply became oblivious to it. I just kept putting one foot in front of the other, placing one suture next to the previous, and taking care of whichever cardiac surgical patient God placed in front of me at the time. I did a lot of praying. Mercifully, the two years flew by quickly.

So it is not difficult to see why the final product of the cardiac surgical training process is a bright, successful, confident and driven person with an intense and highly competitive nature. Graduates of cardiac surgical training programs are goal driven, and by way of the educational process they have survived and thrived in, they are highly successful at achieving their goals. They aren't just survivors, they are conquerors. For their *holy crusade*, they very often have sacrificed considerably—including marriage, family life, non-medical friendships, and all of the fun of the *best years of their life*—and they know it. At the end of the training process it is payback time. They have spent more than a decade selflessly following commands, strictly respecting the lines of surgical authority, serving faithfully, and paying close attention to every clinical detail—all for the good of someone else's patients. Now it is their turn. The promised payback of authority, prestige, and wealth is expected. Anyone who stands in the way of that payback—including his or her fellow cardiac surgeons—had better be ready for a fight.

If you are a hammer, everything looks like a nail. If you are a cardiac surgeon, every relational interaction looks like a fight. That's the world I work in.

CHAPTER FOUR

Out of the Valley

She's been in a low cardiac output state for a long time. This could be rough," said Dr. Samuels, the surgical fellow participating in the surgery.

And she was correct. But with Marjorie Filander's life hanging in the balance, I refused to let anyone in the OR go negative.

"We're moving forward," I replied optimistically. Our patient deserved our very best, and Dr. Samuels was there to learn. She had seen plenty of patients who had been just as sick as—or sicker than—Mrs. Filander at this point in their care. And she had seen many of them recover and go home to their families.

But she had also seen patients who seemed much less ill than Mrs. Filander who had suffered a catastrophic postoperative course resulting in death. So we had a choice regarding our attitude at this point. Mrs. Filander would have zero-percent chance of recovery if we all caved in to the fear of irreversible organ failure and just gave up on her. The only appropriate attitude—until demonstrated otherwise—was that the patient could—and would—recover completely. We owe our patients nothing less than to assume that they can recover, to move forward with a surgical plan that burns no bridges. This plan must be built on the assumption that the patient will be alive twenty years afterward. We—and they—cannot afford to leave anything on the field. We are *all in* until it is clear that we have lost.

But as is so often the case, as soon as I espoused optimism, evidence began to surface of just how severe the patient's preoperative low cardiac output had been.

"Doctor," the anesthesiologist said, "the patient is making no urine. Zero urine since I took over her care in the ICU."

Not good news. Her kidneys were completely shut down.

If the output of the heart and systemic blood pressure was so low that it compromised the kidneys, then other organs were also suffering. If the dissection had sheared off both of her renal arteries, then it was likely that other arteries branching off from the abdominal aorta had also been compromised.

We could use dialysis—either temporary (if the kidneys recover) or permanent (if they do not)—to mitigate the effects of the loss of kidney function, but the compromise of other organs would not be so easily remedied. The compromise of end-organ function by aortic dissections is the most-feared of complications. If your acute aortic dissection shears off the abdominal aortic branch that feeds the blood supply to your liver, you are going to die. If you cut off the blood supply to the small intestine or the colon, you are in deep trouble. Postoperatively, the normal signs of such a catastrophe can be hidden by anesthesia or other dissection-related problems, and when a patient is trying to recover from aortic dissection surgery there is nothing worse than having undiagnosed gangrenous intestine sitting in the abdomen for a day or two.

All of these scenarios ran through my mind that day as I tried to focus on doing perfect aortic surgery. The thought that all your very best efforts on the patient's behalf might be pointless can be incredibly oppressive, and the oppression can spread quickly and heavily through the OR. This is why I refused to let Dr. Samuels or anyone else *go negative* in regard to Mrs. Filander's prognosis. You just can't let a negative thought or attitude gain a foothold in your mind or in the room, or suddenly you'll have a team of usually hard-fighting medical professionals letting a pessimistic spirit rule their surgical decisions.

So I fought back. When defeatist thoughts start to crowd my mind during an operation, I go where I have become accustomed to going under such circumstances.

I remember.

When negative thoughts clamor for my attention during a tough surgery, I *remember* the numerous times I have been in similar situations. I also remember and take great strength from God's promise that He will never abandon me: *Never will I leave you; never will I forsake you* (Hebrews 13:5, NIV).

Indeed, in all the life-and-death battles I have been through, God has never abandoned me. Sure, things have been incredibly tough on many occasions. But I can testify that God's wisdom and grace are always greater than the challenge before me. *My grace is sufficient for you*, He promised us through the Apostle Paul, *for my [God's] power is made perfect in [your] weakness* (2 Corinthians 12:9, NIV). I cannot look back on a single episode in my career in which God's grace—in its many forms—did not overwhelmingly meet the demands of the trial I was going through. As bad as things have sometimes been, God has never abandoned me. I'm confident that if you are honest about your life, you can say the same thing.

Without exception, I've found that remembering God's goodness leads to praise. It happened again, then. I began to praise God for His faithfulness. I remembered the faces of so many little old ladies whose aortic valve disease had led me into the Valley of the Shadow of Death. Then, I had just prayed for God to guide my mind and my hands, put my head down, and plowed forward. One baby step after another—until suddenly I would look up and, by God's grace, things were okay. The patient would survive. Into the Valley and right out again. The little old ladies never knew what hit them. They thought their heart surgery had just been routine stuff, like getting a gallbladder removed.

And the next day I would speak to them in the ICU, where they were sitting up in a chair gumming down their Jell-O, and in the solitude of my mind and heart I would silently sing joyous praises to God. I have told my wife many times how happy I am that God did not go to medical school. Surely, if He had bothered to go to class as I had, He would have known that those little old ladies simply could not survive those operative complications. I am so glad God has not been encumbered with my brilliant medical knowledge!

So right there in the middle of Mrs. Filander's life-and-death surgery, that's precisely where I went. With God, no situation is unsurvivable. I knew that I just needed to keep my head down, stay sharp, use the brainpower and skills God gave me, and keep my faith in His goodness. He loves Mrs. Filander. He loves me. He loves everyone in the OR. So let's honor Him with our very best work, with our very best thoughts for our patient.

We began the planned surgical repair. Aortic dissections are anatomically and physiologically complicated. The surgical therapy in otherwise uncomplicated dissections of the ascending aorta primarily involves resection and replacement of the diseased ascending aorta with a tubular-shaped Dacron graft. This graft basically looks like a 1- to 1.5-inch diameter, thin-walled fabric tube. Replacing the ascending aorta prevents many of the modes by which these patients die. Nonetheless, getting the patient through this complex surgical strategy can be very complicated. The ascending aortic wall's only real strength is in its very outer layer (the *adventitia*). Respect for this thin-but-very-strong layer while suturing the Dacron graft to the aorta is the foundational principle in the successful repair of these disastrous cases.

I should mention that not all dissections require surgical repair. When the dissection is uncomplicated and involves only the distal descending thoracic aorta—the part of the aorta between the curving aortic arch and the abdominal aorta—then the patients are best treated with medical therapy unless complications arise. This nonsurgical therapy primarily involves the use of medications to control heart rate and blood pressure. But when a dissection involves the ascending aorta, as in Mrs. Filander's case, clinical studies show that far better survival is obtained by surgical intervention.

As we began the repair, Mrs. Filander's hemodynamics on cardiopulmonary bypass had stabilized. Despite her instability at the beginning of the procedure, the cardiopulmonary bypass machine did its job as *the great neutralizer* and fixed everything. We were able to support her circulation by draining her blood from the right atrium and pumping the freshly oxygenated blood right back into her arterial system via the right femoral artery. We were in total control of the artificial "cardiac" output to the body that the heart-lung machine so amply supplies and she was quite stable.

As soon as we were stable on the bypass pump, the first stages of the planned surgical replacement of the ascending aorta called for us to initiate the cooling process. This is done by the perfusionist, who resets the thermostat on the heater/cooler attached to the blood reservoir of the heart-lung machine. To cool the patient, we simply run the patient's blood past a cooling coil to lower its temperature before reinfusing it back into the patient. By cooling the blood for reinfusion, we slowly cool the patient.

This cooling is necessary because the safest technique to repair the aortic dissection mandates that we avoid placing a cross-clamp across the ascending aorta. It is precisely the shredded ascending aorta that we must replace, so we must separate it from the rest of the high-volume circulatory system into which it channels the blood that is pumped through it. In the early days of heart surgery, we simply placed a vascular clamp across the aorta between the ascending aorta and the aortic arch. Although this was a bold first endeavor that successfully initiated our first attempts at surgical therapy for aortic dissection, we have since proven that placing the clamp across the aorta not only injures the aorta, but also results in the injury of other arteries in the body.

After many years of performing this repair with a cross-clamp to the dissected ascending aorta, some very smart, very brave heart surgeons proposed a solution to the problems caused by application of the clamp. They proposed that the only way to safely achieve a *clampless* repair was to utilize what is called *deep (or profound) hypothermic circulatory arrest*. This technique is now the standard of care in the surgical repair of aortic dissections. It involves cooling the patient's entire body down to a low temperature, reducing the metabolism of the brain and other vital organs so they will tolerate a period of *no flow*. During this period of no flow, all blood flow to the body is stopped while the operation on the aortic arch is performed.

Once the body reaches the desired cold temperature, the head is packed in ice to add external cooling for the brain and the blood flow to the body is entirely shut off. Yes, you heard that correctly. The body is put into a state where no blood is circulating through the vascular system. Everything comes to a stop. Using a popular term of my childhood, I guess one could say that the patient is placed into a state of *suspended animation*.

We know that when we cool the body to these extreme temperatures we have a good 45 to 60 minutes during which we can completely shut off the blood flow to the brain and other organs and have only a very small chance of brain or peripheral organ injury. During this brief period, we resect the ascending aorta and look up into the aortic arch where all of the major arteries to the head and arms branch off from the aorta. With the circulation shut off, we can see if there are any other tears in the aorta or other problems that need to be repaired.

With Mrs. Filander's circulation shut off, we were operating under a very dangerous time constraint. Even the cooling of the brain won't protect it for long. I praised God for His strength, acknowledged my own weakness, and moved on. I rapidly sandwiched the layers of the dissected aorta together between two Teflon felt strips and sewed the distal end of the Dacron tube graft to the sandwiched end of the aortic arch. I then disconnected the perfusion tubing from the femoral artery cannula and connected it to a new cannula in the Dacron tube graft.

Before I completed the proximal anastomosis (connection), there was more unfinished business that needed tending. Dr. Stillman, Mrs. Filander's ER physician, had heard a heart murmur suggesting that she had developed leaking of her aortic valve. The leaking was so severe that we estimated that almost half of the blood ejected through the aortic valve into the ascending aorta during systolic contraction then immediately leaked back into the left ventricle during the diastolic relaxation of the heart. Along with the pericardial tamponade, the leakage was clearly a major contributor to the cardiogenic shock that had resulted from the aortic dissection.

Luckily, this condition was easily repaired with standard techniques. I simply placed sutures through the wall of the aorta immediately adjacent to each of the three commissures (the junctures between adjoining leaflets that help suspend the valve from the aortic wall) to secure the layers of the aorta firmly together. This prevented the suspension apparatus of the valve from falling away from the aortic wall with resultant prolapse of the valve. Once I had completed this resuspension of the valve, it looked essentially normal.

With the valve re-suspension and proximal anastomosis (connection) finished, I then flushed the air from her *new* ascending aorta and heart and removed the clamp that I had placed across the Dacron tube graft. This resumed the blood flow to the coronary arteries, which branch off the ascending aorta near the aortic valve. The heart developed normal electrical activity within one minute and seemed to jump back to life quite quickly. This was a good sign. As it began to contract rhythmically, I carefully searched all of my suture lines to make sure there were no obvious leaks. Bleeding is the biggest problem after this procedure and I wanted to get a head start on keeping it under control.

Mrs. Filander's heart readily reassumed its blood-pumping responsibilities and she easily flew off of the cardiopulmonary bypass machine.

Everything, for the moment, actually looked quite good.

And then I got that uneasy feeling surgeons sometimes get when their *sixth sense* tells them something just isn't quite right.

My mind went through the usual checklist that I go through as we rewarm an aortic dissection patient following the period of cooling and circulatory arrest. Communication is the foundation of efficiency in the cardiac surgical operating room, so I reflexively voiced my concern as I worked through the first of a long series of checklist items. "We'd better look around," I said.

"Sure," Samuels acknowledged her agreement. She tended to be a woman of few words. The immediacy of her response confirmed that she and I were on the same page.

No sooner had the word left her mouth than we both saw it. "There!" Samuels said, articulating concern for what had simultaneously caught our attention. She pointed directly toward the area of the heart where my eyes were now fixed.

There, in the area of the anterior right ventricle—immediately adjacent to the ascending aorta—was the target of our attention. A small, harmless-appearing bump was beginning to grow. It was a very small *hematoma*—a small collection of blood under the surface of the thin superficial layer (*epicardium*) of the right ventricle. A small amount of blood began to ooze from this hematoma as the thinned epicardium was unable to restrain its growing size. Its initial small size belayed its importance—it might as well have been a runaway freight train. If it continued its growth, as it appeared to be doing, the consequences of this small hematoma would be catastrophic to Mrs. Filander.

The presence of this hematoma *pre*-operatively is not uncommon, and in itself not too much to worry about. In fact, this is often precisely where the preoperative bleeding from the dissection occurs that ultimately fills the pericardium with blood and causes the tamponade that so severely compromised Mrs. Filander. The reason I routinely check this area after repairing an aortic dissection is that the same dissection channel can reopen—even after the ascending aorta is replaced.

I folded a laparotomy sponge (basically an operative gauze bandage the size of a small washcloth) and pressed it against the growing hematoma with my hand. I held the sponge gently but firmly against the hematoma and waited as my team administered the medication to reverse the blood thinners we had given at the beginning of the case. We needed the patient to clot blood normally now.

One good side-benefit of this gentle-pressure technique is that it makes me stop. I have to stop everything else and just patiently hold the sponge against the heart. This is God's rest. About one second into my wait, I was already singing His praises quietly in my heart. *Thank you, Lord, for your love and faithfulness. Thank you for your compassion and mercy. You are a Warrior fighting beside me. Thank you for your Presence. Get us through this. Get this dear woman, whom you love, through this. Guide my mind, my hands, and my heart. Praise. Joy. Rest.* I was overwhelmed by what I can only describe as a warm feeling that everything was going to be all right.

Ten minutes later, I withdrew the sponge from the top of the heart. There was no bleeding. No hematoma. No problem. Skirmish fought, skirmish won—but not by me.

Mrs. Filander's operation had indeed quickly descended into the Valley of the Shadow of Death. I did only what I could do—I praised God, trusted Him for strength and skill, and kept on working. I kept putting one foot in front of the other during that walk through the Valley—all the while trusting that my Lord Jesus Christ knows what He is doing.

Although the bleeding skirmish was over, the war was not. In perhaps no other surgery does the age-old adage *when it rains it pours* so readily apply. No sooner had I successfully buried the fear and oppressiveness that accompanies an operative complication than another one occurred.

"The blood pressure is dropping!" The tone of Dr. Davidson's voice got our immediate attention. He was a superb anesthesiologist with whom I had spent many a late night in the Valley. I had always been amazed at the quickness of his mind. He was a multiprocessor for sure.

"Are you pushing on the heart?" he asked. In a cardiac operating room, this question always follows the all-too-common notification of a soft blood pressure. The tone in his voice was hopeful because an affirmative answer proffered the easiest solution to our problem. Often as we are checking over our surgical handiwork, we have to manually displace the heart to view suture lines on its undersurface. Even gentle displacement of the heart can cause the blood pressure to drop precipitously. It is always a hopeful question because the remedy is so easy—we just have to let go of the heart.

"No," Samuels answered. Her immediate response conveyed our shared concern. We always took drops in blood pressure seriously—they were often the harbingers of impending disaster. A drop in blood pressure can be the first sign of a very serious threat to our patient's wellbeing. The rapidity of her answer told everyone in the room to immediately move on in their search for the responsible culprit.

"What are the pulmonary artery pressures doing?" My words expressed my thoughts—and the thoughts of everyone in the room. Together, we were automatically and efficiently working through the checklist of suspected causes that had been ingrained in our brains by years of battle in the Valley. We all looked up at the large flat-screen monitor on the wall where the patient's vital signs were displayed. Elevated pulmonary artery pressure would signal the deflection of our diagnostic algorithm onto a dangerous track that demanded immediate attention, so this was always at the top of our list. It is amazing how rapidly our minds synchronously worked through the same diagnostic algorithm. We were a team, a unified fighting force with a singular resolve.

"That's a problem!" Samuels snapped. She was often the first to voice the obvious. On the screen was an ominous sign: The pulmonary artery pressures were profoundly elevated.

Everyone in the room knew that the combination of a low systemic blood pressure coupled with high pulmonary artery pressures signaled an impending disaster. The worst-case scenario would be that the left ventricle was failing—thus causing the cardiac output and blood pressure to fall while backing up blood in the lungs, causing the elevation in pulmonary artery pressure. Left-ventricular failure can happen after any operation on the heart—and certainly after a complicated operation like this one.

In emergency situations such as this, physicians focus first on the most dangerous of all the possible causes. In other words, you focus on the possible cause that is going to kill your patient the fastest. This prioritization happens in the minds of every caregiver in the OR, and everyone scurries to their assigned positions to quickly do the exams, blood tests or whatever is necessary to confirm the diagnosis and initiate treatment. In almost all such situations, the more quickly the remedy (presuming there is one) can be administered, the greater its chances of working and that the patient will suffer the least damage from it.

Mrs. Filander was about to die. We simply had no time to spare. A patient who has just had aortic dissection has an extremely vulnerable heart. The low blood pressure had to be remedied immediately.

"Epinephrine!" I went for the reliable *quick fix* to the first three things on our suspect list.

"Quickly!" I added, exposing my heightened anxiety regarding the latest assault on the wellbeing of our very fragile patient. I'd had too many patients immediately spiral, crash, and burn following similar drops in blood pressure. Despite the fact that we had no time to lose, I immediately regretted the second comment. I knew it was unnecessary, and almost insulting.

"Already going in," Dr. Davidson responded calmly. I knew his remedy would be immediate and perfect—it always was.

In fact, Davidson was already administering several other medications into the IV lines that had been placed into Mrs. Filander's heart for precisely this contingency. He and I were both already several decision points down the winding path of the treatment algorithm for precisely this situation. It literally happens that fast. The next several moves all involved the administration of IV medications by the anesthesia team, which has immediate access to the drugs and their administration ports. The catheters that gave Dr. Davidson central access to Mrs. Filander's circulation ensured that the medications reached the heart as rapidly as possible.

As the medications flowed, I reexamined her heart. Although the right ventricle was a bit distended from the high pulmonary artery pressures, the left ventricular function did not look bad at all. Dr. Davidson confirmed this by showing us left ventricular images from the trans-esophageal echocardiographic probe. The echo probe is placed in every cardiac surgical patient for precisely this reason. It gives us great views of the left ventricle since the esophagus lies immediately behind it. This confirmed that the problem was not due to acute left ventricular failure and cardiogenic shock.

The left ventricle was not failing. This was great news.

The next, and most probable, cause was a reaction to the drug that was being slowly administered to reverse the blood-thinning Heparin.

"Did you stop the Protamine?" I asked. Because of the quality of my anesthesia support that night, the question was probably superfluous. But I asked it anyway. This is all part of the *checks and balances* system of a cardiac surgical operating room.

"Already done," Davidson said. "The final drops were infusing as the blood pressure dropped. I'm going to continue to support her systemic blood pressure with the adrenaline infusion."

Slowly the pressure abnormalities began to reverse. Within a few minutes, the patient's BP was back to normal.

Then, just as I was beginning to think we were out of the woods, the anesthesia junior resident peered over the top of the drape that separated the operative field from his work area and timidly asked, "Are you guys having any significant blood loss?"

This is one question a surgeon never wants to hear.

Her hematocrit is only 16," Dr. Davidson confirmed. Mrs. Filander's blood level was less than half of what we expected it to be. Somewhere, she was losing blood.

Once again, it was *all hands on deck* for our operative team.

Davidson queried, "Has her belly always been that distended?"

It took only a sideward glance at her abdomen to confirm our worst fears. Her abdomen was significantly distended—much more than earlier. An aortic dissection can bleed anywhere that the aorta travels. If the pulsating blood of the dissection stream weakens the last thin layer of the aortic wall, then it can give way to the high-pressure blood flow and rupture.

My heart sank. This is every bit as bad as it sounds. Essentially all of the cardiac output that heads down the 1-inch diameter abdominal aorta can suddenly break out of the confines of its conduit and burst into the abdominal cavity. It seemed as if Mrs. Filander, having dodged several well-aimed bullets, would now succumb to massive abdominal hemorrhage. After all we had been through together, this fight was likely going to end in a devastating loss.

The anesthesiology team immediately began to infuse blood that had been typed and cross-matched for our patient—but we knew it would be futile. I began to do what I had to do to confirm the diagnosis. I began extending the incision down into the abdomen. I would open the abdominal cavity, confirm the presence of massive amounts of blood, then make an almost-certainly futile attempt to find the source of the bleeding and fix it—all before irreparable damage was done.

This complication, combined with the severe injury to the organs in Mrs. Filander's body by the low cardiac output, was just too much. Of course, Satan was right there chiding me: *She'll never survive this! Let her die in peace. How could you do this to such a sweet old lady? You are just wasting your time and prolonging the agony for her family.*

Moments before, things had looked so good. Now we were, at best, on the defensive. I had to ask myself where the goodness, faithfulness and compassion of God were in this horrible situation. The battle was lost. This wonderful, sweet lady would die. We had held on as long as possible through the fierce throes of mortal combat, but we had lost.

Satan's incursion into my private battle was a wonderful reminder…to pray. *Bless this dear woman, Lord,* I asked silently as I worked. *Bring her a healing miracle. Strengthen her and us. Guide us.* And then I remembered something else. I remembered…*to praise God.* How many times, by His mercy and grace, had I been inspired by God's Holy Spirit to praise Him for His goodness, faithfulness, and compassion in situations where He did not seem to be present?

So I did exactly that.

As I opened the upper part of the abdomen, I expected a sudden gush of blood. But I was wrong. There was no blood in the abdomen—her tissues were swollen a bit, but overall, things in the abdomen looked good.

"Hematocrit is 40!" Dr. Davidson exclaimed.

"What?" I asked in disbelief.

"Hematocrit is 40," he confirmed, a bit of a lilt to his voice. "I just rechecked it."

Everything was back to normal. I had been so swift to think the very worst. But God was not through with Mrs. Filander—or with me.

To this day, I do not know what happened. Was her swollen abdomen just an illusion? Was the low blood level just a diluted and inaccurate blood sample? Was there a logical explanation for everything? Had we just misinterpreted the clinical data?

Or…had God acted mightily right before my eyes and snatched victory from the jaws of defeat?

Ten days later, Mrs. Filander went home with her husband. She was sore, for sure. But she was alive and her kidneys, liver, and brain all worked fine.

And she never knew how close she had come to not returning from her perilous excursion into the Valley of the Shadow of Death.

CHAPTER FIVE

A Dubious Honor

I will never forget the day I was "appointed" Surgical Director of Cardiac Transplantation. It wasn't exactly a momentous occasion. As dramatic and exciting as it might seem, I can assure you that directing the cardiac transplantation service at a major university medical center had not been a lifelong dream of mine.

As director, whenever a patient's heart failure progressed to the point that all *medical* options had been implemented and surgical assistance was needed, I would get the call.

These situations were always horrifying…and sad. Very often it involved a young adult suffering sudden and profound heart failure, such that he or she was literally going to die within minutes if our resuscitative efforts ceased. In these cases, we often did not even know why the patient suffered such a catastrophic cardiovascular collapse. We just knew that we had only one immediate goal: to stop the young patient from dying by surgically placing one of the short-term mechanical pumps that would take over the work of the failing heart. In these desperate circumstances, we were just trying to save a life. After the dust settled we could determine what had caused the problem—and whether there was any way we could fix it. Exit strategies were often a bit blurry in these emergency situations.

For the decade I served as Surgical Director of Cardiac Transplantation, not only was I included in the regular cardiac surgical call rotation with the rest of my division colleagues, but I also took the great majority of the cardiac transplantation call. As surgical director, it was my responsibility to determine whether a donor heart was in good enough shape to be used. I reviewed the history, echocardiography, and other medical information available about the donor. I also made sure the heart was a good match for the recipient. This matching process was not just about blood-group compatibility, but also took into account such factors as donor/recipient age and size matching. The recipient also had to be checked to make sure that he or she was, at that moment, in good enough shape to tolerate the transplant procedure. Even if I was out of town, if a phone line was available, I took all of these calls.

I had not received training in cardiac transplantation or placement of long-term ventricular assist devices (VADs) during my cardiothoracic surgical fellowship. Currently, if a heart surgeons want to dedicate part or all of their careers to the surgical treatment of heart failure and cardiac transplantation, they do at least one additional year of training exclusively devoted to this subspecialty. The advanced training usually follows a full general cardiothoracic surgical residency. When I was appointed Director of Cardiac Transplantation at my hospital, I was only two years out of my residency and had done no formal cardiac transplantation training.

In fact, at the time of my training there were few, if any, formal transplantation fellowships and VAD placement was in its rudimentary developmental stages. Most of the transplantation and heart failure surgery was done by surgeons who just happened to have done their general cardiac surgical residency in one of the few medical centers that specialized in transplantation and VAD placement. Cardiac transplantation was performed at the university medical center at which I received my cardiac surgical training. Unfortunately, the actual cardiac transplantation service was located at one of the peripheral hospitals to which I had not rotated as a cardiothoracic resident.

At the time I was appointed director, the outgoing director, who had actually initiated the program at our center two years earlier, had just accepted a position as head of cardiothoracic surgery at another prestigious university medical center. A second surgeon in our division, who shared the transplant responsibilities, loved the prestige of being one of the transplant surgeons but absolutely hated being on call and being up all night doing these somewhat stressful procedures. Unbeknownst to me, not only did he not want to accept the position as director of the service, but he also wanted completely out of adult cardiac transplantation altogether.

So one fateful morning I dutifully attended our biweekly cardiothoracic surgical division meeting, where the usual business was being discussed including who would be running the cardiac transplant service. I should have been paying better attention. At the very least, I should have been expecting this. After all, I was heavily involved in the lung transplant program. I had trained at one of the rare institutions that performed lung transplants back then and was a ready and willing participant when the program started at our hospital. I also had made it known that I enjoyed placing mechanical VADs in the acute setting. Besides, I was young and my cardiac-surgical energy and enthusiasm were well known in the division. I really should have seen this coming.

But I didn't.

I remember the meeting well. I happened to be staring out the window of the conference room at a group of workers on the hospital grounds when someone asked, "Who is going to run the cardiac transplant service?"

When I turned back to the table, every eye in the room was gazing *at me*. "Whoa!" I responded to all the smiling faces. "I've never even done a cardiac transplant and I've only seen one!"

Several voices assured me that it would be no problem at all for me to get "trained right up." I should have protested more, but I was a soldier. Surgical training teaches many things, but the very first lesson is that the team is more important than the individual. All through my surgical training it was just assumed that in situations like this, one just *bucked-up* and took one for the team. I had learned through countless similar scenarios to just say "Yes, sir!" and move on. Besides, I figured that they were not really asking me if I wanted to be the surgical director of the heart failure service. They were informing me of my new assignment.

Everyone at the table hastened to commend me as the "perfect" guy to run the service. The reigning director, who had another month or so before leaving our institution, said he would call me for every transplant he did until he left. He would show me how to do them.

He never did.

He did several transplants—all in the middle of the night—but I was never informed until I came in the next day. I should have sensed the purposeful passive-aggressive behavior. But I was so naïve that I just thought he had innocently forgotten to call me.

I later discovered that there was much more to the story and that I was not privy to all that was going on behind the scenes. The departing transplant director had actually been asked to leave our division. It seems there was considerable animosity between him and our division chief and he simply never had any intention of training his successor. There was no personal enmity toward me; he barely knew me. He just had no interest in helping to prevent his departure from adversely impacting the division. In fact, he clearly wanted the division chief to suffer as much as possible. Losing the head of an active transplant service can have a hospital-wide impact—especially back then when we had one of the few cardiac-transplant programs in the country—and he wanted his resignation to have as big an impact as possible. He wanted us to palpably feel his departure, regret his absence, and blame it all on the chief of the division.

Another voice at that conference table assuring me that "everything will be just fine" came from the guy who wanted to exit the cardiac transplant program altogether. He knew all too well that the world of cardiac transplantation could be brutal with its middle-of-the-night urgency. He had no intention of taking on more transplant responsibility. So he saw this as the perfect time to leave the program. Had I known his plans, I would have correctly interpreted his reassuring words. He, too, promised to be available to teach me the procedure and mentor me through the process of taking over leadership of the service. I, of course, thought this meant he would assist me in the first five or ten transplants and remain available through the first year to help me through the difficult circumstances we all knew occur regularly in the world of cardiac transplantation.

Well, his definition of *mentor* and mine turned out to be sizably different. He begrudgingly showed up to assist me during my first transplant procedure. I never saw him again. He made it clear after this first procedure that I was "just fine" to carry on as the new program director without further assistance from him. He essentially said, "Don't bother me unless you have a big problem—a really big problem." But between the lines was the clear message, "I don't want to hear from you ever again." He then informed me that he would no longer be taking any more transplant call at all. He was completely out, and I was completely in.

I couldn't really hold this against him. Heart transplantation can be such a brutal business. Most cardiac transplants occur outside of normal elective operating-room hours. Often you find out you're going to be up all night doing a complex transplant procedure (commonly entailing a *redo* sternotomy, VAD removal, and cardiac transplant combined into one long operation) just as you are finishing up a long exhausting day of elective heart surgery.

It can be incredibly tiring; sleep deprivation among transplant surgeons occurs at a notoriously high rate. Most of the patients are horribly ill before the transplant and equally ill afterward. Most heart transplant patients have had heart surgery before—many having heart-assist devices in place— so their hearts are surrounded by dense scar tissue. Taking down all of the scar tissue without injuring the adjacent structures is tedious and dangerous surgery under oppressive time constraints.

The time constraints are in play because nothing ever goes as planned with the donor-heart retrieval. You are either waiting on the donor heart because of delays in the organ procurement, or the donor heart arrives before you are ready for it. When it arrives early, it sits in a cooler in the corner of the OR accruing *ischemia* (no blood flow) time while you're getting the recipient's chest open, taking down the scar tissue, placing the patient on the cardiopulmonary bypass machinery, removing the socked-in VAD, and excising the native heart.

And if that's not enough pressure, everybody in this group of heinously ill patients expects perfect results. For these and many other reasons, the average heart transplant surgeon's clinical life span is about ten years. It's a brutal business and I cannot hold it against this surgeon for bailing on me—I just wish he had helped me with a few more transplants before he pulled the lever on his ejection seat.

Regardless, immediately after the moving van pulled away from the house of the outgoing director, I was directing the cardiac transplant service at one of the largest hospitals in the country. I had never had plans to make cardiac transplantation part of my career and had never asked to be involved. But despite my lack of training and my not seeking the position, God made sure I entered the world of surgical heart failure. Looking back, it's clear now that the Lord had many difficult lessons for me to learn about trusting Him and humbling myself before Him—and this high-risk, high-stress subspecialty provided the perfect venue, the perfect battlefield. Gunfire was a daily occurrence. God's battle for my heart made sure of that.

Unfortunately, the previous director's hasty departure left me on call—alone—for all cardiac transplants during the entire next year. I had no help, and there was none on the horizon. I was on my own, in uncharted territory, without even a suggestion of the cavalry riding to my rescue. Thankfully, one of my junior colleagues eventually agreed to join me on the call schedule, but for that first long year I was on call every night and I did every transplant. I also participated in every lung transplant—and we were one of the largest lung transplant centers in the world. Needless to say, I was spending a lot of time in the OR during my "off" hours. Nights and weekends of transplantation seemed to fill my life.

By the immeasurable grace of God, I was young, eager, confident, and full of energy. Despite knowing that I was in for a long fight every time I got that phone call, I loved every minute of it. I would be lying if I told you I was not immensely proud of the fact that I was director of the cardiac transplantation and surgical heart failure service at our hospital. I remember that I could not wait to tell my wife (who was the medical director of our cardiac surgical ICU) this grand news the day I was appointed. God, in an undeniable demonstration of His infinite grace, gave me an indomitable spirit and an intense love of everything about cardiac surgery, cardiac transplantation, and VAD placement. I truly felt as if I had been training my whole life for this. I had the right skills at the right time in precisely the right place, and I knew that God was with me. I loved it.

So I charged headlong into the world of cardiac transplantation. Just as I knew He would, God went before me into the fight, and He was also my rear guard. By His grace, our heart failure and cardiac transplant patients did incredibly well despite the fact that I had entered my rookie year with essentially no training.

Besides doing all the transplants, I also determined transplant candidacy and managed the post-operative immunosuppression and post-transplant complications. I did a lot of reading on all of the nonsurgical aspects of cardiac transplantation. I quickly caught up on all the latest techniques and began attending the national heart transplantation meetings.

I rapidly adapted to my new assignment—just like a good soldier.

CHAPTER SIX

Night Fight

It was Friday afternoon. After another rowdy week, I was looking forward to a relaxing weekend. I fool myself like this sometimes. It is one of my ways of dealing with the stress. After all, it absolutely wrecks my weekend—and the weekend of my family and friends—if I dwell on the fact that I am just one phone call away from eight to ten intense hours of cardiac transplant surgery.

I try to fool myself and not dwell on this possibility because I know that once such a phone call comes in, all extracurricular plans are off and the patient's transplant timeline takes over. This transplant timeline is basically focused on only one thing: everything must be orchestrated perfectly to minimize the amount of time the donor heart is out of the chest and not receiving its vital nutritive blood supply. The biggest problem with timeline management is that many factors that impact this *ischemic* period are completely out of the surgical team's control. If, for example, the retrieval of the donor heart is delayed for any reason—and this seems to happen every time—the associated recipient operating room timeline must also be adjusted. Without these continual adjustments and the many resulting critical decisions that must be made, the recipient's operation can be very adversely impacted.

This intensity is what makes being on cardiac transplant call stressful. To deal with this, I have developed my *forgetfulness* into an art. It is one of my primary stress-avoidance mechanisms. I just keep suppressing the thought of being on call until, pretty soon, I forget that I am on call. This is great—until I actually get the phone call from the transplant coordinator informing me of the availability of a donor heart. It is like being awakened from a pleasant afternoon nap by a splash of cold water.

This particular week had been a very busy one; I had done a lot of surgery. I was exhausted. To make matters worse, my wife and I had recently met another young Christian couple at our new church, and we had asked them out to dinner that Friday night.

How silly of me.

We were actually driving toward the restaurant to meet our friends when I got the call. "Doctor," the transplant coordinator said, "we have a donor heart for Brandon."

Brandon Brady was a very ill young man on our transplant waiting list.

My heart sank. I was happy for Brandon, but my restful weekend had just vanished in a puff of smoke.

One of the problems with being on call essentially all the time is that you can't plan things. Having to repeatedly cancel plans really wears you down. It wears on your relationship with your spouse. Your friends say they understand, but they don't. You end up trying not to get excited about any new social plans because such plans have self-destructed so many times before. If you let it, the repeated disappointment can crush your spirit. But I was trying my best to reflect the compassion of Christ in every part of my life, so I tried not to let my disappointment show over the phone.

"The procurement team is just now heading off to Chicago for the heart," my caller continued. "It's about a five-and-a-half hour round-trip, assuming all goes well. We reached Brandon at home and he's headed in."

So I actually had two to three hours before I had to be at the hospital. This might sound good, but it really wasn't.

In fact, the time delay made it worse for me. My choices on how to handle this fell between two unpleasant options.

Option A, I could cancel our dinner engagement and mess up everybody else's evening—which normally would have been my first choice with such a daunting procedure ahead of me. Option B was to proceed with dinner despite my impending ordeal. I had been there many times before, too. I hated sitting at dinner trying to act pleasant while, deep inside, I knew I would be up all night managing a stressful transplant. It is hard to keep your emotions from ramping up as the anxiety grows.

I chose to keep our dinner date. This was a very special couple and my wife really wanted to go to dinner with them. I was trying to learn to love sacrificially, so I kept our plans intact.

Brandon Brady had already undergone placement of an implantable left ventricular assist device (LVAD) several years earlier. For the past three years he had been living with a machine implanted inside him that essentially did all the work of pumping his blood throughout his body. Every second of every minute of every day and night, he was kept alive by the device I had sutured to his heart.

Brandon had not only been horribly ill with heart failure at the time of his device implant, but he also had been somewhat noncompliant with his medical regimen. The medical team had been concerned about listing him for transplantation, and with good reason. They well knew that if you aren't compliant with your immunosuppressive medications after transplantation, you are going to die. We were in the business of doling out a very limited and precious supply of donor hearts to those patients who had the best chance of taking the greatest advantage of them. We wanted recipients who were reliable.

I'll never forget the morning I placed Brandon's long-term ventricular assist device. When I spoke to him in the pre-op room, his cardiac output was so low that he was barely able to answer my questions. He would have died within days, if not hours.

I loved everything about that first procedure. Once again I found myself in precisely the right place with exactly the right technology at precisely the right time to save the life of a desperately ill patient. I felt as if I were born for that moment in time.

For most of our patients, the immediate outcome without surgical intervention is not as predictable as it was in Brandon's case. Most of the time when we agree to do heart surgery on a patient, it is because we're confident that we are making things better for the patient on a *long-term* basis. That was not the case with Brandon. I knew that without my immediate surgical intervention, he was dead. Soon.

After I placed his LVAD, Brandon had proven a model citizen. We were proud of him and the change in his life. Not only had he been compliant with his medical regimen and device management, but he also became a poster child for our cardiac mechanical assistance program. We felt he had proven himself an ideal candidate for transplantation, and we were excited about getting a new heart for him. Unfortunately, getting an LVAD out and a new heart in is complex, tiring surgical procedure. That's what would make this a real fight. As I had feared, the timing was lining up *perfectly*: I would be up all night. And just when I had to be my very sharpest—around 4 A.M.—I would be approaching 24 hours without sleep.

Even more crucial, the combination organ procurement, LVAD removal and heart transplantation begins with, ends with, and is dependent upon, timing. We do not like for the new donor heart to be without its blood supply beyond four hours. The recipient procedure must be perfectly synchronized with the donor procedure (which often takes place in another city) so that when the donor heart arrives in our recipient operating room the recipient's chest is open, the patient is on cardiopulmonary bypass, and the LVAD has been removed. This allows us to excise the patient's diseased heart rapidly and connect the donor heart efficiently, keeping total donor heart ischemia time (time without blood flow) at or below the four-hour threshold. As you can imagine, complications or changes in timing can occur at any of these critical junctures.

So on that fateful Friday evening, as I struggled to maintain a happy demeanor during dinner with my wife and our new friends, I knew I had a slugfest ahead of me. I was sitting and chatting in a restaurant instead of napping. I was expending energy instead of conserving it. Our dinner engagement ended just in time for me to go home, change my clothes, brush my teeth, and head to the hospital.

When I arrived in the operating room, Brandon Brady was waiting for me.

"Hello, Brandon," I greeted him from behind my surgical mask. "Ready for a new heart?"

He was drowsy from his initial round of anesthetic premedication, but he gave me a drowsy-happy smile. "*So ready, Doc. Let's do this*," he mumbled bravely.

I smiled back under my mask, hoping he would see assurance in my eyes. "You're going to be fine," I told him. I nodded at the anesthesiologist and within moments Brandon was enjoying a deep sleep.

And he was ready indeed. Brandon had dealt with the misery of heart failure for several years before his LVAD had been implanted. The despair of heart failure had been replaced by the tedium of being supported by a ventricular-assist device. For three long years an electric cord (emerging from the right-lower quadrant of his abdomen) tethered him to either a battery pack or a bedside power supply. It also meant that his life would be dictated by one simple, morbid equation: *No electricity = No pumping of blood.* And he knew exactly what *no pumping of blood* meant. Whenever he was unplugged from the power console, he was entirely dependent on the batteries that powered his LVAD—and required replenishment every three to four hours. His device had worked well. It had kept him alive until this moment. But Brandon knew when he had the device implanted that he had merely exchanged one medical condition for another. Now he was on the threshold of exchanging that second medical condition for yet a third: the "disease" called heart transplantation.

I call heart transplantation a disease because even though it can quite effectively replace a failing heart, or in Brandon's case a failing heart supported by a machine, it is a benefit that comes with life-long cost. A heart transplant recipient must be closely monitored for any signs that his or her body is attempting to reject the transplanted heart. Back then, the recipients had to return to the hospital procedure room for heart biopsies, initially performed on a weekly basis. A small biopsy forceps is guided into the right ventricle of the new heart via the recipient's neck veins. Several small pieces of the new heart are removed and examined under a microscope for evidence that the body's immune system is attacking the cardiac muscle fibers.

The interval between biopsies is determined by whether rejection has been detected on previous biopsies and by the amount of time that has passed since the transplant procedure. As you might expect, patients are closely scrutinized, especially during the initial months following their transplants.

Further still, the immunosuppression medications needed to keep the body from rejecting the donor heart require daily, weekly, and then monthly fine-tuning for the rest of the recipient's life. These powerful medications have their own set of associated complications. Patients whose wellbeing depends on these medications must be managed closely to optimize protection from rejection while minimizing drug-related complications. Needless to say, cardiac transplant patients get to know their nurse coordinators and medical transplant physicians quite well.

The anesthesiology senior resident's voice snapped me out of my trip down memory lane. "We're ready to rock and roll!"

I loved his enthusiasm.

I nodded to the circulating nurse who began to scrub Brandon's chest with disinfectant.

Game time.

The operation started off normally. Brandon's previous LVAD placement surgery had required a median sternotomy—the chest incision to access the heart by means of a sternotomy (a breastbone-splitting incision) made by a handheld reciprocating saw. This fact, that he had had a previous sternotomy, changed everything in regard to our surgical approach. Brandon's healing response to the previous sternotomy had left thick scar tissue between his breastbone and the structures that reside directly behind it.

In Brandon's case, these structures included not only the heart and its associated major arteries and veins, but also the large tubular conduits that channeled his blood to and from his LVAD. One LVAD conduit was sewn to the apex of his left ventricle. It channeled the blood from his heart to the device implanted beneath his abdominal wall. The powerful, implanted pumping device pumped the blood back to Brandon's body via another Dacron conduit sewn to his ascending aorta. Brandon's ascending aorta then channeled the returning blood to his body via its many branches.

These LVAD conduits are each about an inch in diameter and filled with rapidly flowing, highly pressurized blood. As expected, the thick scar tissue resulting from the previous operation completely enveloped and obscured Brandon's heart, major vessels, and the LVAD conduits. In order for me to do Brandon's heart transplant, this scar tissue had to be taken down so all of these structures were adequately exposed. Only after their full exposure, by first separating them from the scar tissue, could I extract his LVAD and remove his diseased heart.

One technique I adopted early in my transplant career was to establish cardiopulmonary bypass machine support at the very *beginning* of the procedure—before reopening his sternotomy—by placing the pump's blood draining and infusion tubes *peripherally*. Specifically, we place these cannulas in the femoral vein and artery, the blood vessels that connect the body's central blood circulation to the leg. The venous blood returning from the body is drained out of the patient via plastic tubing that is passed from the femoral vein up to the heart. The cardiopulmonary bypass machine oxygenates the blood and pumps it back into the body via another cannula that has been placed in the patient's femoral artery.

By placing these cannulas in the leg, we can support the patient's entire circulation with cardiopulmonary bypass and decompress the heart even before we open the chest. Thus, instead of using this peripheral cannulation after sternal reentry bleeding has already occurred, we use it at the very beginning of the case. This provides a safety net for our patient, should an inadvertent misadventure occur. Further, since it decompresses the bulging heart and vessels, employing this technique can sometimes prevent their injury from happening at all. I adopted this as a routine on all complex *redo* cardiac transplant procedures in which the recipient was supported by an LVAD. Before I reopened his breastbone with the oscillating saw, Brandon was safely on cardiopulmonary bypass with his heart fully decompressed.

Brandon's chest was like a battlefield, and getting in safely required all of the stealth and skill that I could muster. The worst part was the time factor. I had to make rapid decisions at every step. At every stage of the operation I was reminded of the catastrophes that I had encountered there on hundreds of previous heart transplants. When you've done several hundred procedures, something bad has happened at least once at every single step of the procedure. The memories of those cataclysmic events seem very resistant to erasure, even by time and success—and even if they happened only once. These hounding memories are scary and they add to the stress of the procedure, but they also kept Brandon safe. This is why it's always safer to have your heart surgery performed by an experienced surgeon—and for this experience I thanked God. While I definitely had not enjoyed those earlier catastrophic cases, their protective effect during Brandon's surgery was a marvelous demonstration of God's grace.

"The donor heart is in the air," announced Janice Morgan, our transplant nurse coordinator. "It's about an hour out."

The procurement had gone a little long, but now the team was headed back to town with the donor heart packed in a cold preservation solution in a sterile container. They would touch down soon at the local airport, where Janice had a helicopter waiting to fly the procurement team and donor heart to the helipad on the top of our hospital.

I needed to get past the minefield of scar tissue and get Brandon's chest ready to receive its new occupant. With each cut, as I moved my surgical scissors into position, my mind assessed the associated danger. I had been there so many times before. With each cut, I gauged the amount of bleeding. This was all automatic. My mind was a flurry of calculation and command.

The scar tissue was full of small, abnormal blood vessels. If the bleeding got to be too much, I would stop and use the electro-cautery to cauterize the tiny bleeders or a surgical sponge to compress them. The fact that I was peering through 3.5-power surgical magnifying lenses made every drop of blood loom larger. I could not let the bleeding further obscure the geometry of the scar tissue and cloud the data being fed from my eyes to my brain. Bad data leads to bad decisions. I had to move along quickly, but I had to do it safely.

Boom! A spurt of blood—the *big red scream*. I was happy that I had chosen the conservative route of cannulating Brandon's femoral artery and vein for cardiopulmonary bypass. Brandon's long inflow graft coming up from his LVAD to his ascending aorta had migrated over behind the sternum and was positioned directly beneath the midline boney scar. Although I did not hit it with the oscillating saw when I divided the bone, I nicked it with my scissors while dissecting the scar tissue. I had wrapped it in a protective Gortex covering at the time of the LVAD placement to protect it from precisely this occurrence. Unfortunately, a 1-centimeter length of this Dacron inflow graft had become exposed between two sheets of Gortex. There was only a tiny area of the graft exposed but, sure enough, I hit it. The proximity of the graft to the cutting tips of my scissors had been completely hidden by the scar tissue.

By God's grace, I was already on cardiopulmonary bypass and the LVAD pump had been turned off. Otherwise the massive force of the powerful and very efficient device would have painted the ceiling with Brandon's blood. Because his blood was under less pressure, I controlled the bleeding easily with my index finger, then fixed it with a single suture. *Thank you, Lord*, I said silently. *Thank you.* God's presence had long since become a comfort for me during these stressful procedures. Ever since I had decided to place my trust in Him for every surgical procedure and decision, Jesus had gone before me into these battles. I sensed His presence in the middle of this fight.

Brandon's heart and LVAD inflow/outflow cannulas were now cleared of scar tissue, so I turned my attention to removing the device itself. Because Brandon's body had worked for more than three years to lay down a healthy, thick layer of leathery scar tissue, it took me more than thirty minutes just to extract the device. By then the donor heart had arrived, and I was ready to excise Brandon's diseased heart and swap it for its healthy young replacement.

The excision of the diseased heart is straightforward, aimed at optimizing the subsequent implantation of the new, healthy heart. After placing an aortic clamp, cutting through the walls of the deflated collecting chambers of the heart, and transecting the aorta and main pulmonary artery, I lifted the diseased heart from Brandon's chest.

Despite the fact that I had done this hundreds of times before, the scene that filled my high-powered surgical glasses at this point never failed to take my breath away. This time was no different. In Brandon's chest, where I would normally see a full beating heart, there was simply a large, hollow cavity. It's an eerie sight. I was deep in the Valley.

If our timing was on track and things had gone well with recipient preparation, I always breathed a big sigh of relief at this critical juncture. It was another reminder that I was not alone in this fight. Our team double-checked the donor identification and blood typing. I then lifted the donor heart from the cold preservative solution that filled the sterile travel container and gently placed it in a large basin of cold sterile saline. There I prepared the vascular and atrial cuffs that would be the attachment sights for Brandon's new heart.

The donor heart looked great. Carefully, I wrapped it in a cold saline surgical pad and lowered it into Brandon's chest. "All yours, Doctor Mason," I said to one of our superb cardiac surgical residents. He had procured the heart in Chicago and flown back with it. Under my watchful eye, he would do most of the actual suturing. He was tired, but reenergized by the task before him.

"I'm all over it," he responded confidently, as he replaced me on the surgeon's side of the table. "It is a great donor heart. Brandon is going to love it." His positive attitude was contagious and the whole operating room received a much-needed middle-of-the-night boost from his enthusiasm. He had sewn in many donor hearts with me and I knew he would do a great job.

My job was to maintain perfect exposure so Dr. Mason had a direct line of sight to suture the four connections. Mason was a sewing machine. I had never seen him suture more accurately and I was glad he was on call that night. I was confident that he would be a world-famous surgeon someday.

As Mason came across the top of the left atrium with the suture line, I reminded him of the importance of perfectly placed sutures. If that suture line leaked, it would be incredibly difficult to repair later. It had to be sewn perfectly right then while we could see it well—and it was.

We quickly moved on to the right atrial suture line. Mason continued sewing rhythmically, skillfully. I thought how strange it was that we routinely sutured in this manner— with a small curved needle on the end of a long, delicate clamp-like needle driver—but it was working perfectly. The thin strand of suture—as thin as a hair—would be charged with holding the donor and recipient right atrial walls together until Brandon's body was able to meld them into a single wall channeling the blood returning from his body.

We sutured the donor heart's ascending aorta to its recipient counterpart. This would mark another critical juncture, because it allowed us to remove the aortic cross-clamp and reestablish the nutritive blood flow that had been denied Brandon's new heart during its four-hour out-of-body experience. The moments following this introduction of the recipient's blood to its new pump are always tentative for the operative team. Sometimes the heart does not respond and remains lifeless, even after the nutritive blood supply has been reestablished. I had been there many times. That kind of early response usually meant that you were in for a long night.

But, before our eyes, Brandon's new heart sprang to life. *"Yesss!"* someone exclaimed.

"Looks good!" another added.

The immediate resumption of normal cardiac contraction is always a moment of exhilaration. I praised Jesus for being there with us, as I usually did when we passed critical points in an operation. It is so soothing to be reminded by the Holy Spirit to praise God because it is also a reminder that I am not alone.

But we needed to move on.

The rest of the implant procedure is comprised of completing the unfinished right atrial and pulmonary artery connections. The operative field often gets a lot bloodier—and becomes a moving target—once the blood flow to the heart is restarted and the heart reanimated. That's why we complete the deep posterior portions of the right atrial and pulmonary artery anastomoses (connections) before we resume the blood flow to the heart. These suture lines are located behind the heart where we cannot easily place repair sutures, so we perform their delicate suturing with a dry and motionless operative field. The heart's resumption of its normal contraction is no impediment to accurate suturing of the *top* portions of those anastomoses. The pace of the operation even slows a bit since the critical ischemia time of the heart has passed. So I was in a great mood, and it spread throughout the OR. Things were going very well so far.

I checked all of the completed suture lines that comprised the four critical connections and was delighted to see that there were no leaks. Now we needed to wean Brandon's new heart from the heart-lung machine, stop the bleeding, and carefully scrutinize the management of his blood pressure, heart rhythm, and intravenous fluids. This was the point in the eight-hour operation when I asked God for a special dose of strength. 3:30 A.M. I was exhausted and I was about to hit the dreaded 4 A.M. wall—always my worst time, and precisely when I needed to be at my very best.

I can't tell you how many times I had hit this 4 A.M. wall over the preceding three decades—each time wondering how I would get past it. So often had I prayed for supernatural strength, and every time God had answered.

I have never been much for *casting Satan out* of situations like this. I have lots of friends who are always *binding* him and *casting him out* of everything. I don't do that because I have never been a middleman kind of guy. I always go to the guy in charge, and it's no different in the middle of the slugfest of a heart transplant. I am all efficiency in the cardiac operating room. I don't mean to be flippant about it; I just don't have time to waste on Satan. Although he may indeed be trying to mess things up, God is still sovereign. Jesus is still on the throne. It is Jesus I go to in these situations and it is His will and the power of His cross that I seek.

The time had arrived when we would see whether our efforts on Brandon's behalf would pay off. I turned to Jermaine, our perfusionist, who was in charge of monitoring and controlling the heart-lung machine. "Leave a little blood behind."

"You bet," he responded. He, like everyone else in the operating room, was ready to see what this new donor heart could do. He placed a clamp partially across the venous return line traveling from Brandon to the heart-lung machine. By doing this, less blood was drained into the pump and more was left behind for Brandon's new heart to pump to his body. This is how we gradually wean the new heart from the support of the heart-lung machine. At this point, Brandon's new heart needed to take over the full-time job of meeting all of the blood pumping requirements of his body.

"The heart looks good, Jermaine. You can leave a little more blood in the heart."

"Got it," Jermaine said. "Leaving more blood behind." Jermaine's response, just like those from all members of the team, parroted back the command I had given him. This is how every member of the operative team notifies the cardiac surgeon that the command was received and is being carried out. There can be a lot of noise and distraction in the operating room in the middle of the fight and, especially in regard to time-sensitive commands, the cardiac surgeon needs to know that his command was received and is being carried out.

My eyes, my mind, and my heart were focused intently on the young heart that lay empty before me. From the corner of my eye, I saw Jermaine making the adjustments to carry out my command. Even though we were all pleased with the immediate return of electrical and contractile activity, the real test of this new heart comes when it is called upon to fully support the circulation of the recipient. During this critical weaning time, my eyes bounced back and forth between Brandon's new heart and the flat-screen monitor that electronically displayed his EKG and blood pressure.

I never consciously meant to, but I often held my breath at this point. I usually didn't even realize I was holding my breath until afterward, when I practically had to remind myself to take a breath. This was, after all, the most critical time for the new heart. Despite the fact that millions have ascribed much over many millennia to that fist-sized lump of muscle called the heart, at its basic level it is still only a pump. If his new donor heart could not do this job, it was worthless to Brandon—and we were all in a lot of trouble.

"Perfect, Jermaine. Bring us off. The heart looks terrific." I signaled success to the entire team.

"Venous line is clamped, pump is off," responded Jermaine.

B randon's new heart was what I call a *snapper*. As the bypass pump was turned down and more and more blood found its way to the new heart, it started *snapping*. It looked magnificent. It appeared more than strong enough to handle the blood-pumping responsibilities of Brandon's body. Once again, this brightened the whole demeanor of the operating room. Of each of the critical milestones, this was the most important, and everyone knew it. The complex operation at which we all had labored through the night was going to be a success. We were not completely out of the woods, but we knew Brandon was going to live. As everyone in the operating room smiled behind their surgical masks, my heart silently praised the name of Jesus. As far as I was concerned, this moment was all His.

I was exhausted, and yet my exhilaration reinvigorated me. I needed that, because I knew our battle for Brandon was not over yet. Surgeons who bail out—physically or mentally—at this point by leaving the care of the patient to assistant surgical staff have always left me perplexed. After spending that much time, sweat, and emotional and intellectual capital on behalf of the patient, why turn the outcome over to individuals who have less experience and less surgical knowledge and skill? I know in my heart that God is always faithful to let me know when it's time to relax.

Otherwise, I'm all in. I'm in the middle of the fight until it is over. If there is still gunfire, I belong in the middle of it.

Despite my elation, several critical issues still loomed menacingly over the operating room that early Saturday morning. The continued successful adaptation of the donor heart to its new environment is not just a one-time event occurring during the initial wean from the heart-lung machine. An example of an ongoing issue that can show up minutes, hours, or even days after the successful introduction of the donor heart is right ventricular failure. Fear of this complication mandates continued vigilant monitoring of the pressure catheter in Brandon's lung arteries. This pressure, in combination with the right atrial pressure, is a critical metric to assess the adaptation of the donor right ventricle to the recipient lungs, through which it must pump the patient's blood.

Looming in the forefront of my memory were those times when the donor right ventricle began to fail. It's an insidious setback. The central venous pressure slowly starts creeping up as the right ventricle slowly weakens. If you haven't picked up on the problem before the struggling right ventricle begins to dilate like a balloon, your patient is in more than just a little trouble. The early postoperative period is a very dynamic time when you can go from looking spectacular one minute to having severely compromised cardiac function in the next.

So I watched Brandon's new right ventricle closely. My eyes searched for the sentinel signs that things might be drifting in the wrong direction. After all we had been through together, I wasn't going to let him slip away from me. We were battlefield brothers.

Things continued to look good. Even as I went about the *tidying up* that must done before the chest can be closed, one eye was always on that new heart. I also continued watching for any evidence of perhaps the most feared of all complications after heart transplantation: hemorrhage. Almost all heart failure patients are taking systemic anticoagulants, or *blood thinners*. They have either very low contractility of the heart or an implanted LVAD or both. These conditions predispose the patient to systemic embolization, a.k.a. *throwing blood clots*. Blood thinners reduce this risk. Most commonly, they take the form of Coumadin—an oral medication that *thins* the blood so there is a lower propensity to form clots in large dilated hearts or in assist devices.

When these patients come in for their transplant, they are, of course, still anticoagulated because the effects of these long-acting blood thinners often do not wear off for days. Add this to the full anticoagulation required for the long cardiopulmonary bypass time and you have a patient with a uniformly compromised ability to clot blood. Clotting blood is critical when you have just taken down the scar tissue (with all of its small abnormal blood vessels) surrounding the heart and LVAD. In addition, the many arterial and venous connections required to complete a heart transplant are all holding back a pressurized bloodstream—thus making the setting ripe for bleeding. This is why postoperative bleeding is the most common and sometimes most devastating of post-transplant complications.

So, I could not let my guard down. Because of the risks of sudden hemodynamic change and postoperative hemorrhage, the transplant surgeon can't just close the patient's chest and hope for the best. Sure, in the majority of cases, things would turn out just fine. Nonetheless, in a finite number of cases, bleeding results in pericardial tamponade—just like Mrs. Filander experienced. The undrained collection of blood inside the pericardium presses down on the donor heart and impairs its filling. A pump that cannot fill adequately cannot be expected to pump adequately. The consequences can be even more threatening after a heart transplant, where the donor heart function is so critical.

Dr. Mason and I searched diligently for any sign of bleeding from the long suture lines. Things looked great. It was time to close. Using heavy wire sutures, we pulled the two halves of Brandon's breastbone together. Then we closed the superficial layers of his chest and groin incisions—all while keeping one eye out for any sign of deterioration in the pulsating waveforms on the monitoring screen. By the grace of God, Brandon stayed rock stable and we transported him up to the cadre of superb critical care nurses in our ICU.

It was 5:45 A.M.

Back in my office, I collapsed into my desk chair and dictated Brandon's operative note. Once finished, I wanted to circle back to the ICU for one final check on him before I headed home. When going to see a patient immediately post-op, I always prayed as I walked to the ICU. Bad stuff can happen in those first several hours. And over the years, I have learned that prayer truly matters. I must admit that on this morning I prayed as much for myself as for Brandon. I was seriously exhausted and the thought of dealing with a major complication at that point was onerous, to say the least.

In the ICU, Brandon's cardiac rhythm, blood pressure, lung pressure, and cardiac output were textbook perfect. The nurses were very happy with his progress. There was only the normal scant amount of bloody drainage from the chest tubes I had inserted into the operative site before closing his chest. There would be no postoperative bleeding complications for Brandon.

The head of Brandon's bed was elevated. Beneath the gradually waning fog of anesthesia, he was able to slightly open his eyelids and give my hand a squeeze. At that moment, I experienced what can only be described as one of those intangible *paybacks*, where God flies by so close that you can feel the warmth. I knew my night was over. It was as if I could hear the soft words of my Savior, Jesus, saying, "Go on home. I will take care of him."

I was always extra careful on the drive home after being up all night. The fatigue can overtake you without warning. I was physically drained and my muscles ached as if I had been stacking bricks all night. My back felt like it was out of joint.

None of this mattered. I was heading home to *morning-after-being-up-all-night-fighting-the-fight-for-someone-who-can't-fight-for-himself* sleep. Such sleep is nothing less than a very special gift from Jesus. It is made special by that bond of fellowship and camaraderie forged between warriors who go into battle together. If you have ever suffered with a fellow warrior through a very difficult time, you know the bond to which I am referring. We experience very similar fellowship and camaraderie with Jesus when we stand together with Him in battle, when we trust in His strength alone. The moments that follow are very special. They make me think building that bond is one of the reasons God allows these difficult times—these battles—into our lives. This is where God builds our faith in Him. The camaraderie we develop with our Savior as we stand back to back with Him in the fury of a fight simply cannot be duplicated elsewhere.

But rejoice that you participate in the sufferings of Christ, so that you may be overjoyed when his glory is revealed. (1 Peter 4:13, NIV)

Jesus is there in the middle of the fight with us when we fight like warriors of God—when we forgive the unforgivable, give to the ungrateful, and love the unlovable. He is there with us when we venture into the Valley of the Shadow of Death on behalf of others. He is there when we turn and move toward the gunfire. There is nothing like sharing the joy of a hard-earned victory with a fellow warrior after an exhausting fight. And there is nothing like the sleep that follows. I had been to war alongside Jesus, and flopping down on my bed felt so very good. Soon I was enjoying the sweet slumber of a warrior of God.

My wife *gets* this. On many occasions in her role as an intensive-care specialist, she has herself been on the receiving end of *up-all-night-saving-a-life* sleep. Mercifully, that morning she closed the bedroom door behind her on her way out and guarded the immediate vicinity from the noise of marauding children.

CHAPTER SEVEN

First Defeat

A discussion of warfare in the Valley of the Shadow of Death would be incomplete if exclusively focused upon the cardiac surgical operating room. After all, gunfire in the Valley comes from many directions and so far we've only talked about *surgical* battles. We need to address the *real* fights, the interpersonal, relational fights.

In this regard, the great relational battle campaign of my cardiac surgical career, carefully crafted by God before time began, has had great purpose behind it. Relational warfare has been a primary part of my sanctification process over the years. In fact, whatever progress I have made in the promised sanctification transformation of my mind has, to a large degree, been stimulated by relational battle. This is not surprising since a mandatory first step in teaching is to get the student's attention—and nothing gets my attention like a good fight. I share this trait with the ancient nation of Israel. As one might therefore expect, my battle history resembles theirs: God has had to hit me with some pretty big sticks. These big sticks—these fights—have come in the form of what the world would call *interpersonal conflicts* in my professional and personal relationships.

Through these interpersonal conflicts, fight after fight, God slowly began to show me that the fighting techniques I had adopted during my youth were not His way of doing battle. Indeed, God has a unique method of waging war. His tactical battle plan for daily living in the world of cardiac surgery is actually the polar opposite of the strategy that I had adopted during my early life and mastered during my decade of surgical training. There was a sizable amount of teaching to be done in the case of this young warrior—and I was a particularly recalcitrant learner. Needless to say, the resulting battle campaign was long and bloody.

To this end, God has placed some very interesting people in my life over the past three decades. Many of these people were easily and immediately defined and recognized as my "enemies" by my extensive, worldly warrior training. The reconnaissance on them was easily acquired and straightforward in its interpretation. Encounters with them evoked that visceral feeling that we all experience when we feel threatened: anxiety, fear, and apprehension—emotions that engender a purely defensive posture. Our responses to these so-called "enemies" are, therefore, most often reflexive. My reflexive responses, just like yours, had been engrained from years of training in the worldly ways of war. They were based upon the lies of this world, and they needed to change.

This first story is a story of failure—my failure. I totally blew this one. The Lord pretty much let me have my way with this first battle. He may have been speaking to me, but I obviously wasn't listening. The hardness of my heart, built up from a life of ignoring Him, had pretty much left me not listening to anyone—let alone God.

Hindsight is so clear. When I look back, I can clearly see that I had been getting some serious battle lessons for quite sometime. But I had my head in the clouds and I was not learning from God's tactical lessons. I was doing things my way—the way that I had been taught, the way that was comfortable. Before the necessary changes could be brought about, God definitely had to get my attention.

At the time of this first battle, I was still in a church that only gave lip service to reading the Bible. I was not reading the Word faithfully and there was woefully little foundation for the Lord to build upon. Thankfully, He is a patient and compassionate God. The Good Shepherd knew that one of His most rebellious sheep had gone rogue and wandered far from the flock.

And Jesus had come back to look for me.

This episode began a year after I started cardiothoracic surgical practice at my current location: a large university-based, academic tertiary-referral hospital. When I first joined this group of heart surgeons, they really were a nice bunch of individuals. We all got along well and there was very little, if any, conflict. This was all about to change. We brought one of our resident trainees on as an attending surgeon within a year of my arrival. There was considerable evidence of his intermittent duplicity prior to his hiring, but he was a very talented cardiothoracic surgical trainee and we were all willing to give him a try. I'll call him Dr. Rock.

Despite the fact that I had personally witnessed multiple manifestations of his intermittently questionable temperament when he was a resident in training, I bent over backwards to support Dr. Rock when we first brought him on. I wasn't totally ignoring God. I knew He had been gently tugging on my heartstrings. I knew that loving my neighbor was a priority of His. Dr. Rock was now supposed to be a partner in our cardiac surgical practice, a university academic colleague, and very possibly a friend. So I gave him the benefit of the doubt. By worldly standards, I really was quite naïve in this regard. I optimistically did not think there would be any problems and, in fact, decided that he deserved to be treated like a friend right from the very beginning.

Several months after settling into our group, however, Dr. Rock began to show his true colors. He began to use any and all means to raise himself above the rest of the members of our division in the eyes of the referring cardiologists. You may note this as a recurring theme among heart surgeons as we go through these stories. Securing cardiothoracic surgical cases is critical to all of us. After all, heart surgery is what we do. The referring cardiologists are our lifeblood since they diagnose patients with cardiac ailments that require surgical intervention and then refer them to us for their surgical procedure.

If the cardiologists like you and your surgical results, they send lots of patients your way. If they don't like you or don't trust you, then you get to sit in your office all day instead of operating. Since we all wanted to be doing plenty of cases, we were therefore in direct competition for the favor of these referring cardiologists. Dr. Rock was all over this. He knew that whenever any of his partners had a bad surgical outcome, it was his card to play. He was quick to take advantage of any such missteps and would seize any available opportunity to make his competing partners look bad.

One morning, Dr. Rock and I were in a discussion with several of the referring cardiologists after a combined cardiology/cardiac surgery conference on mitral valve repair techniques. In the course of the discussion, Dr. Rock brought up a particularly difficult mitral valve repair technique. He then smoothly steered the discussion toward the fact that one of our partners had recently had to re-operate upon a patient in whom this particular mitral valve repair technique had initially been attempted. Two days postoperatively, a follow-up echocardiogram had demonstrated that although the repaired mitral valve was leaking less, it still had severe regurgitation. The surgeon—one of our senior partners in the division—knew that he could not leave the patient with that degree of mitral regurgitation. He took the patient back to the operating room and replaced the patient's repaired valve with a prosthetic valve. It is of course less than ideal whenever a cardiac surgeon must return a patient to the operating room following a cardiac surgical procedure. As a result, when this patient's postoperative course was brought up in the discussion, Dr. Rock deftly seized the opportunity before him. I saw him roll his eyes and give one of the cardiologists a *knowing* look.

I know you are familiar with this *look*. It spoke volumes to the cardiologist. All with the simple widening of the eyes, raising of the eyebrows, and cocking of the head, a clear message was sent. This message was not subtle and not misinterpreted. It said, *Wow! That is unfortunate. I certainly would not have had to take that patient back for a second surgical procedure. Of course I am not surprised. He has always been a careless surgeon. I hope you remember this next time you have a patient with mitral valvular regurgitation who needs a valve repair.*

I really don't think I read too much into what I saw. I was an experienced street fighter myself. I knew that Dr. Rock's maneuver was as effective as it was stealthy. He didn't even have to say a word. Nonetheless, the damage was done. The blow was dealt. He had successfully torpedoed one of his senior partners. I can assure you that this had an immediate impact upon further referrals from that particular junior cardiologist to that senior cardiothoracic surgeon in our division.

There was only one problem. During the conversation, Dr. Rock had failed to mention that the patient in question had a very complex valvular problem for which most cardiac surgeons at that time—including Dr. Rock and myself—would not have had the surgical skillset to even attempt a repair. Mitral valve repairs are almost always preferred over outright replacement with a prosthetic valve since a repair avoids many of the problems associated with prosthetic valves, such as blood thinners and prosthetic valve degeneration. The surgeon involved had considerable skill in this area and had tried his best to prevent the patient from needing a complete replacement of his valve.

In my judgment, not only had our partner surgeon not done anything wrong, he had done a superb job. Sometimes things just don't work out. This was in the early days of valve repair and the techniques were still being ironed out. In this case, an attempt at repair was a reasonable bet and the patient would have been much better off had it worked. Despite having to undergo the second procedure, the patient did very well after the replacement procedure and was discharged home. Since Dr. Rock did not have the skills to even attempt such a repair, the patient ended up no worse off than if Dr. Rock himself had just replaced the valve in the first place.

What surprised me the most was that Dr. Rock knew I was standing there and involved in the conversation. He knew I had seen his expression. In fact, right after he rolled his eyes and gave the cardiologist that knowing wink, Dr. Rock looked directly at me. At first I thought that he had just forgotten that I was standing there. But the expression on his face when he glanced at me was not one of repentance. It was an expression of defiance. His eyes confirmed that I was not misinterpreting his intentions. He wasn't the least bit apologetic.

I had no doubt from that moment forward that if Dr. Rock would do that to one of the senior members of our group—a far more experienced heart surgeon than either of us—he would surely do it to me. Dr. Rock wanted to be doing the majority of the mitral valve repairs that were done by our group and the only way to reach that goal was to corner the referrals from the cardiologists. He had a plan, and he obviously wasn't going to let me or any of the other partners—who had welcomed him into our surgical group less than a year earlier—get in his way. From that moment onward, I knew I could not trust Dr. Rock. He would stop at nothing to secure surgical referrals.

It quickly became apparent that a change in the state of the group had occurred with the hiring of Dr. Rock. On his part, unbeknownst to most of us, there had been a declaration of war when he arrived. My response to this threat was not a good one. Once his plan became apparent, the gloves came off and things got quite ugly.

I'm sure I was getting lots of messages from Jesus during this initial phase. I am sure He was telling me to trust Him through all this. On the surface I gave it my best. But in my heart there was no trust, no forgiveness, and definitely no love. There was only judgment for Dr. Rock and his scheming activities. In my mind, he was two-faced, scheming, dishonest, and a threat—and all of the worldly training that I had obtained to that point spoke only of a warrior response. There was considerable fear and anxiety—I was under attack—and these feelings generated hate. Like a good little boy (more like a good little passive-aggressive warrior), I was able to cover up and contain my anger during most encounters. But, when ambushed—when caught off guard in meetings and other surprise encounters—the words of my mouth directly reflected my heart.

The good man brings good things out of the good stored up in his heart, and the evil man brings evil things out of the evil stored up in his heart. For out of the overflow of his heart his mouth speaks. (Luke 6:45, NIV)

My thoughts, words, and actions reflected what was in my heart—and I most certainly did not love.

This was warfare pretty much as usual for me. The new guy on the block threatened everything I had established at my new professional home. Obviously, things were clearly already escalating after the previously described event involving a senior partner. But that escalation was only the beginning. Soon, an objective third party presented unquestionable evidence that Dr. Rock had also lied about me to my partners. I felt that he had significantly damaged my reputation by his lie. He was very good at dealing out reputational damage while all the while covering his tracks in feigned innocence. The world said that I had every reason to hate him and to go to war with him. My resistance to this logic was low and I bought into the declaration of war. I fell into my routine manner of handling this sort of issue—battle according to Satan. I was clearly choosing to do things my way, not God's way. I don't remember ever actually stating this, but my actions spoke louder than words: *Thank you very much, Jesus, but I think I can handle this one on my own. No need for me to trust in you and do things your way right now...because I have this covered.*

Unfortunately—or fortunately—this guy was an animal. He was a battle-hardened warrior from the city streets. I was no match for his street-wise battle tactics. The result, in hindsight, was predictable. He tore me apart—and that made things even worse.

There was a lesson to be learned here and I, by God's grace, actually learned it. This was the first time in my many battles in the world of cardiac surgery that I acknowledged that the world's grandiose promises regarding its method of war were false. The world's method of handling this situation was not the answer to my problems. It only made things worse. All that this approach of plotting, scheming, and hating had accomplished was to entangle me further in the mess. For the first time, God really got my attention. My reconnaissance of the post-conflict battlefield left me with the very strong feeling that there simply had to be a better way.

I was not very familiar with the real paradigm change that is to be found in the words of the Bible because I was not reading it faithfully at that time. Although this would soon change, at that time I simply had no idea the Bible promised that God would go before me into battle if I would just do things His way. I had no idea that I could trust in and enlist the power of my Creator in my daily interactions with the people in my life. There was so much that I needed to learn. I was not yet demonstrating the love of Jesus Christ to those around me because I had not yet really turned over the reins of my heart to Jesus. I had invited Him in for sure. But in regard to my actual daily life, I was not yet letting Him *steer the cart*. Obedience in loving the unlovable, based upon trust in God (the action that turns belief into faith), was woefully lacking.

As time went on, there were many lessons learned and God began to reach into my life in many different areas to make fundamental changes. Gradually, I began reading the

Bible—sporadically at first and then more consistently. I was beginning to pickup hints regarding where God wanted me in this fray. But, for the most part, I still did not have the big picture. It was a very frustrating, very painful time of my life. There was a lot of suffering and, overall, I took a real pounding—both personally and in my career as an academic cardiac surgeon.

All of this had a predictable result. It led to the feeling that I was not where I needed to be in regard to my relationship with God. I realized that my whole approach—including the choice of the church that my family and I attended—was wholly inadequate. This was a radical feeling for someone who had been raised under the thumb of intense legalism in my childhood church. I am a black and white kind of guy, nonetheless, and it made no sense to me to be *halfway* on the matter of God. If the God of the Bible was really there, if Jesus was really who He said He was, and if God's written word was really true, then my relationship to Him had to be the only thing that mattered in this life.

Thus, it was in this first major inter-relational battle with one of my cardiac surgical partners that I finally truly squared off with possibly the most profound of life's fundamental questions:

Who is Jesus Christ?

Jesus is either whom He said He was, the only Son of God, or He isn't. It is our mandate to make the call. One way or the other, we must make the call. This, the most discussed question in history, demands an answer. In fact, by God's design, a response to this question during our life is compulsory. God relentlessly puts it in front of us. It *can* be avoided, but to avoid it—once again by God's purposeful design—is, in fact, to answer it.

To me (and my black and white mind), the logic used to formulate an answer to this question is clear. This logic necessarily forms the foundation of any decision we make in regard to this question and it is inexorably life altering: *Jesus is either nothing or He is everything.* Logically speaking, there can be no safe middle ground. It became readily apparent to me that avoiding the question and simply never answering it—which I had been doing all my life—required no life altering changes, but nonetheless clearly still answered the question. To proceed on without changing my life was clearly to decide that Jesus was nothing.

On the other hand, I knew that if I were to come down on the side of *Jesus is everything*, then that decision *should* unquestionably be life changing. That decision shouldn't just command my life for an hour or two on Sunday morning, it should rule every moment of every day from the first fluttering of my eyelids in the morning until my last glimpse of light at night. To me, this was pure logic, and to that point in my life, I had worked very hard to define my life by what I perceived to be purely logical choices.

Back to Dr. Rock. Because of our daily encounters in the operating room suites, as well as the proximity of his office to mine, Dr. Rock's presence seemed to dominate my professional environment. As a result, I spent a lot of time thinking about our professional relationship and the associated hostility. Unfortunately, I fell into a pattern of dwelling on my less than charitable thoughts in his regard. I was not controlling the thoughts that entered my mind and they began to control me. That is how it works. The more of Satan's nonsensical *logic* that I allowed in, the more I dwelt upon it—and the more I let him control my mind. I was resisting very little. I had taken the first steps in a vicious cycle that can spin rapidly out of control.

How true the Bible rings when it speaks of the dark pathway that we tread when we dwell on the hate for our enemies and the anxiety that accompanies these thoughts. The word of God tells us exactly what we can expect when we choose this behavior. In this regard, I sometimes feel as if Psalm 73 was written specifically with me in mind. Actually, I am sure that it was. It was written for all of us worldly warriors who long to be warriors of God. It describes the results of worrying about the apparent prosperity of the wicked.

> *But as for me, my feet had almost slipped; I had nearly lost my foothold. For I envied the arrogant when I saw the prosperity of the wicked. They have no struggles; their bodies are healthy and strong. They are free from the burdens common to man; they are not plagued by human ills. Therefore pride is their necklace; they clothe themselves with violence. From their callous hearts comes iniquity; the evil conceits of their minds know no limits. They scoff, and speak with malice; in their arrogance they threaten oppression. Their mouths lay claim to heaven, and their tongues take possession of the earth. Therefore their people turn to them and drink up waters in abundance. They say, "How can God know? Does the Most High have knowledge?" This is what the wicked are like— always carefree, they increase in wealth. Surely in vain have I kept my heart pure; in vain have I washed my hands in innocence. All day long I*

*have been plagued; I have been punished every
morning. (Psalm 73:2-14, NIV)*

This Psalm really hit home with me during my battle
with Dr. Rock. Asaph, the recorded author of this psalm, and
I obviously have a lot in common. Asaph had clearly been
hammered by Satan's lies. Satan tried to convince Asaph of
the same thing of which he tries to convince all of us when
problems arise. He had Asaph convinced that the way of the
world (the way of the wicked) led to prosperity and was
obviously and logically the desired path. *After all, just look
at all those other people who have accepted the world's
answer and how well they are doing!* Satan was trying to
convince Asaph to quit relying on God, take the steering
wheel back, and get this cart back on the road *by himself.*
Asaph's mistake (and mine also with Dr. Rock) was to dwell
on the apparent success of his enemies and worry about his
own lack of success. He (and I) initially defined success only
in worldly terms.

Asaph admitted that he didn't understand how this was
God's plan or how God's heart for him could really be good
if He in fact allowed this to happen. But, then, just when he
was about to falter, Asaph returned to God's sanctuary.

*When I tried to understand all this, it was
oppressive to me till I entered the sanctuary of
God; then I understood their final destiny.
(Psalm 73:16-17, NIV)*

Asaph returned to the *sanctuary of God*. He went back
to the place where the real *reality*—the eternal reality—can
be seen; back where the blindness could be washed away as
he focused his eyes upon the only thing that really matters—
God, and God alone. With the resulting change in
perspective, Asaph then understood the destiny of the

wicked—just as I have also come to know the destiny of those who choose the path of the worldly warrior.

> *Surely you place them on slippery ground; you cast them down to ruin. How suddenly are they destroyed, completely swept away by terrors! As a dream when one awakes, so when you arise, O Lord, you will despise them as fantasies. (Psalm 73:18-20, NIV)*

The best part of Psalm 73 is yet to come. Asaph then describes what happens to us when we dwell upon and envy the victories of the wicked: we plot and scheme against them, we become as *a brute beast.*

> *When my heart was grieved and my spirit embittered, I was senseless and ignorant; I was a brute beast before you. (Psalm 73:21-22, NIV)*

What a perfect description of me when I was not faithful to cast these evil thoughts from my mind. What a perfect description of me when I got down in the dust of the street to fight with Dr. Rock. I was wallowing around in my worry and self-pity, butting up against everything and every one. Just like a brute beast, I was no longer able to see or hear, let alone be guided by, the truth. But God, as shown in the words of Asaph, does not leave us in the utter hopelessness and despair of our plight. His story is a story of hope.

> *Yet I am always with you; you hold me by my right hand. You guide me with your counsel, and afterward you will take me into glory. Whom have I in heaven but you? And earth has nothing I desire besides you. My flesh and my heart may fail, but God is the strength of my heart and my portion forever. (Psalm 73:23-26, NIV)*

I'm sure you have heard the Bible referred to as the instruction manual for the human heart. Truly it is. The Holy Spirit perfectly describes the situation we are in, tells us where God's heart is, and then tells us of the plan for the rescue—if we will only listen, if we will only obey.

Gradually, in my conflict with Dr. Rock, I began to realize the error of my ways. I began to try to get along with Dr. Rock. I tried desperately to clean up my heart. But, in the heat of battle in the tumultuous world of cardiac surgery—when I was reminded of the seemingly real threat—I must admit that I fell back on the old tried and true worldly warrior methods. In my lame efforts, I truly redefined the term *backsliding*. I dwelt on thoughts of revenge and ways to take Dr. Rock down—secretly, of course. I schemed. I worried. I wallowed in self-pity. I, for sure, became precisely that *brute beast* described by Asaph. I truly considered Dr. Rock evil. In the depths of my failure, I even fooled myself into believing that I was on God's side and the logical plan was for me to righteously stand up to the evil that Dr. Rock represented. Surely, I was walking a dark path down a slippery slope.

Thankfully, God in His endless mercy, saw my desperate plight—saw that I was taking this entirely in the wrong direction—and lured Dr. Rock away from the institution with a lucrative job offer elsewhere. I had not done well in choosing the path of a worldly warrior, but at least I began to recognize the futility of the path that I had chosen. As I mentioned, I also began to read the Bible regularly near the tail end of this battle. The ground was being set for the Lord to get my attention on a new approach, a new battle plan. His tugging on my heartstrings was becoming strong and sustained.

I proceeded to my next life lesson in what I can only describe as an optimistic, and yet moderately confused, state. My deep heart kept telling me that the words of the Bible, as frustrating as they might be, were nonetheless pure truth. In fact, everything made perfect sense to me during my Bible reading time early every morning. Unfortunately, I still had to go to work in the "real" world immediately afterwards. I descended into the Valley of the Shadow of Death every day—where the likes of Dr. Rock awaited me. Sure, Dr. Rock was gone. But my days in the Valley of the Shadow of Death were always faithful to deliver up a continuing stream of challenging relational conflicts. After all, Jesus and I descended into that valley together every day for a reason—and there was so much more work to be done.

CHAPTER EIGHT

Stress

Every job has stress. Surely, with various jobs there are differences in type, source, and severity—but every job has stress. To understand cardiac surgeons, and why they think and act the way they do, we must gain a familiarity with the unique brand of stress that accompanies daily descent into the Valley of the Shadow of Death. After all, stress shapes the perspective with which surgeons view their patients and every associated relational milieu within which they take care of those patients.

Some stresses are obvious and acute, while others are subtle and brewing, but either way, they can be brutal and take their toll upon even the most resilient of cardiac surgical warriors. As I take you through the many medical, academic, and social venues in which I have found myself submerged over the last three decades, understanding these stresses may help you grasp why my colleagues and I act the way we do. The foundational first step in understanding why cardiac surgeons sometimes behave so badly is to determine what exactly generates stress in cardiac surgery. Without this, it would be very easy to misinterpret the motives and thought processes behind the observed behavior in this sometimes-inexplicable world.

The first and foremost source of the stress associated with the clinical practice of cardiac surgery is founded in a fairly obvious fact: we are doing high-risk surgery on living human beings. It is nearly impossible for one human being to take control over the critical management of another human being's cardiac health decisions without having a natural empathy that is derived from similar life experiences. With heart surgeons, this natural empathy can play a critical role in shaping the way they do heart surgery. These are not dogs, cows, sheep, or pigs that we are operating upon. These are living, breathing human beings with fathers, mothers, spouses, children, and friends. Our patients are just like us. I can't speak for all of my cardiac surgery colleagues, but for me it is impossible to enter into my patient's world of medical hurt without having empathy for the fact that *there, but for the grace of God, go I.*

Once again, there is something very special and unique about the covenant that a patient and their surgeon enter into when both agree to proceed with cardiac surgery. Literally half an hour after we meet them, we are asking the patient and their family to entrust us with their most prized possession—life. They put their trust in us and the last thing in the world that we want to do is to break that trust and fail them. And, let there be no question about this, major complication or death following cardiac surgery equates with breaking that trust. Major complication or death is precisely how cardiac surgeons define failure.

As we have already discussed, the severity of the patient's medical condition, and therefore the critical nature of the care that must be provided by a physician, varies in every situation and lies on a broad spectrum in the expansive scope of the world of modern day medicine. Some young physicians abhor the very thought of accepting responsibility for the outcome of another human being's life and death struggle. They deal with this stress by simply avoiding it. They choose low-risk subspecialties where the worst that can happen to the patient is a worsening of their skin rash, the mal-alignment of a bone, or a slight deviation of the nasal septum. However, to many other young physicians, dangerous medical situations and high-risk decisions are precisely what drew them to the practice of medicine in the first place.

Cardiac surgeons certainly fall into this latter category. This is dangerous stuff that we do. When things go bad, lives are altered and all-too-often come to an end. There are very few medical subspecialties whose hallmark procedures have as high an associated risk of life-altering complication or death as that of the subspecialty of cardiac surgery. In a university-based, tertiary referral practice, cardiac surgeons not only perform the standard fare of CABG (coronary artery bypass grafting) and valvular surgery, but also take on the high-risk redo operations, major aortic surgery, heart failure surgery (including cardiac transplantation and ventricular assist device placement), and a high volume of advanced endocarditis (valve infection) cases—all of which are most commonly referred from other hospitals. Depending on the setting, overall cardiac surgical mortality can run into the 5%-10% range. This means that one out of every 10-20 of their patients will not make it out of the hospital alive.

Even cardiac surgeons with so-called *boutique* cardiac surgical practices (a predominance of straightforward coronary bypass and valvular operations) have patients who don't do well following their surgery—and when patients don't do well after cardiac surgery, even in these so called "straightforward" cases, it is not pretty. After all, this is the heart we are operating upon and we aren't born with a *backup*. When things go bad, no matter how simple the procedure seemed to be, death is always a possibility. Even the most straightforward cardiac surgical case can go awry, and when things go awry, people die. As every cardiac surgeon can tell you, "Beware the *routine* CABG patient!"

Further compounding this stress is the fact that high-risk cardiac surgery does not take place in a social vacuum. Quite to the contrary, it is only in very rare circumstances that a cardiac surgeon doesn't fully engage not only the patient, but also the patient's entire family and collection of close friends. We simply cannot avoid the human factor in the world of cardiac surgery. Even in the direst of emergencies, when we do not actually meet the patient (because they are already sedated and on a mechanical ventilator), they usually still come with a number of family members or friends.

Moreover, the majority of our patients, by any standard, are nice people with nice families. It is very easy to get attached to them. Despite the fact that we do cardiac surgery every day and see patients like this all the time, it is very hard to not have deep feelings of empathy for endearing people who are desperately ill with cardiac surgical diseases. It is too easy to see yourself in their shoes—especially since most of us have either had heart disease ourselves or at least had family members and friends afflicted by this most common killer of Americans. We, like them, have spent our time in waiting rooms anxiously praying for our dear friends and relatives. As a result, we cannot help but become emotionally invested in every patient. More than anything, we want them all to do well and their families to not suffer.

Another factor that adds to the stress of cardiac surgery is the broad spectrum of clinical presentation that is associated with cardiac surgical patients. Certainly, some cardiac surgical patients are admitted to the hospital *on death's doorstep*, in horribly critical cardiac condition. Others are chronically and miserably ill for long periods of time prior to their admission for cardiac surgery.

But, unfortunately, a large portion of our patients are often minimally symptomatic or even completely without symptoms of any kind. Even though they may have a critical cardiac condition that will most assuredly take their life if left unattended, many have no related symptoms at the time that surgery is recommended.

For example, I can't even begin to number the patients upon whom I have performed emergency coronary artery bypass surgery who were essentially without symptoms despite having a 99% near-total *widow-maker* occlusion of their left main coronary artery. This utter lack of symptoms means that they have the potential to electively walk into the hospital with their wife, husband, family, or friends for elective surgery—looking just as normal as anyone you might pass on the street—and exit the hospital in a body bag. Because they look so normal, nobody is thinking or talking about being dead. Besides being a horrible outcome for the patient, this is simply brutal on their poor families. Their expectations for a good outcome could not help but be high, because their loved one looked just fine to them. They simply didn't look like someone who was precariously balancing on that narrow precipice between life and death. As if the loss of an asymptomatic patient is not bad enough, the cruel toll that it takes on the patient's unsuspecting family and friends has, on far too many occasions, crushed the life right out of me.

As if that were not enough, another undeniable fact is clearly at play in these difficult situations. Even though innumerable healthcare professionals populate the complex world of cardiac surgery, the buck still stops with the cardiac surgeon. When there is a bad outcome after heart surgery, the responsible person who must step forward and answer the tough questions is the cardiac surgeon. When somebody has to deliver the bad news to the family after a bad cardiac surgical outcome, it is clearly the cardiac surgeon's responsibility. Some cardiac surgeons try to avoid this responsibility, but their efforts are futile. When one assumes authority in the cardiac surgical arena, which all cardiac surgeons must, responsibility cannot be avoided. Authority and responsibility are inseparable and this is just a fact of life.

This responsibility can take a heavy toll on cardiac surgeons. There is simply nothing as heartbreaking as delivering the news of a patient's death after heart surgery. I have had to tell spouses of half a century that their beloved life-partner had died. I have told parents about their children and children about their parents. I have told nearly inseparable brothers and sisters of the death of their siblings—who are also often their closest friends. I have walked into crowded waiting rooms and I have walked into empty waiting rooms—I'm not sure which one breaks my heart more. I have spoken to 30 people at a time and I have looked into the eyes of a single forlorn person waiting alone for news of a loved one.

I have also dealt with every kind of response to the bad news—although it is never anything less than traumatic. I have seen way too many tears well up in waiting room eyes in my career—I can see them right now as I write these words. I have felt the pain of enough broken hearts to fill a thousand lifetimes. I have seen people faint. I have had several waiting family members themselves go straight from the waiting room to our hospital's emergency room after I delivered bad news. One even had a heart attack. One ended up having heart surgery himself a day later. One woman literally leaped—in a single convulsive response to devastating news about her mother—across the waiting room floor, only to land in a pathetic pile of shrieking humanity. It was an astonishingly athletic act and it was simply heartbreaking.

And then there are those family members who respond to their grief with anger. This is one of the most difficult things that I have encountered in my career as a cardiac surgeon. It can be such an ugly scene. After having just spent 8 horrible hours trying to save their desperately ill family member, I am met with raging anger—toward me.

I understand how this can happen. Many people are just naturally suspicious of things that they do not understand. Some patients are transferred to our cardiac surgical care after mismanagement at outside referral hospitals—and their family members know it. They know that their loved one did not receive the care they deserved and they understand that their dire situation is at least in part due to this negligence. They can be very angry. Some just feel so overwhelmed, so out of control, all they can do is attack. Many are warriors like me and their natural first response to almost any emotional situation is anger. Since they are in an unfamiliar social environment, at first they may bottle up their anger. Sitting in the waiting room, they are like a bomb waiting to go off. They are so full of suppressed anger that they cannot help but vent it toward the first responsible person they encounter. All too often, am that person.

These attacks always catch me off guard. Despite the fact that they are not uncommon, I never expect them to occur. I guess I have always assumed the family and I are on the same team. On more than one occasion, these attacks have actually gotten physical, with family members expressing their grief by threatening me with visually intimidating posture and gestures. On one occasion I had been communicating with a very pleasant family member for several days during the course of a critically ill patient's preoperative workup, only to have a completely different family member also show up in the waiting room immediately after the surgery. As I began to address the familiar family member, the unrecognized family member pushed his way to the front of the crowd and got right in my face. He began shouting truly horrible things with his face about 3 inches from mine. He was incredibly angry.

I just stared at him. I myself was grieving over the outcome and I was completely caught off guard. I had been brokenhearted over the impact that I knew it was going to have on this very pleasant family. I was vulnerable and simply speechless. I just stared at the guy. Luckily, another family member stepped up and pulled him away. The loss of the patient had broken my heart and the vitriolic attack by a grieving family member had broken my spirit. There are many wounds delivered to both sides during these difficult episodes.

Another factor that amplifies the stress of losing a patient to a bad cardiac surgical outcome is intrinsic to our hearts: *rescue*. *Rescue* is important to all of us—it is precisely what Jesus Christ did for you and for me on the cross of Calvary. He made it very personal. We are the objects of the Greatest Rescuer's greatest rescue. We are the hostages who were set free. We have been rescued and in humble recognition of that which has been done for us, we desire to rescue.

Since the focal point of the entire creation was our rescue, it is safe to say that God places a lot of importance on being a Rescuer. This is not surprising since righteousness, compassion, selflessness, justice, mercy, and love are all intrinsic to both rescue and to the nature of God. Since we are in fact made in God's image, rescue has been written on our hearts from the very beginning, even before we were rescued. Christians love to rescue in grateful response to our rescue—but even non-Christians love to rescue because every one of us is made in God's image. And He *loves* to rescue.

As a result, our hearts assign great value to the act of voluntarily stepping into the fight on behalf of individuals who cannot fight for themselves—and that is what cardiac surgeons do every day. We cannot help but have a visceral reaction to our patient's helpless plight when the *slimy pit* of death has entrapped them in its *mud and mire* and they are going down for the third time in the throes of cardiovascular disease. We inherently desire to step in and lift them out:

> *I waited patiently for the LORD; he turned to me*
> *and heard my cry. He lifted me out of the slimy*
> *pit, out of the mud and mire; he set my feet on a*
> *rock and gave me a firm place to stand. He put*
> *a new song in my mouth, a hymn of praise to*
> *our God. Many will see and fear and put their*
> *trust in the LORD. (Psalm 40:1-3, NIV)*

Our patients tread that thin precipice between life and the oblivion of death. They see the problem that threatens their very existence—it is hard to miss—but have no power to fix it. They have no knowledge. They have no experience. They have no skill in this arena. By our knowledge, experience, and skill, we have the God-ordained power to bring them back from that edge, to lift them from the bottomless pit. That inner, deep-heart desire to rescue is exactly what drives us to step into harm's way—to drag ourselves out of bed in the dark hours of the night to take on an 8-10 hour operation under the most desperate and trying of circumstances. We fight to save a life and when it works we enjoy that very special feeling that belongs only to the few who not only go into harm's way to attempt rescue, *but who also succeed*. We walk in the victor's parade as heroes.

But equally so, when we fail to rescue, the wound is especially deep. We have no choice in these feelings. God has written this all over our eternal hearts.

Although true personal grief is the predominant emotion experienced by most cardiac surgeons after losing a patient, there is also a less humane and somewhat darker side to *losing* in the world of cardiac surgery. This more malevolent shroud of emotion that too often veils our intellect and clouds our judgment has its foundation in one simple fact. We didn't become doctors to lose. We became doctors to help our patients get well. There is therefore only one metric by which we are judged in the world of medicine—and most certainly in the world of cardiac surgery—and that is whether our efforts return a well patient to a reasonably normal life style. Death, no matter what the circumstances, is always tallied as a loss.

We take this loss personally, because it has always been personal. Cardiac surgery is our world. We have invested our entire adult lives in it. It is all too often our sole provider of what psychologists term *ego support*. Unfortunately, we all-too-often build our entire existence upon cardiac surgery. We simply can't live without it. This is why cardiac surgeons find it so difficult to retire. Our entire life has rotated around the idol of cardiac surgery and we, very literally, have nothing left when cardiac surgery is withdrawn from our world.

Further, since we have made cardiac surgery the center-stage idol among our many life idols, it becomes the foundation of our appraisal of our self-worth. Gradually, a permanent change in our perspective occurs. In our minds, we believe that we are certified valuable by society only because we are cardiac surgeons. Far too many of us find our *total* value in the fact that we are cardiac surgeons. Echoes from our past further support this encumbrance. That little voice in the back of our head that reminds us of our many childhood father-wounds cynically asks us whether we truly are the *real-deal* or not. For many that question remains unanswered. That skeptical little voice is always there and with many of us it carries far too much weight.

That drive to be good at what we do is especially critical in the world of cardiac surgery for another very pragmatic reason. If you aren't a good cardiac surgeon with good results—the lone metric being whether your patients live or die—then you will not be a cardiac surgeon for long. There are too many interested parties with oversight authority who are tracking our surgical results. Death is their primary metric. String together too many bad outcomes— even in high-risk cases—and the red flags will be waving.

We all, in the back of our minds, fear those red-flag-waving oversight authorities. Some have the clout to literally take the world of cardiac surgery away from us. The presence of these oversight authorities rouses that age-old fear of *not being good enough*, which rears its ugly head with incredible ferocity. We fear that they will take from us this world in which we find our identity—and in which we have so heavily invested. We desperately need our presence in cardiac surgery to continue—so it obviously follows that we absolutely must have good patient outcomes. So, it is not just patient and family empathetic grief that drives us for good outcomes. Unfortunately, it is not just *all about the patients*; it is very often *all about us*.

The bottom-line of all this: I, and every heart surgeon I know, have been on the losing side of things too many times. In our minds, nothing good ever comes from losing in the world of cardiac surgery. Yes, there are many conflicting motivations behind our fears, but no matter which is dominant, the specter of losing a patient is an ever-present and sometimes overwhelming burden. We hate it so much that we will do almost anything to avoid it. And in that effort to avoid death is found the stress that accompanies a heart surgeon into every single operation that he or she may perform.

Our previous forays into this valley of death compound the stress. These previous trips have taught us the importance of being adequately prepared for every possible turn of events during the course of an operation. Anticipated operative complications are always more efficiently and effectively dealt with than unanticipated complications. As a result, a normal part of our preoperative routine is a mental visualization of the course of the planned procedure. Just like an athlete anticipating a competitive event, we play the surgical tape forward with all contingencies. Those contingencies must include all of the possible pathways—even those that lead to a bad outcome. Even as we begin and progress through the operation, we are continuing to replay the tape over and over—and with every hit on the *replay* button, the stress continues to multiply.

As you read the rest of this book, the ever-present stress-induced dread of taking on the emergency high-risk cardiac surgical patient will become painfully obvious. You will encounter this dread in every one of my cardiac surgical colleagues and you will certainly see it in me. Understanding the stress associated with the care of our patients may give you a better grasp of the source of this dread. With every emergency high-risk cardiac surgical procedure comes the amplified potential for loss and all of its weighty baggage. It is no wonder that as the initial cardiac surgical thrill wears off, most (if not all) cardiac surgeons begin to populate their practice with risk-avoidance behavior.

Each cardiac surgeon builds into his or her every day, countless mechanisms for dealing with the associated stress of their career. Some try to avoid emergency high-risk cardiac surgery altogether. They make a career of dumping the high-risk cases that arrive on their doorsteps onto the operative schedules of their junior (and sometimes senior) partners. These same surgeons may even try to avoid taking emergency call at all. When difficult cases do arise, they try to transfer them to other hospitals. When they work at tertiary referral hospitals like ours, they make up all sorts of excuses that allow them to refuse to let those difficult cases be transferred to their care.

To add to the problem, these evasive surgeons often correctly note that as long as they are in the operating room, they have stress. Being concrete thinkers, their solution is straightforward: *Get out of the operating room as fast as you can.* Thus, from the moment their foot first steps across the operating room threshold, they are trying their hardest to get out of there as quickly as possible. Soon, getting out of the OR becomes their top priority, surpassing even the patient's wellbeing. To these surgeons, speed is of the essence. In fact, operative speed becomes the primary metric by which they judge their surgical skill. Anyone who happens to get in the way of this primary goal will most deservedly feel the wrath of pent-up stress. These cardiac surgeons are easy to recognize. They tend to be very vocal, yelling at everyone who stands in the way of their rapid exit from the operating room.

These same individuals tend to deal with stress that occurs outside of the operating room in a similar fashion. Problems that arise in the ICU or on the wards may threaten their patients just like those that arise in the operating room. As one would expect, the stress can be rekindled with the same intensity as in the operating room. Just like in the operating room, they want the most expeditious solution to each problem that arises. Their solution is to tell the other involved physicians, resident staff, and nurses to *just deal with it!* The tone of their voice makes it obvious to everyone—usually because it is loud, demeaning, and intimidating—that they do not want to be involved with the details. *Just fix the problem!* These surgeons are masters of what I call the *ostrich head in the sand* technique. They believe that if they just ignore the problem, surely it will go away.

Unfortunately, this behavior just increases the chances of a bad outcome, since someone with presumably less skill is therefore made responsible for dealing with the problem. Then again, these surgeons have an answer for that also. If a bad outcome occurs, they just yell more. The house-staff, nurses, and other physicians may even be told that their actions resulted in the patient's death, that they *killed* the patient. As I said, these cardiac surgeons tend to be very vocal. As scary as this seems, I have seen this particular methodology played out in hospitals across the continent on countless occasions.

Most cardiac surgeons readily acknowledge that they cannot realistically avoid all of the stress. Their goal, then, becomes controlling the stress when it occurs. Often they deal with all of the other stresses in their life in a similar fashion. We all know these people—and most of us *are* these people at least some of the time. When the stress occurs, they—we—just bottle it up inside. The problem with this approach is, of course, that most of us have a limit to how much stress we can bottle up before we must vent it, often in the form of an explosion.

These explosions are infamous in the world of cardiac surgery, since most cardiac surgeons rely upon this technique to some degree in their practice. When stress begins to build up, propriety, behavioral standards, and university ethical mandates all tell us to *behave* ourselves. We do. Until we reach our capacity. Then the smallest little thing sets us off. I do not know a single cardiac surgeon—myself included—who hasn't exploded in anger at their fellow caregivers. Even the very nicest among us explode when the stress overwhelms us. And most of us hate ourselves for doing it.

There is one more "solution" to the problem of cardiac surgical stress that deserves a final comment. There are many sociological theories that are applicable to this innovative solution. I will not bore you with their detail, except to tell you that when human beings are unrelentingly subjected to repeated high-intensity stress, which continues to occur no matter which path they choose, there is another classically human method used to offload it. The sociological theories tell us that in those cases, the repetitively stressed individuals ultimately reach a point where they simply abandon all social mores. They altogether quit worrying about what other people think or what standards they will be held to, because they simply reject all outside standards. They run on their own behavioral *code*.

This perspective is further reinforced in these cardiac surgeons when they realize that indeed there is *no* stress if you *just don't care*. As a result, *not caring* becomes their new norm. Their evaluation of patients for surgery, their operating room technique, their postoperative care, and their dealings with family, friends, and fellow caregivers just becomes rote routine, *no big deal*. They go through the motions and seem oblivious to the outside pressures that want to fill their life with stress. They have abandoned the standards and metrics by which society in general, and cardiac surgery, specifically, judges them. They just don't care.

The abandonment of the norms and standards that are associated with the normal practice of cardiac surgery has many interesting consequences. Unlike the rest of us, these surgeons really don't mind the high-risk emergency case. From their distorted perspective, there is simply no human being attached to that emergency surgical case. Likewise, there is no family in the waiting room—or even if there is, this brand of cardiac surgeon just doesn't care what those waiting family members think of him or her. There is no bond with the patient or family because these surgeons never *allow* such a bond to develop, let alone seek one! These surgeons feel that they are somehow above all that emotional mess with which the rest of us seem so embroiled. They feel that they, by whatever great skill they may possess, have raised themselves above the metrics by which other cardiac surgeons are evaluated. They are no longer accountable to anyone but themselves and their own *code*. To them, the death of a patient is nothing more than a speed bump.

A good analogy that illustrates this approach to stress avoidance is found in the world of videogames. Most of our kids' action videogames allow them multiple *lives*. When they lose a battle, they just get another *life*. It is, therefore, no big deal when they lose. They almost always get another chance. Even when they run out of *lives*, they just reboot the system and move on to the next game.

In a similar fashion, when these surgeons lose a patient, it is no big deal. They seem to think they have infinite *lives*. They just reboot and move on to the next patient. In their minds, there is no accountability. The feeling that they themselves are the only individuals qualified to sit in judgment of their work allows them to simply *un-assign* death as a metric. A death is no longer a loss. It is just an expected part of the game. The world of cardiac surgery has become the equivalent of a videogame to them. They accept the deaths just like they accept the successes. There is no positive feedback and there is no negative feedback. There is nothing. In regard to patient outcomes—in regard to the humanity of cardiac surgical patient care—they have lost all sensation. They are no longer connected. These surgeons have gone rogue. They have fallen off of the social and inter-relational grid of the world of cardiac surgery. As you can imagine, they are an intriguing group of individuals when encountered in the clinical setting.

With this information as a background, most of us can readily appreciate why cardiac surgeons respond the way that they do when the ominous battle sounds of an emergency high-risk case begin to echo down the towering walls of the Valley of the Shadow of Death. To most it sounds like an ambush. To most it sounds really bad. To most it sounds like a chance for loss, defeat, and pain. All too often the idealistic enthusiasm for another opportunity to save a human life has been slowly eroded by the siege of persistent and unrelenting stress. Whatever high ethical and moral commitment they may have had is gone. The altruistic feelings they had in the beginning have given way to the unrelenting barrage of emotional and physical pain. All too often, they find themselves conjuring up excuses as their legs reflexively carry them out of harm's way. All too often, moving toward the gunfire is the last thing on their minds.

Cardiac surgery is high stakes battle in which the plunder is human life—and it is simply never easy to lose a life. This loss of human life is special—every time—and it takes a horrible toll on cardiac surgeons. There are very few chosen careers that can so easily and deeply wound you on such a regular basis. This is life, however, in the world of cardiac surgery. If you engage powerful enemies in big battles in the Valley of the Shadow of Death—which we do every day—the losses come very hard and the wounds are deep. After all, if there were no risk in moving toward the gunfire when the bullets are kicking up the dust at your feet, everyone would do it. As every cardiac surgeon can tell you, if you habitually and reflexively move toward the gunfire, sooner or later you will be shot.

CHAPTER NINE

A Cardiac Surgeon's Prayer

Jesus.
I stand before this operating room,
this battlefield to which You have led me.
You planned this day before I was born.
I see before me a patient inflicted by an enemy
who is dangerous, shrewd, powerful,
and better prepared for this battle than I.
I admit that I am afraid of making mistakes—
that hurt my patient.
I admit there is a part of me that wants to turn
and walk away—
and let someone else fight my fight.
Instead, I will do the only thing that I can do.
I cry out to You alone, Jesus.
Yours is the *only* Name upon which I call.
Give me the strength to move toward the gunfire.
Give me the courage to turn into this battle.
Give me the audacity to charge boldly into this fight—
despite the full knowledge of my weakness.
For I have no power to face this vast army
that is attacking me.
I do not know what to do, but my eyes are upon You, Jesus.
I declare to all my reliance upon You alone, Jesus.
I trust in Your sovereignty over these events
and in the goodness of Your heart—
and therefore the goodness of the outcome of this operation
because I know You love me.
Yet still I must actually fight this fight.
I have to step onto the field of battle.

I must stay focused, be strong, persevere, and
operate as efficiently and skillfully as I can…
You have made me a skillful surgeon.
My senses must all be alert, my reactions swift,
my mind calm, and my hands sure…
You have given me great hands.
Jesus I need You to help me keep the eyes of my heart
focused only upon
You
during every moment of this great battle.
When it is over and I walk from this operating room,
win or lose,
let me know that I stood back-to-back with You alone
in the fury of this great day.
In eternity that is all that will be remembered.
Jesus, let me remember that I knew only Your strength.
And let it be known by all who gaze upon this field of battle
that the glory is
Yours
and Yours alone.
My Lord, my Savior, my Redeemer,
and my Strength in battle,
Jesus.

CHAPTER TEN

Battle Plan: Surrender?

Following the embarrassing defeat in my first major interpersonal battle as a cardiac surgeon, I did not have to wait long until I encountered yet another challenging relational confrontation. My first fight with Dr. Rock had been a disaster, but in its illumination of my humbling mismanagement, it had served God's purpose well—it got my attention. Just as God had planned, it was an awakening. Right on its heels came a second pivotal battle that would completely restructure the way I would approach battle for the rest of my life. At the time, I had no idea that this second interpersonal confrontation would initiate a complete realignment of my priorities in strategic and tactical battle planning.

Dr. Bull, another junior cardiac surgical faculty member, had joined the division simultaneously with my arrival. We immediately became good friends. We interacted well on a professional and social basis. For the most part, things went very well for quite some time. The occasional problem would arise and we would deal with it in a congenial fashion. Slowly, however, our relationship began to morph into something altogether different. Our innate and easily triggered *threat* alarms began to sound all too frequently in our interactions as each of us felt more and more threatened by the other. We were very competitive people trained at similarly competitive surgical programs. Unfortunately, this meant that our response to the threat we posed to each other was also similar.

War was never really declared. That is often how these things begin. The battle was mostly covert and had an almost insidious onset. A few small skirmishes along the common frontiers were the first signs of things to come. We began, in a very subtle way, to take each other on. A mild form of *tactical taunting* might be a good way to describe our professional interactions. This was in my nature and, as I have discussed, had been refined by my training. Not surprisingly, I initially I found myself once again relying upon my old battle habits. As a result of my first battle with Dr. Rock, I had been convinced of the necessity for change and had tasted the goodness of that change, but relational battle is complex. I had not had enough battle experience flying my new paradigm to deal with all of the nuances of these complex interactions. When I found myself on unfamiliar relational ground, the old battle tactics manual was dusted off and, sure enough, I went back to my old way of handling things.

I know what you must be thinking. *Not again! What a loser!*

Surely you are correct. There is a common thread running through all of these stories. That thread would be *me*—and my less-than-Christ-like attitude! Maybe, you must be thinking, there is nothing wrong with all of my partners, just something wrong with me. Not only are you correct in your supposition, it's even worse than you might suspect!

This *taunting* was business as usual for me. I was quite good at it—too good in fact for my own good. Sometimes I would slip into the attack mode without even realizing it— that is the way it gets when you have been practicing the art of battle your whole life. Battle tactics become automatic. Just like the well-trained special ops warrior that I was, engaging the enemy no longer required cortical thought processes or reason. There was no room for wisdom. Instead, my relational responses were occurring as an automatic reflex. The cerebral cortex was simply not involved. This is precisely the goal of the realistic and repetitive training of any special ops combatant—and all cardiac surgeons! This automatic response works to your advantage if you are a Navy SEAL in a firefight or a cardiac surgeon responding to a sudden intraoperative catastrophe. It is, nonetheless, a disaster if you are trying to get along with your cardiac surgical colleagues. My reaction to Dr. Bull's taunts was reflexive. Because it occurred immediately and without thought, Satan must have just loved it. Reaction without thought in relational situations is the goal of his deception. Although reflexive reactions may work for the worldly warrior, acting without thinking is not good for the young warrior who is desperately trying to do things God's way.

The subtle battle tactics that I employed are easy to recognize. Of course, we "Christians" never say anything bad about anybody. So, I never said anything bad about Dr. Bull. There are, of course, much more than just words involved in our day-to-day interactions. As we have discussed, so much more can be communicated by the casual winks, *knowing* nods, or even tactical silence during conversation with others in the hospital ward hallways or the operating room. Let me be plain about it. When others said critical things about Dr. Bull, did I come to his defense? No chance. Did I agree with their statements by my silence? You bet. You know the routine.

Slowly but surely, things were gradually spinning out of control. There was initially only the very rare episode of open conflict in which testy words were exchanged. But, for the most part, there was just silence. In fact, despite my continued acknowledgment of him, Dr. Bull began to completely ignore me. He would simply not speak to me. I remember several occasions when our eyes would meet as I walked by him in the office or hospital hallways. My "Good morning!" was met by utter silence. He just looked away— not even a nod of acknowledgment. It was as if I was not even there.

Dr. Bull was very good at this silence tactic. It was another form of tactical taunting. His expertise with this technique was getting to be very well known by all of the members of our division. I was not the only one who was on the receiving end of his silence treatment. Apparently, this was Dr. Bull's way of dealing with tension in professional relationships.

Dr. Bull's tactics worked well. I felt isolated and helpless. Similarly, my tactics of fake Christian love further contributed to the growing rift. It seemed as if I could not help myself. When operating room staff gossiped about him—for I had not been the only target of his wrath—I would listen intently. It was as if I was comforted by his misfortune—almost like I truly believed that his continued *acting out* made me look good.

I know what you are thinking. This was third grade thinking, for sure. Nonetheless, his angry outbursts made mine look relatively benign and trivial. I must admit that I did take some comfort in this—admittedly a very human response, despite its third grade tactical level. Despite all of my rationalizing, however, deep in my heart I knew that this just wasn't right. It was precisely then, in the depths of my intense relational mediocrity, that God again touched my heart.

I don't mean to be overly melodramatic in its description, but what occurred next really shook me up. Surely this really was a moment of divine intervention— one of many in my sanctification process. I claim absolutely no credit for it. That which occurred was not only *not* of my doing, it was surely the farthest thing from my heart. Admittedly, by then I had reconfirmed my commitment to Jesus and had truly asked Him to take command of my heart—but I had absolutely no capability in this situation. I had reached that *bankruptcy* described by C.S. Lewis. It was all too clear to me that I could never manage to love Dr. Bull on my own.

Never.

In fact, I actually remember consciously acknowledging after rereading the words of Christ in the gospel of John—*Love one another* (John 13:34, NIV)—that I could simply never do what God was asking in regard to Dr. Bull. I guess I considered him unlovable. I had reached a truly pathetic state.

Then, right in the middle of my utter bankruptcy, Jesus made His move. He gave me a nudge in the right direction. Actually, He mainly just nudged me out of His way. He took command of my heart. Despite the fact that I could not love Dr. Bull, Jesus informed me that He could.

Right now—with the aid of perfect 20/20 hindsight—it is readily apparent that up until that point I was like a blind rat wandering through a maze. It was as if the Lord knew I had absolutely no chance of finding my way out unless He intervened. He put it lightly on my heart that perhaps there was another way. The words of scripture that I had read before with minimal impact suddenly began to hit very hard.

In that amazing moment, I knew in my heart that I had to end this war. Not only that, but I also knew precisely how to do it. I knew that it took two to fight and that either contestant in a fight had the ability—at a moment's notice—to end the fight. I knew exactly what I had to do. There was no reasoning or discussing or "working through it" left for me to do. The answer was straightforward. The call—directly from the word of God—was simply for me to completely humble myself before Dr. Bull in utter surrender.

Total surrender. I was to totally surrender to Dr. Bull. Obviously, I was no longer controlling my thoughts. I knew I was incapable of coming up with that sort of plan. Jesus was in control and, for just a moment, I was standing back in utter amazement—and delight.

My first *brain* reaction (up to this point, the amazement and delight were pure *heart* reaction) was from my warrior nature and was totally predictable: *Whoa—I'm not sure that I'm ready for that! Surely there is another way.*

But there was simply no denying the source of this command. It was straight out of the Bible. This utterly alien thought from an altogether different dimension was clearly from the Lord. Jesus had invaded and was now imparting His signature wisdom from the control center of my heart. Under His direct command, my heart seized control of the situation. Love, not "logic" would rule the day.

I am incapable of adequately describing what followed. This was a very emotional moment for me. It was like a wave washed over me. I literally shuddered. I was in the middle of a fight that was causing me no little bit of anxiety and all of the sudden…it was over. It was as if a great load had been lifted from my shoulders, like a great feeling of relief suddenly descending upon me. I knew that the fight would continue indefinitely like it was—or even escalate further—if I didn't take extraordinary measures to stop the vicious cycle of accelerating expressions of anger. These skirmishes were taking a toll on me. They were wearing me down. They were distracting me from my primary mission. I was ready for the fight to be over. I knew that I had to stop the fight and that God had just revealed how I to do it. I had a God-approved battle plan. I was to fight the fight His way for the first time in my life. I was to fight and win…by losing.

I admit that immediately following my realization that this thought was from God, that it was totally consistent with the Bible, that it was the right thing to do, and that I needed to do it right now, a bit of subtle confusion smothered my enthusiasm. I knew I had to do something called *surrender*. There was only one problem. As an academic cardiac surgeon, I had never before voluntarily surrendered. I did not even know what that looked like in real life. I knew it had to involve humbling myself before Dr. Bull. But, once again, I had no idea what this was actually supposed to look like.

My mind was a jumble of thoughts. Admittedly, I had humbled myself to my wife and family before. That was tough enough, but this was much different—and much worse. Dr. Bull was a real cold customer. I figured it was probably unrealistic to expect any kind of a reciprocal response from him. Actually, I *knew* that I could not expect any kind of a reciprocal response from him. Carrying out God's command was not going to be straightforward.

Then, in the middle of my confusion, God struck again.

This had to be entirely one-sided.

I can assure you that one-sided commitments have never been—and still aren't—easy for me. Nonetheless, God's holy Word was blazing in my mind now and God let me know that my inexperience at this method of war—His method of war—did not matter and certainly was no excuse. I knew that my commitment to Dr. Bull could be one-sided because God's commitment to me through the shed blood of

Jesus was one-sided. (Praise God that my eternal salvation is not dependent upon *my* efforts.) This wasn't really about what Dr. Bull thought and it certainly wasn't about what I thought. It was about what God sought in my life—plain and simple. As I worked further through this and began to fill in the gaps, God began to remind me of a profound truth that I had been ignoring: I had made very significant contributions to the riff that existed between Dr. Bull and I.

In fact, in the course of several little *reminders*, it became quite clear that in regard to my relationship with Dr. Bull, it was I who was not right with God. The mess in this relationship was, in fact, of my own doing. Things were starting to clear up in my mind. The fog of my sin and self-deception was beginning to lift. It became readily apparent that I could have stopped this mess early in the fray and that I had chosen—by my own free will—to continue the fight. God showed me that indeed, despite my feelings to the contrary, Dr. Bull was not the only one at fault in this relationship. I had been the perpetrator of plenty of that which was worthy of sincere repentance. In fact, I had been in the wrong much more than I had been in the right. What an eye-opener! This is clearly addressed in God's Word, and the course of action is clearly spelled out.

> *My son, if you have put up security for your neighbor, if you have struck hands in pledge for another, if you have been trapped by what you said, ensnared by the words of your mouth, then do this, my son, to free yourself, since you have fallen into your neighbor's hands:* **Go and humble yourself**; *press your plea with your neighbor! Allow no sleep to your eyes, no slumber to your eyelids. Free yourself, like a*

gazelle from the hand of the hunter, like a bird from the snare of the fowler. (Proverbs 6:1-5, NIV; emphasis added)

I knew I had to take this radical step. I also knew that before I could ever go and surrender to Dr. Bull, I had to get my heart in the right shape. Dr. Bull was no dummy. He would see right through a fake surrender. Before I could ever march into his office and surrender, I had to completely forgive Dr. Bull. I had to recognize that he was just another guy trying to get along in a tough job—just like me. I realized that his personal attributes were God-given, just like mine. God made him just the way he was, just like God made me the way I am. I had no grounds for judging him and certainly no basis for raising myself above him. Before anything else was discussed in the meeting that I was planning, I needed to apologize to him for my initiation of the fight, escalation of the conflict, and my stubborn refusal to back down. And, above all, I had to really mean it in the depths of my heart. Total surrender. God let me know that total surrender was the only thing that was going to work.

It seems so simple now, but it was anything but that back then.

It was a very humbling experience to come to the realization that Dr. Bull's offenses toward me were no worse than mine toward him.

I care very little if I am judged by you or by any human court; indeed, I do not even judge myself. My conscience is clear, but that does not make me innocent. It is the Lord who judges me. Therefore judge nothing before the appointed time; wait till the Lord comes. He will bring to light what is hidden in darkness and will expose the motives of men's hearts. At that time each

will receive his praise from God. Now, brothers,
I have applied these things to myself and
Apollos for your benefit, so that you may learn
from us the meaning of the saying, "Do not go
beyond what is written." Then you will not take
pride in one man over against another. For who
makes you different from anyone else? What do
you have that you did not receive? And if you
did receive it, why do you boast as though you
did not? (1Corinthians 4:3-7, NIV; emphasis
added)

I was, also by God's grace, reminded that forgiving
Dr. Bull was a trivial thing compared to the forgiveness that
my Savior had already shown me. I had to repent before my
righteous God of the many contributions to the problem that I
had made along the way—then I had to repent before Dr.
Bull. How silly it is when we harbor hate in our heart while
simultaneously professing faith in Christ. How hypocritical
to think that we can praise God together with the members of
the Body of Christ on Sunday morning, all the while
knowing full well that we harbor hate in our heart for another
individual.

Jesus knew precisely what my response would be on
that fateful day when He laid out the battle plan for my next
interaction with Dr. Bull. He knew what I would be thinking.
He knew exactly where my struggling heart would go with
this. But, Jesus had a plan to counter the immediate second-
guessing that He knew would fill my weak heart. In fact,
Jesus made sure that the battle plan for my next skirmish in
this *Great War* got written down in black and white—just for
me.

"Therefore, if you are offering your gift at the
altar and there remember that your brother has

something against you, leave your gift there in front of the altar. First go and be reconciled to your brother; then come and offer your gift.

"Settle matters quickly with your adversary who is taking you to court. Do it while you are still with him on the way, or he may hand you over to the judge, and the judge may hand you over to the officer, and you may be thrown into prison. I tell you the truth, you will not get out until you have paid the last penny. (Matthew 5:23-26, NIV)

My pride-filled ego told me that this was going to get ugly.

As unbelievable as it seems, however, as soon as God led me to His conclusion, framed it out, and countered my second-guessing, I was ready for a fight—God's way. I knew the plan was right—and I couldn't wait to implement it. *Whoa! Where did that come from?* I am sure that you know exactly what I am talking about. I am sure you have experienced that feeling also—when something hits a chord that resonates in those very deep secret chambers of your heart. As I look back on it, that moment of revelation was truly one of those moments in my life when I can absolutely say that God passed palpably close to me.

The feeling was unmistakable. I knew that this course of action was right. I prayed, got my heart in a truly contrite state, and then prepared to walk boldly into Dr. Bull's office and spill my guts all over the place. I can't begin to tell you how outright scary this was for me. After all, this was the *real* world here. It was one thing to decide to do it in the 06:00 AM quiet of the early morning after spending time in the written word of God—and a whole other thing to actually go and do it in the real world of academic cardiothoracic surgery. At the same time, however, it somehow felt totally right and utterly freeing.

I almost ran down the hallway to Dr. Bull's office. There is just something special about knowing absolutely—beyond any shadow of any doubt—that what you are about to do is unquestionably dead center in the will of Almighty God. It is invigorating. Rarely, in my entire life, have I been so sure as I was at that moment. I was totally committed to this course of action, no matter what the consequences.

I was practically out of breath when I reached his outer office door. As I stepped confidently through the threshold of his office, a cold icy sensation hit me like a winter gale. The feeling took my breath away. For a moment I froze in my tracks. I was overwhelmed with the feeling that I should turn around and retreat back out into the safety of the hallway. The icy fingers of true spiritual warfare gripped my heart.

I pressed forward into enemy territory.

Dr. Bull's secretary rose to greet me. "He's expecting you. Go right in." She hesitated and then motioned with her hand toward his office door—almost as if she was afraid to open it herself.

"Thanks," I responded with as much politeness as I could muster in the thick of battle.

As I swung the door open, I immediately knew the source of the winter chill that had hit me on the way into the office. Dr. Bull was sitting behind his desk. His hands were hidden behind the desk and he was motionless. He was not smiling. He was not frowning. His facial features were without emotion. Nothing. He did not greet me. He did not shift in his seat. Absolutely nothing. Classic Dr. Bull.

How I wished I had not even darkened his office door.

"Can I come in?" I asked as I moved into his office. I was glad I had continued to move into his office, because Dr. Bull did not respond. He just sat there with that blank, icy look on his face.

It suddenly dawned on me. He wasn't angry with me. Nor was he happy or sad or anything. It was much worse.

It was as if I did not exist.

He was letting me know that to him I simply did not exist. To him, I was not even worth the effort of a standard greeting.

My thoughts raced through my mind in what seemed to be an eternity of time. Maybe I was reading too much into this. Still, I wondered whether it was too late for me to just bolt out his office door. Then I wondered whether I had thought that question *out loud*. I did that sometimes. I glanced at Dr. Bull. Nothing. Luckily I had not. This time I had contained my thoughts.

I steeled my resolve. I was committed. I was going to do this—come hell or high water. I reached for the back of the chair sitting in front of his desk and pulled it back. I realized how telling this was. I had just signaled Dr. Bull that I wanted to be as far away from him as possible during this conversation. No doubt this was true. He just stared at me, motionless. He missed nothing. I noticed how dark the room was. It was cold. I think it was cold. I know there were goose bumps.

"I just wanted to discuss things with you," I started.
Nothing.

"Actually, I wanted to apologize." My voice quivered and trailed off at the end.

Nuts, I thought to myself, *did I really just do that?*

Nothing. Even the word *apologize* triggered no response. This was going to be ugly.

I went on. "I wanted to tell you how sorry I was that things have gotten so difficult between us. I also wanted you to know that I recognize that this is *my* fault. I started this and I am to blame for things getting so bad. I really am sorry that I have been such a creep to you."

Nothing. His expression never changed. He did not even shift in his seat. I decided to go for it. "I have been unfair and self-centered in my dealings with you. I have been very wrong and very mean and I hope you will forgive me."

This was a huge step for me. I held nothing back.

I suddenly realized that my entire apology had been spoken with my head down, staring at my hands in my lap. I looked up. He was staring at me and his eyes were looking right through mine! Dr. Bull was trying to read my intentions. *Whoa! This is like dealing with an alien being. He is trying to read my thoughts!* I realized that this is why I had been staring down when I apologized. *He was trying to read my heart—and he wanted my soul! He was from another dimension and he wanted control of my mind!* Still nothing registered on his face. He was a cold customer.

I decided to go for the total commitment that my Savior had shown on the cross and that I knew He expected of me. I wanted Dr. Bull to know that this was not just about asking forgiveness for past offenses, it was also about permanently and completely changing the future course of our relationship. This was a course reversal and I wanted him to know it.

I began slowly, "I also want you to know that I will try as hard as I can to never *jack* with you again. If you ever hear about bad things being said about you, I will never be the source." I silently asked for God's strength to not trip over this promise. I knew it would be tough, but I also knew that it was God's will.

I continued, "I am human and I will screw things up in the future. I am asking for you to forgive me and count on the fact that I will make this right."

Dr. Bull shifted—ever so slightly, but there *was* movement. And yet the expression on his face never changed. He just stared right through me now as before—as if I weren't even there.

And then he nodded. That was all. He never said a word. He just nodded. He didn't admit to any part in the situation or to any contribution to the problem. It was clear that in his mind, I was in fact totally the problem and could not be trusted. This was clearly going to be—just as I had already been convinced—a one-sided covenant. Dr. Bull offered nothing and agreed to nothing.

Silence followed. Just silence—a long, drawn-out, awkward silence.

I knew that I could expect nothing more. This conversation was over.

But, this was totally okay.

Let us therefore make every effort to do what leads to peace and to mutual edification. (Romans 14:19, NIV)

This was not about me—or even about Dr. Bull—this was about Jesus Christ. My Savior had given the commands in His Holy Word and I wanted very badly to try to follow them. I didn't want just a passing grade; I wanted an A+. I didn't want to just please Jesus; I wanted to make Him rock back on His heels in pure joy. I didn't just want to just trust Jesus a little bit; I wanted to leap off of the precipice into my Savior's waiting arms. I was going for the gold. I knew, as I know now, that there were not any contingencies built into His commands to love our enemies. The covenant that I was entering into was not really between Dr. Bull and I. It was (and always is) between Jesus and I.

That covenant is very straightforward: I do what Jesus says to do and He takes care of everything else.

Awesome.

The more I thought about it, the more I realized that any such covenant must, by definition, be utterly one-sided, since I have no chance—in my strength alone—to do what my Savior asks anyway. Bankruptcy. That is a good word for it (God bless you, C.S. Lewis). The facts are quite clear. I need God's help on every part of this deal. And that is exactly what He offers to me—and to you.

When the awkward silence had become intolerable I stood up. I glanced at Dr. Bull one last time and said, "Thanks."

His eyes were unchanged. I pushed the chair back toward his desk and turned to walk right out of his office. They were the longest four steps of my life.

I was glad it was over. I was a little embarrassed—his response had not exactly been positive—but in my heart I was delighted with what I had just done. It felt very right.

I left Dr. Bull's office bound and determined to obey. I was determined to only say good things about Dr. Bull. I was determined to pray for Dr. Bull. I was determined to never contribute to any bad conversation in his regard. In fact, I was determined to *build him up* in any conversation where his name was mentioned.

Each of us should please his neighbor for his good, to build him up. (Romans 15:2, NIV)

Dr. Bull actually had many endearing qualities and it was quite easy to sway the conversation onto these things. I must say that God was faithful to help me in this endeavor—

I simply never could have done it on my own. I felt only sorrow that Dr. Bull refused to be my friend. But, from then on, in the operating room or any other venue where Dr. Bull's plight was discussed, I spoke up on his behalf. I raised him up. By God's unending mercy, I found myself praising Dr. Bull's good qualities. This had been so difficult to do before and was so easy now, by God's grace—but only after I humbled myself before God and before Dr. Bull.

Unfortunately, Dr. Bull remained completely unrepentant. It seems that God gives our enemies a choice also. Just like we have the choice to choose to love our enemies or not, our enemies have the choice to build peace or make war in response to a one-sided, gut-wrenching offer of surrender. Dr. Bull chose to make war. He stayed my enemy. He never smiled or said anything to me from then on. He continued to just walk past me without even lifting his eyes when we encountered each other in the hallways. To my knowledge, I never said anything but good things about him from then on. Nonetheless, our past history was such that he simply could not trust. He could not believe that I could ever be a friend, despite the fact that we had been friends before all this happened.

To make a long story short, Dr. Bull had chosen his own destiny. God struck with the intensity and finality that characterizes His warrior interventions in the Old Testament. I'm pretty sure He sent His *hornet*:

> *"'Then you crossed the Jordan and came to Jericho. The citizens of Jericho fought against you, as did also the Amorites, Perizzites, Canaanites, Hittites, Girgashites, Hivites and Jebusites, but I gave them into your hands. I sent the hornet ahead of you, which drove them out before you—also the two Amorite kings. You*

*did not do it with your own sword and bow.
(Joshua 24:11-12, NIV)*

Truly I did not do any of this by my *own sword and bow*. God was teaching me how truly weak I was when I ventured into battle without Him—and how truly strong He is when I get my ego out of the way and allow Him to go into the battle before me. If there is ever anyone that you want to stand back-to-back with in the throes of pitched battle, it is Jesus. Anyway, within months, Dr. Bull's operating room behavior caught up with him. I think the stress got to him. He had a lot of stored up anger. When he finally let go, it was ugly. Unfortunately, this time he aimed it at the chief of the division. Before I knew it, he was gone.

The LORD is a warrior (Exodus 15:3a, NIV)

God surely had a plan for Dr. Bull, but that plan did not include his continuing as a member of our division. Jesus had kept His promise and stepped right into the middle of the fight on my behalf. His first kept promise was that He would pour into my stubborn heart the vast quantities of grace that were obviously necessary to empower me to get out of His way! That was the first and certainly the most difficult of the skirmishes that took place in my heart. For me to be receptive to His suggestion that there was indeed a better way was unprecedented and represented an almost insurmountable obstacle. And yet His faithfulness was literally on parade in my life back then. He changed my heart. He promised that He would go into the battle with me if I would just do things His way and then—amazingly—*He* gave me the heart to do things His way. Jesus did it all, from start to finish. Only I know the depths my wretched heart had reached—and, therefore, how powerfully God had acted in my life. Only I know what a miracle this was. This was grace, pure grace.

My second major relational battle in the Valley of the Shadow of Death had ended. In it, God had clearly demonstrated my need for *real* battle experience. Sure, I had been moving consistently toward the gunfire in the cardiac operating room for years. I always had a real warrior attitude in regard to cardiac surgery. I felt battle tested and battle proven. But God wanted more. He wanted me to move toward the real heart of warfare in this life, *relational* conflict. He wanted me to move toward that conflict armed with the subservient, sacrificial love of utter surrender. This is the gospel of Jesus Christ and its actual application in my life was new stuff to me.

CHAPTER ELEVEN

Ambush in the Valley

I can't even begin to tell you how many times God has rescued me from that which can only be described as utter disaster in the operating room. Surely, it has been far too many times to recount. When we start talking disaster in the world of cardiac surgery, we are talking real disaster. We are talking about catastrophic times when all hope seemed to be lost. These were times when, based upon my training and experience, I believed there was very literally no chance that the person undergoing the cardiac surgical procedure was going to get through the operation alive. Zero chance.

These were times in the operating room when complication after complication piled up, one on top of the other, to an almost ridiculous level. These were times when everyone in the OR just looked at each other with looks of bewilderment and incredulity—as if they simply could not believe how bad things had gotten. These were times when the wheels were not just off the cart; the cart had flipped over and was somersaulting down the hill.

And then, in the midst of utter disaster, the dire situation had dramatically, or even not so dramatically, reversed by what every witness readily acknowledged was outright, undeniable, and near-cataclysmic divine intervention. I literally could write a whole book filled with nothing but these episodes—a book full of eyewitness accounts of the endless mercy of God displayed in the every-day episodes that fill the life of any heart surgeon.

A representative example occurred several weeks ago. I had volunteered to help one of my partners out of a bind by doing a complicated heart transplant on a day that I was not on call for transplants. My operative and academic schedules were very full that day. My secretary had pointed this out to me. She reminded me of how much pain my good deed had just sent in her direction. She had to reschedule my whole day—everything from elective coronary bypass surgery to research meetings.

On the other hand, my partner who was on transplant call that day had already had a fairly miserable week. He was feeling incredibly beat-up as a result of several recent unfavorable outcomes in similarly difficult cases. When the transplant coordinator called him about the available donor heart, she said he had just audibly moaned in pain over the phone. He had clearly reached a point that we all occasionally reach. He needed a rest from the staccato of pain bolts that were being so regularly served up on the heart failure service at our institution. I heard about the transplant by way of a cautiously inquiring phone call from the transplant coordinator and agreed to help. I heard the gunfire echoing through the Valley. By the grace of God, I moved toward it. My partner did not even try to hide his relief. He was fried.

I was actually feeling pretty good about the fact that I had gotten out of the way and let Jesus formulate my response when the gunfire reverberated through the Valley. As a result, I was feeling confident as I walked into the operating room that day. In the back of my mind I remembered all the times God had so blatantly and unabashedly honored similar decisions of mine. I expected to feel His palpable Presence during the difficulty that one can reasonably expect when one sews a new heart into a critically ill patient. I'm not saying I didn't expect it to be challenging. Most are. But I honestly expected things to go well.

In this case, however, it was simply not going to go down that way. In God's perfect sovereignty, He decided that after I had slogged through this mess of a transplant procedure, the new donor heart that I had just sewn in was simply not going to work. We had overcome countless challenges during the procedure and I felt things had, by the grace of God, gone quite well. All of the suture anastomoses had been completed and there was no bleeding. The donor heart had been reperfused within a reasonably short time. When it was finally time to wean the patient off of the bypass pump and let the new transplanted heart take over the recipient's circulation, everything appeared to be just fine. Instead of jumping up and immediately resuming its vigorous pumping activity, however, the donor heart just laid there like a little puddle of soft muscle. We tried every technique and trick among the vast array of those available in an experienced cardiac transplant facility. The heart simply did not respond. Our patient was in big trouble.

Unfortunately, this sort of thing happens not uncommonly in the world of heart transplantation. It even has a name: *primary graft dysfunction*. As we have discussed, there are many variables in donor heart evaluation and procurement, all of which cannot always be controlled. Sometimes the hearts just don't work. After exhausting all possible resources, we had to resign ourselves to the fact that this donor heart was just not yet ready to handle the load of supporting our unfortunate patient's circulatory needs. We were therefore forced to support the patient's circulation using a very invasive mechanical pump to take over the work of the failed heart. This support, called ECMO (extracorporeal membrane oxygenator) support, is used only as a last ditch rescue option.

Needless to say, I was distraught over my patient's plight. My thoughts nonetheless stayed focused upon the mercy and provision of God. As I look back on my years as a cardiac surgeon with the perfect 20/20 vision of hindsight, I can honestly acknowledge that things have always just seemed to *work out*. Surely in my early days as a heart surgeon, surgical disasters like this one were reason for much angst. But over time I began to understand—even in the middle of the mess—that by the grace of God, *it was going to be okay*. In fact, that became a motto for me back then. I used to say it frequently in the operating room when I found myself in the middle of a fight that I was losing.

Things are going to be okay.

I knew it then—and certainly I know it now—not only because of the revelation of the written word of God, but also because of my years of experiencing the hands-on, day-to-day mercy of God. I am not saying that every one of my patients survived to live a normal life after I operated on them. I am just saying that when I look back in hindsight, I can see that God had a plan and was at work in every situation. God is ever faithful and despite my feelings at the time, I now acknowledge that He was right there in the middle of things every single time.

Because of this real life experience, I have hope in every disaster. I know that if God is there, which He always is, then *things are going to be okay*. How can it be any other way? With this knowledge, I have joy in the middle of the fight that I simply never experienced in my very early days as a heart surgeon. I have peace that is founded in the knowledge that God's heart for us is good. The word of God says it and my years of cardiac surgery have proven it.

I am not saying that it is always *easy* either. This is especially true when I'm knee-deep in the fury of the fight.

As we have discussed, at times it has been very long, very tiring, very difficult, and very stressful. I can't even begin to number the times I have walked out of the operating room mentally, physically, and emotionally spent after a 10-12 hour ordeal in what can only be described as an operative slugfest. There is pain, anxiety, and injury abounding in these daily battles that God sends into each of our lives. And several weeks ago in the middle of all of this transplant misery, I had indeed cried out to the Lord in my heart in a fashion that would have made Jeremiah wince. I had waited and waited for that last minute save at which our awesome God is so very good.

Indeed, I had been in almost continual prayer during and following that transplant procedure. The Holy Spirit was faithful to keep my mind focused on the only true source of rescue. In this, I had indeed experienced the hope and joy and peace that are available in the knowledge of the attributes of God.

And still I felt very alone.

I was palpably experiencing the absence of God's intervention despite the fact that I knew then what I know now—that He was and is so very close. In fact, I am confident that He is closest when I think He is not there, when I cannot feel His presence at all.

So, in the middle of that very special brand of desolation that is unique to the world of cardiac transplantation, I did what I always do when God's rescuing intervention is absent or delayed. I just kept plowing forward through the surgical procedure. I did what I know how to do. I did what years of standing at my patient's side had ingrained as reflex. I just put my head down and kept sewing. I put one surgical foot in front of the other and kept the procedure on a path that *could* end in success. I counted on

God for the *exit strategy*—and I just kept marching forward. I kept on working even as the complications piled up like cordwood around me. I kept on working and praying instead of fretting, yelling, and blaming like I had done so routinely in the early days.

I think that this—continuing to move forward while trusting God for the outcome—is all that God asks of us in these difficult situations. I was overwhelmed with the feeling that what I was doing was honoring and bringing glory to God despite the fact that it was not going well—and, honestly, I expected Him to show up at the end of that long day leading the cavalry. But that day would not end with rescue—and still I know that God's awesome purpose ruled in that operating room.

My other ever-present thought today—now that the operative dust has settled a bit—is of the complete and absolute sovereignty of God. He is God. I am not. He is in charge. I am not. He has true wisdom. I have a cheap worldly imitation of true wisdom. I am so glad that I am not in charge. I am so glad that I can so completely rely upon Him. I find immeasurable peace in this: I know that Jesus has our perfect eternal wellbeing as His number one goal—and that I, in my great wisdom, have only messed things up every time I have *taken charge*. Even though my patient was still in a world of hurt after her cardiac transplant procedure, I knew that God was there by her bedside. I knew that He was watching very closely and that He had a plan.

We waited and waited for that heart to recover. For the next three days following her surgery, she remained fully supported on the ECMO mechanical support system that we implanted the day of her transplant. Being on ECMO is almost exactly like being on cardiopulmonary bypass, which I have previously described in detail. We had a large venous return line in her right atrium that drained blood into the blood pump that sat next to her bedside. The venous blood was oxygenated by the membrane oxygenator and then propelled by the centrifugal pump back into her body via a plastic cannula placed in her ascending aorta.

We have several alternatives when it comes to mechanical support immediately following a failed heart transplant. I chose ECMO support that day because I felt that it offered the best chance of keeping my patient alive for the short-term *wait-and-see* period with the lowest risk of complications. The *wait-and-see* terminology refers to the fact that we did not know whether the contractile injury of the donor heart was just a temporary problem or whether the heart muscle had suffered a devastating irreversible injury. Either is possible when we procure, preserve, and transport a donor heart for transplantation since the procurement process for a donor heart can be quite complicated with many uncontrolled variables. It requires that we administer cold preservation solution to arrest the heart in the donor procurement operating room, pack it in ice, and transport it across the country to the recipient operating room. There are many opportunities for things to go wrong.

Our initial inclination at the time of the transplant was that it was the former, a temporary *reversible* injury. We felt this way because the heart did not *look* that bad. It had not developed the *stone heart* configuration of a severely injured heart. In such cases, the heart contracts into a hard little ball—thus the term *stone heart*. This is always irreversible and when this is observed, your recipient is in big trouble. Fortunately, this is very rare.

My hope on the day of the transplant procedure was that the donor heart injury was just a temporary *stunning* of the myocardium and that its contractile recovery would return the next day. A temporary, recoverable injury following donor heart procurement is not that unusual. My plan was, therefore, to let the mechanical pump do all the work of keeping her body alive until her donor heart recovered.

Nonetheless, in the back of my mind I knew that sometimes these hearts never get better. I recognized that the trade-off for the simplicity of placement and management that was offered by ECMO was countered by its limited support duration. Patients just don't do well for very long when supported by a non-pulsatile system with a long blood tubing circuit and strict anticoagulation requirements—all of which are characteristic of ECMO support. The general consensus is that adult patients *ideally* have 5-7 days on ECMO before the complications begin to outweigh the advantages.

As time progresses without donor heart recovery, the exit strategy of course changes. If no recovery is seen within the first several days on ECMO support, the patient is commonly relisted for another attempt at cardiac transplantation. If 5-7 days passes without improvement, the patient is returned to the operating room to replace the ECMO circuit with a long-term mechanical support option. In this patient's case, this would entail placement of a left ventricular assist device (LVAD) like Brandon's. If the injury was severe and also involved the right ventricle, then it might also require a right ventricular assist device (RVAD).

Once the long-term support devices have been placed, there are two possible exit strategies. The first would take place if the heart eventually recovered. Most commonly, if the heart is only *stunned*, recovery occurs within the first week. In fact, it is quite rare to see significant recovery of the donor heart if none has occurred within the first week. Nonetheless, if our patient's donor heart later recovered enough cardiac function to adequately support her, we would take her back to the operating room to remove the support devices. If her donor heart did not recover, she would, as mentioned, be relisted for re-transplantation as long as her course on the devices did not result in a complication that compromised her transplant candidacy.

Following the transplant, the method utilized to assess the donor heart functional recovery each day involved the placement of a special echocardiography probe down the esophagus. Transesophageal positioning of the echocardiographic ultrasonic transducer immediately behind the heart gives us the best view from which to assess its contractile function. Echocardiography can serve many critical diagnostic purposes. In addition to visualizing all of the cardiac valves quite well, it also allows real-time visualization of the contractile function of all regions of both ventricles.

The transesophageal echocardiography (TEE) performed on the first morning after the transplant procedure was not promising. It demonstrated little, if any, cardiac contractile recovery. That first morning, we in fact already knew that the heart had not recovered even before we placed the TEE probe. We had tried turning down the ECMO pump support, which left more of the venous blood return in the donor heart. Her heart was not even able to develop enough contractile pressure to produce a *bump* in the arterial pressure line tracing. A hard knot tightened in my throat as my disappointment manifested itself viscerally. This was a very bad prognostic sign. Not only was the contractile function not adequate to support our patient's circulation, this donor heart was doing nothing.

The echocardiography on day two revealed similar results. I cannot even begin to tell you how depressed I became that second morning when I viewed the poor contractility of her heart on the TEE. Her donor heart should have been recovering by then. I knew that the overwhelming majority of hearts that *would* recover showed at least some improvement by day two. Hers demonstrated none. It looked horrible.

Needless to say, I was crushed by the severity of donor heart contractile injury. I was having ongoing discussions with the patient's family to keep them informed of our progress and plan. I prepared them for the fact that we would need to take her back to the operating room for the big challenge of surgically exchanging the ECMO circuit for biventricular assist devices. I was still just moving forward, putting one foot in front of the other, trying to keep in step with whatever God's plan was going to be for this patient. Obviously His plan was not the same as mine. I put her in God's hands, but I cried out to Him for her—and also for me. I needed the strength of the cross of Christ to hang in there and make good decisions for my patient. It was a time of great distress, but I must admit that it was simultaneously an amazing time for me. I was in a desperate fight. Still, for some reason, my heart was at rest and I had a reassuring peace about my critically ill patient. I didn't know God's plan. I just knew I could trust Him and that my job was to just keep moving forward each day, placing one foot in front of the other.

I was in the operating room the morning of day three when the ICU staff and heart failure cardiologists performed the transesophageal echocardiography in the intensive care unit. They called me in the operating room with the results. The fact that they called me while I was in the middle of another cardiac surgical procedure was never a harbinger of good news. They knew I was focused on the care of another critically ill patient. I knew they would not interrupt without good reason. If the results were as expected, they would have told me after I finished my case. Indeed, they had called because there was very bad news. It is hard to believe that things could get any worse, but they had. It is like that sometimes when you move toward the gunfire in the Valley of the Shadow of Death.

Not only had there been no recovery of contractile function on day three, but, in addition, my transplanted patient's donor heart was now *full of clotted blood*. This was truly a disastrous turn of events. As disastrous as it was, it was not entirely unexpected. We had been concerned with this possibility. Whenever a heart shows little or no recovery, we have to divert almost all of the returning venous blood to the ECMO pump. This results in a relatively small amount of blood moving slowly through a weakly contracting heart. The interior surfaces of the heart are thus no longer being flushed with the normally large volume of blood. This results in stasis, or slow movement, of blood in the heart. This is a setup for the formation of intra-cardiac clot. Blood stasis leads to activation of the coagulation system—and that means clot formation.

This stasis of blood is not usually a problem in most applications of ECMO for cardiac support, because there is usually some residual left ventricular contractile function. In other words, the contractile function of the injured left ventricle is unable to support the full circulatory requirements of the body, but can still eject a portion of the blood. The ECMO circuit does the heavy lifting, but a decent amount of blood can still be circulated through the heart.

To prevent clot formation in these patients, therefore, we routinely and purposefully do not allow all of the returning blood to be drained into the ECMO circuit. This allows a significant amount of the returning venous blood to go into the heart and be ejected by the left ventricle. This keeps the left ventricular surfaces well washed by moving blood and helps prevent the areas of blood flow stasis that predispose the patient to intra-cardiac clot formation.

Unfortunately, this maneuver was not possible in this patient with the failed donor heart because her new heart was so severely injured that it was incapable of ejecting even small amounts of blood. When we tried to restrict the return of blood to her ECMO circuit, thereby leaving blood in her heart, her left ventricle just became dangerously distended.

The tendency toward clot formation in poorly ejecting hearts can be at least partially countered by the use of blood-thinners. These are routinely administered during ECMO support as long as bleeding is not occurring. Although this anticoagulation is aimed primarily at the prevention of clot formation on the artificial surfaces of the ECMO circuit, it also helps prevent intra-cardiac clot formation. Unfortunately, it had not been enough to prevent clot formation in my transplant patient's injured heart.

Like I said, this was incredibly bad news. In fact, many would consider this a death knell. First of all, if clot is forming in the presence of anticoagulation, the heart is really not moving at all. This means that there has been essentially no recovery. To be three days out with no recovery at all suggests that the heart has sustained a severe, unrecoverable injury. As discussed, the exit strategy at this point is beginning to change.

Further, the presence of clot inside of any cardiac chamber anytime predisposes the patient to a high risk of this clot being ejected to the vital organs of the body. This is called *embolization*. If the ventricle does develop enough contractile force to eject the clot into the ascending aorta, it will be carried by the ECMO blood stream in the patient's arterial system until it reaches a branch vessel that is too small to allow it to progress further. At that point, it can occlude the branch vessel thereby cutting off the blood flow to the vital organ it serves. This of course can be catastrophic. Once again, if the clot gets into the main blood stream it can go to the brain and cause a stroke, the kidneys and cause kidney failure, the liver and cause liver failure, an extremity and cause muscle death, and the intestine and cause intestinal gangrene. Needless to say, any one of these possibilities in a fresh post-transplant patient would be very bad news.

I must admit that I was horribly affected by this new turn of events. My spirit was crushed in empathy for my poor patient. I had really thought there would be a rescue. Instead, things were now spinning horribly out of control. After receiving this news from the operating room circulator nurse who had taken the phone call, I could do nothing but continue on with the coronary bypass surgery that I was performing. I tried to concentrate on making sure that everything went perfectly for the patient I was operating upon at the time. I did not want there to be two casualties associated with that phone call. Once again, I cried out to God. In the quiet recesses of my heart, I again asked Him for a miracle. Then I went back to work on my patient. It was all I could do. Later in the case when I was finishing up that procedure and things were quieter, my mind kept wandering back to my patient in the ICU. I kept trying to think and pray and praise my way through the various therapeutic alternatives that were available to deal with the new problem.

Just as I was finishing the chest closure on my CABG patient, the phone on the wall of the operating room rang again. It was one of the intensive care specialists from our ICU and he was frantic. He insisted on speaking to me. My assistants would finish the skin closure on my CABG patient, so I scrubbed out and took the phone. "What's happening up there?" I asked apprehensively.

"You're not going to believe this!" he yelled into my ear.

"What?" I asked, fearing the worst.

He was out of breath as he blurted back, "Not long after they finished the transesophageal echocardiography this morning, the nurses repositioned her slightly for bedsore prevention. When they did this, they noticed that *bumps* suddenly appeared in the patient's arterial line trace!"

"What?" I asked, "I thought you told me there was no improvement on the echo this morning!"

"There wasn't!" he shouted back. He was practically gasping for air. This had obviously been a very shocking turn of events. To say that this was unexpected is an extreme understatement.

Then he related the rest of the story "When I saw the bumps, I immediately called the cardiology fellow who had performed the transesophageal echocardiogram earlier in the morning. At first he refused to come back down to repeat the echo. He said he had just looked at the heart just two hours earlier and had clearly seen that the heart was not contracting and that it was filled with clot. He told me that there was simply no way that the heart had significantly recovered contractile function in that short of an interval!"

"Tell him to get himself and his echo machine in that ICU right now!" I yelled. I could not believe it.

"Already did!" he explained. "The fellow obviously thought about the implications and he came right down. I did not have to explain the potentially grave implications of increased contractile function in the presence of a heart full of clot. He was back down here in 15 minutes and repeated the TEE."

"Excellent!" I exclaimed in between his hurried statements.

He went on, "We were both stunned at what we saw. The walls of both the right and left ventricles were moving quite well. The clot appeared to still be present in both the upper (atrial) and lower (ventricular) chambers of the heart despite the fact that blood was swirling around it and being ejected by the heart. I couldn't believe it! The clot is still sitting there. It appears to be adherent to the walls despite their vigorous contraction."

"I can't believe it." I said. "This is a miracle." I was the first to voice what we were both thinking.

"This is amazing!" he yelled back.

"And potentially disastrous at the same time." I voiced my thoughts again.

He knew exactly to what I was referring. Even though the improved cardiac ejection represented by the bumps in the arterial line tracing suggested that the heart was recovering—which truly was very good news—it also had very grave implications.

"The heart could eject that huge amount of clot and occlude every blood vessel in her body, including those going to her brain." I said.

"No doubt," he responded. "That's why I interrupted your surgery. It's decision time."

"Get her ready for surgery," I snapped without a further thought.

"I'm on it!" He exclaimed as he hung up.

I turned to the circulating nurse in the operating room. "Tell the front desk that I need an operating room prepared *stat*." She had been listening to my conversation and had pieced the puzzle together from the cryptic words of my side of the telephone conversation. She was out the door before I could say another word.

This turn of events immediately solved my dilemma regarding therapeutic choices for my heart transplant patient. Now—by God's grace—my hand was forced. I loved it. It smacked of the distant and ever-so-faint sound of a cavalry bugle. A rescue was afoot in the Valley of the Shadow of Death.

> *Strengthen the feeble hands, steady the knees*
> *that give way; say to those with fearful hearts,*
> *"Be strong, do not fear; your God will come, he*
> *will come with vengeance; with divine*
> *retribution he will come to save you." (Isaiah*
> *35:3-4, NIV)*

I had never heard of anyone performing such a procedure, but my plan was to take her back to the operating room and take a first hand look at the function of the heart. If it was as good as suggested by the report I had received, then I would switch the patient's ECMO circuit for a regular cardiopulmonary bypass setup, stop the heart with cardioplegia, make an incision in the left atrium, extract the clot from both the left atrium and left ventricle, and then boldly try to wean her off of the cardiopulmonary bypass machine.

The reason that I had never heard of anyone attempting such a bold move was because we had never encountered such extensive intra-cardiac clot in a transplant patient on ECMO. Nonetheless, I was emboldened by what I felt was a clear indication of divine provision. This was not a time for hesitation. If she ejected the large volume of clot in her heart, she would die—plain and simple. I definitely also considered the option of just extracting the clot and leaving her on the ECMO circuit. After all, if her heart function had improved enough, we would then be able to keep the heart well flushed by reducing the ECMO flow and letting the donor heart do some ejecting. This was definitely an option if my visual inspection of the donor heart left me with doubts about its ability to support the patient's circulation.

And yet I felt emboldened to do more. I do not know from where my boldness came. I just felt as if this was not the time for hesitation or timidity. I felt that it was time for an *end run*. To expand the football analogy, this patient needed for us to bust past the linebackers and do a little *open field running*. The longer she stayed supported by the ECMO machine, the higher the risk that she would never make it through this ordeal. Unless the heart looked worse than I anticipated, it was time for us to cut and run.

Admittedly, there were significant risks with either of these choices. With the machine in place, she had *backup*. She had the reserve blood pumping capabilities of the machine should the donor heart begin to fail again. But, she also has the well-recognized risks of ECMO, with its many complications—such as the development of more clot in the heart. On the other hand, with the machine out, her little donor heart (that admittedly had been through a major ordeal) would have to carry the load alone. Tough call, but I felt it was time to get her off the machine if at all possible.

Once again, as is the case so many times in the world of cardiac surgery, I was reminded of the famous quote of Adlai Stevenson: "On the plains of hesitation lie the blackened bones of countless millions who at the dawn of victory lay down to rest, and resting died."

It was time to go. I felt that God had provided a pathway and it was time to unhesitatingly attack with everything that I had at my disposal. The facts surrounding her near miraculous recovery of cardiac contractile function following three long days of dismal contractile function bolstered me. I had been praying for and expecting a miracle. For three long days, I had kept one ear cocked, listening for the sound of the thundering hoof beats of the cavalry riding to the rescue. I was almost expecting to see Jesus in His glorious war chariot, the Shekinah Glory itself, circling above and supplying air cover for the rescue of my heart transplant recipient. It was another one of those Holy Spirit fly-by moments. It was going to be okay and somehow I knew it. Jesus had clearly gone before us into this battle and I knew He would also be our rear guard.

They were already setting up the operating room when I arrived at the patient's bedside. The family could sense the urgency in my voice as I explained the plan. Within 30 minutes, we were in the operating room. I was concerned about subjecting this healing heart to yet another period of ischemia (no blood flow), which would be required to extract the clot from the donor heart. Nonetheless, once I had sterilely prepped, draped, and reopened her chest, my fears were eased. Both the transesophageal echocardiography that we repeated in the operating room and the visual examination of the donor heart confirmed nearly normal cardiac function. Of course, this nearly normal function was with the full support of the ECMO circuit. Hearts can look remarkably normal when they do not have to do all the work of ejecting blood against a normal systemic blood pressure. The real test would come when the clot was extracted and I could then proceed to try to wean her from the bypass machine.

The clot extraction went well. The two large clots were easily removed intact and we carefully examined every aspect of the inside of the heart to make sure that no fragments of the clot were left behind. The left atrial clot had been attached to the left atrial suture line that connected the donor left atrium to the recipient left atrium. The formation of clot on exposed suture lines after cardiac transplantation is a well-recognized possibility. The left ventricular clot was attached to the parachute-like support structure of the mitral valve—the chordae tendinea. After extracting the clots, we closed up the heart, rested her for about 30 minutes on full cardiopulmonary bypass support, and attempted to wean her from the heart-lung machine.

I was praising God near continually. I had gotten into a habit of trying to maintain as much continual praise as possible while in the operating room. Praise is the best prayer. It confirms my acceptance of God's will in this and in all situations. It confirms my recognition that His heart is good for me and for my patient. It confirms that I realize that everything that I have, know, can do, and believe in, is directly from Him. And it confirms that no matter how this particular day ends, when my life is over, it will end well for me. All of this is in His hands and not in mine. And how I praise Him for that!

As we have previously discussed, weaning the patient from the cardiopulmonary bypass machine is just the simple process of letting less of the returning venous blood be drained off into the heart-lung machine. This leaves more blood in the heart for it to pump. In hearts with borderline contractile function, this process progresses slowly until the cardiopulmonary bypass venous drainage cannula can be completely clamped and the donor heart is handling all of the returning venous blood. Needless to say, I took my time weaning this wounded donor heart. But I was amazed at what I saw. The donor heart sprang to life. The more blood we left in this miraculously rejuvenated donor heart, the more it perked up. By the time I finally put the clamp on the venous drainage cannula to divert all of her venous blood into her new heart, the blood pressure was 130/82 and the heart looked essentially normal.

Wow. I was speechless. I just stared at that heart and in my heart sang the praises of a merciful and compassionate God. The anesthesiologist confirmed with the transesophageal echocardiography that not only was the heart function normal, but there was no evidence of any residual clot in the heart. Everyone in the operating room that day knew they had witnessed something special.

With the odds stacked so heavily against us that day, I don't know how I had seen this coming—but I had. I had expected this blatant divine rescue and my heart simply rejoiced in the grace of God that filled the operating room that day. I also humbly recognized that even if this wonderful outcome had not occurred, I could still rejoice in the compassionate mercy of God. I don't know why God chose to bless my heart transplant lady—and to bless me—that day, but I do know that He did. I was as high as a kite when I walked out of that operating room that afternoon. And my patient went home with her new heart only ten very short days later.

CHAPTER TWELVE

Behind Enemy Lines

For a swaggering young buck looking to establish himself as a warrior, there is certainly no shortage of worthy opponents in the world of cardiac surgery. The Valley of the Shadow of Death is abundantly populated with outlaws like me. Indeed, I did not have to wait long for the old relational radar screen to light up with yet another impending *threat*. Although I was still reeling from the impact of my first two pivotal battles, I admit that I was still acting a bit like a young gunfighter looking to make a name for himself on the streets of Dodge City. Unfortunately, the change that God requests from us doesn't happen overnight.

Still, although I didn't really understand the mechanism behind God's intervention in the first two battles, I did know one thing for sure: in both, God had acted powerfully in my heart and palpably in my life. I was excited about this. I had felt His presence. Despite my tendency to still swagger a bit more than I should, I was again hungry for that feeling of a high-speed Holy Spirit flyby. I knew something incredible had happened that day when God's grace poured down and constrained me to humble myself before Dr. Bull.

It soon became readily apparent who would step forward as my next and most worthy adversary in the Valley of the Shadow of Death. I will call him Dr. Butkis. This encounter mirrored that with Dr. Bull in many respects. In fact, Dr. Bull, Dr. Butkis, and I all entered the division with a year or two of each other. We were all three very similar in our training, capabilities, and interests. I cannot imagine a milieu more likely to generate conflict than throwing three young cardiothoracic surgeons who had all just finished their training and all had academic aspirations into the competitive environment of a large university-based medical center. Needless to say, we did not fail to meet expectations.

Dr. Butkis was a good man. He really was. He had a good heart and I truly think his intentions were good. He worked at an adjacent hospital in our large university medical complex that was also staffed by members of our cardiothoracic division. His boss at that hospital was a nationally well-known surgeon with incredible influence throughout the medical center. I knew Dr. Butkis was continually on the defensive from attacks that came primarily from his own boss. His boss seemed to be at continual war with most of the members of the division that worked at our hospital also, as he saw us as *the competition*. This was, of course, despite the fact that we were all members of the same university surgical group.

Needless to say, much plotting, scheming, and manipulation routinely took place behind the scenes—on both sides of the street that separated our hospitals. My colleagues and I at the main university hospital were repeatedly caught off guard by ambushes from our "friends" at the other smaller hospital—and visa versa. To say that Dr. Butkis worked in a hostile environment at the other hospital would be an understatement. He was continually caught in the crossfire between our hospitals. It was an outright toxic environment—and all too typical of the Valley of the Shadow of Death.

Overall, I was pretty successful at flying below the radar and staying out of these fights. I just kept my head down, did my work, and avoided the conflicts. For the most part, so did Dr. Butkis. Most of the divisional interpersonal battles were fought at much higher levels than ours and were noteworthy for their occasional outright viciousness. Eventually and despite our best efforts, the fallout from one of these skirmishes nonetheless pitted Dr. Butkis and I against each other. I honestly don't think either of us saw it coming.

Dr. Butkis's boss at the other hospital—we will call him Dr. King—had performed a routine cardiac surgical procedure upon a patient who unfortunately had developed the most devastating of complications. The patient had been admitted for an elective operation for garden-variety atherosclerotic occlusive disease of his coronary arteries. Once again, the coronary arteries are the small and yet vitally important arteries on the surface of the heart that are the conduits for the blood flow that meets the high metabolic needs of the vigorously and continually contracting heart muscle.

There are two high-risk, invasive, and yet very commonly employed solutions to the cholesterol plaque that blocks the coronary arteries of so many Americans. The most common solution is the trans-catheter placement of tiny metal *stents* that are balloon-inflated inside the arterial blockages to hold them open. These coronary stents are mounted on tiny balloons on the tips of catheters that are passed up to the heart vessels from the femoral (leg) or arm (radial) arteries. They are passed through the branches of the coronary arterial system until they reach the blockage. The balloon is then inflated thereby pinning open the walls of the blockage with the metal stent.

This stent procedure is much less invasive than the well-known coronary artery bypass procedure, or *CABG*, which involves making an incision in the chest to operate on the heart directly. A CABG procedure most commonly starts with the surgeon splitting the patient's breastbone with a handheld reciprocating band saw. The thin sac that surrounds the heart, the pericardium, is then opened and the heart exposed. This gives direct access for the surgeon to place the tiny bypass grafts that will serve as new alternate routes for the blood flow by simply *bypassing* the coronary blockage and perfusing the distal heart muscle with a vigorous supply of blood.

These new blood flow conduits that serve as bypass grafts are provided by the body's so-called *extra* blood vessels, such as the left and right internal mammary arteries (LIMA, RIMA) from the inner chest wall, the radial arteries from the forearms, or the saphenous veins from the legs. The internal mammary artery is the best of all the bypass grafts. It is a small branch off of a larger blood vessel, the subclavian artery, and it runs parallel on either side down the full length of the breastbone. Its location on the inside of the chest wall between the ribs and the lungs make it easily surgically accessible. It is most often utilized as a bypass graft by leaving it connected proximally to the subclavian artery while the rest of the vessel is detached from the inside of the chest wall. The distal end of this artery is then swung down on a pedicle and its tip sewn beyond the blockage on the targeted coronary artery.

The LIMA is most commonly placed to the left anterior descending (LAD) coronary artery, arguably the most important of all of the coronary arteries. Blockages of this coronary artery have perhaps the most potentially devastating consequences and placement of the left internal mammary artery, the best of the bypass conduits, to the LAD is the perfect match. This is the most celebrated of all of the bypass grafts that we commonly construct. The LIMA is the bypass conduit that is most resistant to atherosclerosis and its use in specifically bypassing the LAD has been clearly demonstrated by many large studies to improve the patient's chances for a long life.

The next two most commonly used bypass conduits, the radial artery and saphenous vein grafts, are taken from other parts of the body as *free* (or completely detached) grafts and therefore must also have the proximal end of the vessel sewn to the ascending aorta. This proximal connection supplies a high-pressure source of blood for the graft. The other end of the conduit is sewn on the targeted coronary artery, once again, beyond the atherosclerotic blockage. This is all basically just plumbing—admittedly complicated plumbing—but still just plumbing. These extra blood vessels become the bypass grafts that are the new pipes through which the blood supply is rerouted around the atherosclerotic obstructions in the patient's *clogged* pipes.

The heart-lung machine is usually used to perform the work of the heart and the lungs while this heart revascularization is being completed. As its use in Mrs. Filander's and Brandon Brady's procedures demonstrated, this heart-lung machine can be used for any number of operations where the function of the heart or the lungs (or both) must be temporarily interrupted to perform needed heart or lung repairs or replacement. Nonetheless, cardiopulmonary bypass is not needed for all heart operations. Cardiac surgeons have cleverly devised techniques to avoid some of the complications of the heart-lung machine by doing the heart surgery without it. The most common is called *off pump* coronary artery bypass graft surgery (or OPCAB), which uses special techniques, retractors, and cardiac immobilizers to allow the procedure to be done while the heart is beating and the lungs are inflating (without the heart-lung machine). During these procedures, the heart and lungs must continue to do their job *while* they are being operated upon.

Getting back to our story, things had not gone well in the "routine" heart surgery that Dr. King had performed. As sometimes happens in the world of cardiac surgery, things had been anything but routine. The patient had been placed on the heart-lung machine and the coronary artery bypass grafts had been sewn into place. When it came time to wean the patient off of the heart-lung machine, however, the heart muscle was too weak to support the circulatory needs of the patient. The cardiac output and blood pressure were low and the heart became quite dilated with very poor contractile function.

When this happens in the course of elective heart surgery, the usual plan involves the placement of some sort of mechanical support. As discussed, we use mechanical support only in a last ditch effort to keep the patient alive. The need to resort to mechanical support means that the surgeon and the anesthesiology team have maximally exploited all routine and heroic measures to get the heart to support the patient's circulation by itself. This means that intravenous medications to make the ailing heart beat stronger, such as adrenaline, will have already been started and an intra-aortic balloon pump will have been placed. The intra-aortic balloon pump is a machine that assists the pumping of the failing heart, but it will not perform the entire job of supporting the circulation.

Only when all of the heroic measures to strengthen and support the heart in this endeavor are exhausted, is it time to resort to mechanical support. Because of the dangerous nature of their inherent complications, the use of temporary electromechanical pumping machines truly defines the patient's plight as desperate. Unfortunately in the case of Dr. King's patient, both the right and left ventricles were failing and could no longer support their respective circulations. Without the use of mechanical support, Dr. King's patient would have died right there on the operating room table.

Two small, short-term ventricular assist devices (VADs) were placed, each being charged with taking up the slack for one of the two failing ventricles. Dr. King called Dr. Butkis in to place these devices, presumably since Dr. Butkis had more experience in this area. Placing these complex machines in this setting can get very ugly very quickly.

The configuration of these short-term assist devices is similar to that described previously for the heart-lung machine and for the placement of the long-term assist devices, such as that used in Brandon Brady's case. Placement of the short-term devices requires that plastic drainage tubes be placed in each of the collecting chambers for the respective ventricles: the right atrium for the right ventricle and the left atrium for the left ventricle. Placing these drainage tubes is relatively straightforward. A purse-string suture—circular in shape—is placed in the atrial wall, a hole is made in the middle of the circular suture, and the hollow plastic cannula is passed into the chamber. The purse-string is then cinched down to hold the inflow cannula in place and to prevent bleeding around the cannula. These cannulas channel the blood into their respective mechanical pumps with the blood being returned to the pulmonary artery (RVAD) and ascending aorta (LVAD) through two separate tubular Dacron grafts sewn to the side of the main pulmonary artery and ascending aorta, respectively.

These sutured connections between human and machine tend to bleed a lot because of the high pressures and oscillating movement of the pumps. Obviously, these cases can be challenging. Dr. King had another straightforward elective case to do that afternoon and he was ready to move on to it and let Dr. Butkis handle the VAD implants. Ultimately, the hope for this unfortunate patient was that his heart would heal and recover enough of its pumping capability to keep him alive on its own. If the heart recovered, no bridges had been burnt—the two machines could simply be removed during another relatively straightforward surgical procedure.

This was a long day for Dr. King's patient. The procedure, including both the CABG and the placement of biventricular assist devices, took over 9 hours. They did a great job and the patient got through the procedure and the predictably complicated early postoperative course.

Plan A, as mentioned, was to support the patient with these two devices (both of which together handled 100% of the blood pumping responsibilities of the heart) until the heart recovered enough contractile function to handle the job on its own. Unfortunately, this particular patient's heart never recovered. The patient remained completely dependent upon the two devices to stay alive.

When recovery does not occur, if the patient is deemed a suitable candidate for such advanced therapy, they can be listed (after a complex evaluation) for cardiac transplantation. As we have discussed, using the ventricular assist devices to support a patient until a suitable donor heart is obtained for transplantation is referred to as *bridging* to transplantation. This is a common technique that is utilized at most major medical centers.

As more time passed following that initial surgical procedure, it became obvious that the patient's heart was not going to recover. As expected, the surgical team requested that the patient be evaluated by our cardiac transplant service at the main hospital. This is precisely the point where my plan to avoid getting drawn into a conflict with Dr. Butkis or Dr. King began to fall apart. After all, it is impossible to continue to fly undetected beneath the radar when you are the surgical director of the cardiac transplantation service and their patient has no other options.

To make a long story short, the patient was rapidly evaluated and immediately listed for transplantation. He went to the bottom of the local transplant list because transplant priority back then was based primarily on the time accrued on the waiting list. Since I was the surgical director of the cardiac transplant service at the main teaching hospital, I had therefore become this unfortunate patient's *exit strategy*. Cardiac surgeons (and all physicians for that matter) are usually taught early in their training that every therapeutic plan for every patient must have an exit strategy. An exit strategy is the plan that moves the patient on to the next stage of their recovery (out from under the cardiac surgeon's care) and on to the rest of his or her life—whatever life that may be.

There is much practical utility in the clinical determination of exit strategies. They mandate that the patient's physician begin to address possible outcomes early in the course of a patient's illness. They require that the physician project, to the best of his or her ability, where initial therapeutic decisions are ultimately going to take the patient. The point is obvious in regard to cardiac surgery. If you are going to proceed with a cardiac operation on a patient, whether that operation is elective or emergent, the surgeon must play the tape forward to each of the possible outcomes.

This conversation must include both good and bad outcomes—both the likely and the unlikely. When the possible outcomes of the procedure have been addressed, the surgeon must devise a plan—an exit strategy—to move the patient along to the best possible exit strategy. There needs to be a visible light at the end of the tunnel. There needs to be a plan to get the patient out of the Valley of the Shadow of Death. With every patient, with every planned procedure, with every contingency, you must have an exit strategy. To enter into the surgical care of a patient without an exit strategy is like planning a raid to free captive hostages without including a plan to get them and the rescue team out of harm's way. The absence of an exit strategy turns a rescue mission into a suicide mission.

In the world of cardiac surgery where the patient's life is dependent upon a good cardiac surgical result, the *early* development of an exit strategy is critical. The lack of an exit strategy early in the patient's course increases the likelihood that you will paint yourself—and your patient—into a corner. You may find yourself having to deal with a dying patient with no good therapeutic alternatives—in other words, a nonexistent exit strategy. For example, the assumption that cardiac transplantation is an option in a patient who is not a candidate for cardiac transplantation would be considered a flaw in exit strategy management. As you can imagine, such a critical tactical error can lead to a huge clinical dilemma with patient, family, and medical caregivers all suffering the heartbreaking consequences.

The VADs that are in use today are more durable and allow for long-term support and the *destination* therapy option—where the patient lives the rest of his or her life on the device with no hope of transplantation. Back in those earlier days when Dr. Butkis placed two VADs in Dr. King's patient, however, VADs capable of such long-term support were under development, but not yet widely available. Thus, to have a person who is *not* a candidate for transplantation supported on devices that are only capable of temporary support leaves the patient with very limited therapeutic options—and no viable exit strategy.

Dr. King's patient serves as a perfect example of appropriate exit strategy management. In this patient's case, before Dr. King performed the original CABG procedure on this patient, he had VADs as one of several exit strategies. In other words, if the patient's procedure had gone as originally planned, the exit strategy would have been normal postoperative care and out-the-door. If things did not go as planned, which they obviously had not, the exit strategy for Dr. King was to call Dr. Butkis to put VADs in the patient. Then, in turn, Dr. Butkis needed a new exit strategy following the VAD procedure. After VAD placement, the possible outcomes considered are twofold. First, the patient's heart recovers and Dr. Butkis removes the VADs—and the patient goes back to routine postoperative care and the *out-the-door* exit strategy. The second possibility was that the patient's heart would not recover. This is what happened and this is where I became a part of this story. I was Dr. Butkis's exit strategy.

With Dr. Butkis's patient listed for transplantation, we then played the waiting game. This is usually the part of the transplantation ordeal with which patients and their families deal quite poorly. We do not have the luxury of having transplant donor hearts sitting on the shelf ready for use when the need arises. As we discussed previously, transplantation occurs only in the circumstances when an unfortunate donor suffers brain death without cessation of cardiac activity. This irreversible injury to the brain is most often due to an intracranial bleed, a stroke, anoxic injury, or trauma. Then the local organ procurement agency must obtain permission from the family, assess the donor for communicable diseases (such as AIDS or hepatitis), and make sure that the donor heart has normal contractile function—all prior to listing the donor patient as available for organ procurement. As soon as the organ procurement agency does its work and all of the organs that are suitable for transplantation are lined up with suitable donors, the donor OR time is scheduled. As previously discussed, all of the various organ procurement teams then assemble, sometimes from across the United States and Canada, to perform the procurement procedure.

For all practical purposes, in order to obtain a donor heart for Dr. Butkis's patient, we had to wait until the patients who were of similar size and blood group on the list ahead of him were all transplanted. Then we had to wait until another suitable donor of similar size, of compatible blood group, and with great cardiac function became available. This takes time.

Not long had passed, however, before Dr. Butkis's boss, Dr. King, came to the conclusion that we, the transplant team, had not been *trying hard enough* to quickly obtain a suitable donor heart for his patient. The patient was quite stable, actively rehabilitating, and regaining his strength while being supported by the devices. The family, whose expectations had always been somewhat overly optimistic, rapidly grew impatient. To state that they were not a happy group would be a sizable understatement.

It is hard to hold the family's impatience against them. This particular family had believed, after all, that his first operation would be *routine* with their loved one home in 5 days. To maintain such optimistic expectations on every case, as every heart surgeon can readily attest, is unrealistic in itself. As I mentioned, experienced heart surgeons don't consider any heart surgery to be *routine*. We have all had too many so-called *routine* cases that became anything but routine. All it takes is one small problem and suddenly the ship is taking on water. The next thing you know, the "pleasure cruise" upon which you thought you had booked safe passage is threatening to slide beneath the surface of the water.

Additionally, Dr. Butkis's boss was feeling considerable heat from the referring primary care physicians—who were also being pressured by the family of the involved patient. This pressure had the expected results. Dr. King was not subtle in making statements that suggested we didn't care about his patient as much as we cared about the other patients we had listed for transplantation at the main university hospital. This was, of course, complete nonsense. As director of the heart transplant program at that time, I was nonetheless the lightning rod for his comments.

I tried to reassure him. If a good quality heart of the right blood type and size became available—and was designated for his patient by the organ procurement agency—transplanting his patient would, because of the presence of the ventricular assist devices, be a top priority. I assured him that I just took the calls on the donor hearts as they came and delved them out to the patients for whom they were designated by blood type, size, accrued waiting list time, and acuity. Other than a tiny bit of leeway in certain rare situations, the actual availability of a donor heart for Dr. King's patient was out of my control.

Despite the barrage of academic gunfire—most of which seemed to be aimed at taunting me into a fight—I initially avoided conflict and things remained calm. Then, one unfortunate day, I was blindsided by an assault from Dr. Butkis that was clearly initiated by his boss. Actually, it was a roundabout stealth hit that was aimed at my boss (at the main teaching hospital) by his boss. The two bosses really disliked each other and covertly fought all the time. As mentioned previously, this level of animosity at the highest levels of leadership is certainly not unusual in the world of academic cardiac surgery. After all, the individuals who rise to the top of this academic fistfight—the *Chiefs* of cardiothoracic divisions—are, by definition, the very best of the very best pugilists. They are not just competitive; they are masters at tactical battle. In this battle, Dr. Butkis and I were merely pawns in their most recent power chess match. This firefight at the highest levels supplied the battlefield, the fierce academic backdrop, and the angry milieu in which Dr. Butkis and I had the pleasure of interacting every day.

As one might expect, the withering barrage of fire between the two chiefs inflicted considerable collateral damage. With the fire being poured on from above, our lower level battlefield also soon erupted in fire. A semi-fierce firefight developed between Dr. Butkis and myself. It was bound to happen. I had initially been able to avoid outright conflict, but rapidly found myself stumbling into the crossfire.

Don't get me wrong. I am not displacing blame onto Dr. Butkis. In fact, I have no doubt that the whole thing was my fault. Surely I knew exactly what was going on.

Nonetheless, it has always been incredibly difficult for me to remain disengaged with a firefight erupting all around me. I was, after all, still very much a warrior and I have always found it very hard to walk away from a taunt, let alone a full-fledged fight. And I was really tired of being blamed for things that were out of my control.

Anyway, I allowed myself to become a part of the fight and then, of course, made major contributions to it. When I look back upon this not-so-bright spot in my career, I am so embarrassed. I am also struck by the mercy and faithfulness of God. When He says He will be there, He will be there. He wasted no time in showing me that I had turned away from Him again in my interactions with the people that He had brought into my life.

Then, once again, God struck my heart with the stunning clarity of a lightning bolt across the midnight sky. By His abundant and continuing grace, my eyes were opened. It became clear to me that if things continued to accelerate on their projected trajectory, there would be serious consequences from this evolving fight. The two bosses were squaring off behind their two protégés. They were clearly playing us like the two low-level chess pieces that we were—and a fight of near Biblical proportions was about to occur. The current trajectory of this fight was one of escalation to levels that were clearly not in line with the goal of my sanctification.

Thankfully, the Lord was, as always, generous and forgiving. He reminded me that I was only going to get hurt by this. He also softened my heart and reminded me of that which I knew before my warrior mentality had blinded me: Dr. Butkis was not a bad guy. He and I had been friends before—good friends. In the midst of this evolving fight,

God reminded me that I had once again lost sight of the big picture.

Then it happened again.

Just like in the previous battle, and once again by God's grace, a feeling of *what had to be done* swept over me like a tidal wave.

In retrospect the solution seems so obvious. But it was still anything but obvious to me back then. In fact, it was preposterous. I remained blinded by my sin, and without the lightning bolt, I never would have figured this out on my own.

God gently reminded me that I once again had the power to stop this fight. This is His undeniable truth in all such contentious circumstances. It takes two to fight. If one party refuses to fight, there is no fight. The fight is over just that quickly. I knew that I could end this fight before it even happened.

Once again, the path was crystal clear and there was only one. I had to go over there and humble myself in Dr. Butkis's office and admit my transgressions and contributions to the problem. I had to unconditionally apologize. I knew in my heart—and I praise God for this—that going over and sitting down in his office and trying to travel the middle ground, to *rationalize* and *compromise*, was doomed to failure—as it always is.

In my life, attempts to travel this middle ground of lukewarm commitment to God's clear request for total commitment have always spiraled into more hurt feelings and more conflict. The so-called *middle ground* is always a position of compromise. It is like balancing on a steep mountain peak with only the two opposite slippery slopes for footing. Picture that. It never works. The middle ground never stays middle for long. I am convinced that God designed it that way because that choice—of partial and incomplete commitment to His plan of total commitment—is never that which He desires in our life.

To drive home this point, God gave us the perfect example of total commitment. In fact, God *became* the perfect example of total commitment. He took on the flesh of mankind to show us the way by perfect example. With Jesus—as He demonstrated on the cross—it is and always has been *all or nothing*. It is black and white. Jesus left no doubt available to us in this regard: it is a full commitment or no commitment because anything less than a full commitment is, in fact, no commitment at all.

I was overwhelmed by this eternal truth. Anything short of complete surrender—completely humbling myself before Dr. Butkis—was going to fail. Further still, I knew that I had absolutely nothing to lose here by humbling myself before Dr. Butkis.

After all, would God abandon me if, in the Name of His Son Jesus, I totally humbled myself before an enemy?

Is there any possibility that God would be sitting up there on His throne, scratching His head, and wondering what had gotten into me? *Boy what a stupid cardiac surgeon. I thought I gave him more brains than that. I think that am just going to let Him get plastered in this fight for doing such a stupid thing.*

No chance.

The written words of God (especially the clear and direct teachings of Jesus Christ Himself) repeatedly admonish us to humble ourselves before our enemies.

"But I tell you who hear me: Love your enemies, do good to those who hate you, bless those who curse you, pray for those who mistreat you. If someone strikes you on one

cheek, turn to him the other also. If someone takes your cloak, do not stop him from taking your tunic. (Luke 6:27-29, NIV)

Jesus told us to love and forgive them just as we have been loved and forgiven. And then He became our perfect example. He humbled Himself to the point of being crucified for the salvation of the very individuals who have gone to great lengths to designate themselves as His enemies—you and I.

Nope, I reasoned, God would surely go before me into this battle. I was to turn toward the gunfire and fight this fight the hard way: like God wanted me to fight it. I knew that He would stand back-to-back with me in this fight if I obeyed and did it His way. God would never abandon me, I reasoned, on the very battlefield to which He had sent me in the first place. God would never abandon anyone who humbled himself and called upon His holy Name.

The LORD sustains the humble but casts the wicked to the ground. (Psalm 147:6, NIV)

For the LORD takes delight in his people; he crowns the humble with salvation. (Psalm 149:4, NIV)

Despite my earlier success with Dr. Bull, this was still an utterly outrageous line of thought for an experienced cardiac surgical warrior like myself. Surely, it is one thing to be struck by the "logic" of these things during your quiet time in the morning while reading the Bible—and altogether another thing to actually go out and do it in the real world. After all, I was pretty sure that the rest of the cardiac surgeons in the world had not gotten this same message that morning over coffee and Bible study. To them, it was battle as usual.

I tell you this as a warning. As easy as it is to write these words, the memories of the reality of that morning testify in stark clarity to the 180-degree difference between God's plan and the world's plan, God's reality and the *reality* that has pervaded our every breath since our birth. Although I speak boldly as I write these words, I was utterly terrified that morning.

After all, God's plan called for me to go into enemy territory. God's plan called for me to surrender. God's plan called for me to move toward what I expected to be a maelstrom of gunfire—all aimed directly at me. My fear of the consequences led to hesitation. My hesitation was just the opening the real enemy—my rationalizing self-life—wanted.

Surrender? No chance. He had attacked me! Why should I be the one to give in?

All of my worldly training kicked in with full intensity.

Win by surrendering? That's preposterous. This is the world of cardiac surgery. You can't show weakness. It is a world of swagger and boasting where any evidence of weakness most certainly sends a signal to the enemy—a signal to attack!

All of the world's usual scripts were swirling through my mind that morning. Satan was busy hammering away at me by bringing up the fears that he had taught me—with which he had imprisoned me—for my entire life.

Nonetheless, along with this plan came an incredible feeling that countered my fear. Once again, I really don't know how to describe it. I had felt it before—most recently before my encounter with Dr. Bull—and by God's grace I have felt it many times since. It is so hard to describe—it was almost like a feeling of victory, only *before* the battle. It was warmth, comfort, and peace—and simultaneously it was also battle. And yet it was also victory. It was irrational. It was victory by surrendering. It made no sense and yet somehow it made all the sense in the world. I was overwhelmed with peace because despite the fact that it flew in the face of all *rational* thought, this plan felt very, very right. It felt like truth. It felt like really bright light in the depth of palpable darkness. Despite the anticipated pain of the encounter ahead of me, it was a feeling that surrender was exactly what God wanted from me—and that in surrender was an eternity of victory.

I could sense a close-in, low-level Holy Spirit fly-by heading straight toward me.

As a result of these feelings, once again, I almost rushed to make this happen. Every time I thought about what I was about to do, I was very literally giddy. Like I said, the feeling was simply irrational. Yet somehow the ferocious warrior in me knew that this was precisely the correct battle plan. I felt like this might have been another of the very few times in my life when I knew exactly what God wanted me to do—and I was ecstatic. There was a quiet inner voice encouraging me and whispering that this "battle" plan was not just okay, it was, indeed, very right. Logically, I knew it was right because I knew in my heart that it mirrored my Savior's battle plan. It was the very same one that He had used on the cross of Calvary. This was fighting a fight while not depending upon the strength of horses, chariots, or warrior's bow, but upon the Spirit of the Living God.

> *So he said to me, "This is the word of the LORD to Zerubbabel: 'Not by might nor by power, but by my Spirit,' says the LORD Almighty.* (Zechariah 4:6, NIV)

I knew then, in that precise moment in time on that field of battle with the enemy lying in wait for me, that I was privy to nothing less than the thoughts and wishes and will of Almighty God in my life.

And there is nothing like it.

I look back on that day and I know that my faithful Savior Jesus once again stood very close to me. I felt His presence and it was overwhelming. Just as before, this was a feeling that struck to the very core of my being. It resonated throughout my heart. This was definitely the kind of feeling that makes you want to move in that direction again. This was the sanctification process happening right before my very eyes. This was a step forward in my transformation by the renewal of my mind—and all occurring by Jesus resident in my heart. It was palpable. I could feel it deep in my heart and it made my bones ache with anticipation. It was almost like a very troubling question, from deep in my heart, had been answered.

God's Holy Spirit immediately went to work on me in preparation for battle. I asked for God's strength and for God's wisdom to allow me to identify, acknowledge, and own the very significant contributions that I had made to the contentious nature of this confrontation. Unlike before, I actually *wanted* to know the fullness of how I had contributed to the problem. I also asked God to help me truly forgive Dr. Butkis while helping me to be truly repentant for my own transgressions. God did not let me down. I knew I had been wrong. That which I had never been able to do—acknowledge my contributions to the escalation of a simple disagreement into a full-fledged fight—I was now doing in a fashion that scared me. Honestly, I was almost afraid of what was going on inside me.

A longing fulfilled is sweet to the soul. (Proverbs 13:19, NIV)

I genuinely repented before God. And along with that repentance came the recognition that it was now time to repent before man. I knew that this chance to worship God—in a manner actually prescribed by God—would be utterly incomplete without the *repenting before man* part. My heart was ready for this battle.

> *He shall say: "Hear, O Israel, today you are going into battle against your enemies. Do not be fainthearted or afraid; do not be terrified or give way to panic before them.* **For the LORD your God is the one who goes with you to fight for you against your enemies to give you victory."** *(Deuteronomy 20:3-4, NIV; emphasis added)*

Once again, I couldn't get into Dr. Butkis's office fast enough. I made the phone call to tell him I was coming over. As I hung up the phone, however, the icy cold fingers of reality once again overwhelmed my initial exuberance. This was, after all, a foray deep into enemy territory. Dr. Butkis's office was right next to his boss's office—and that was *ground zero*. Their entire office very literally went to *DEFCON 1* when they heard that I had called and that I was on my way over to meet with Dr. Butkis. This simply was not done. No one invaded *the sanctuary*. If there was to be a fight, it was to occur on a designated battlefield, not in the sanctuary of their academic offices. Showdowns like this always took place in the traditionally neutral venues like a division conference room—the *OK Corral* of the academic cardiac surgeon.

That analogy was closer to the truth than I appreciated at the time. Dr. King's office staff was in an uproar and the impending encounter was being billed as an Old West style shootout. Apparently my call had triggered a frenzy of chatter and activity. I'm sure that before I got there they had all prepared for what they figured was going to be a knock-down, drag-out, fists-flying, furious, screaming-and-yelling fight. They were probably selling tickets.

In sharp contrast to what I expected, when I actually walked through the office door I was met by utter silence. I was immediately ushered into Dr. Butkis's inner sanctuary by his secretary. She kept her head down and her eyes averted. She said nothing. She moved quickly like an innocent bystander—trying to remain calm. She had obviously been in these situations before. I'm sure she was terrified with the possibility that she would become collateral damage in a fight she wanted nothing to do with. She promptly exited, shutting the door behind her.

I can still picture the scene in my mind. When I finally turned and looked at Dr. Butkis I was met by a stone cold stare. He was an imposing figure, a large man with thick bones. His furrowed brow almost completely hid his narrowed eyes. Dr. Butkis was sitting behind his desk in a position of pure defense. He was leaning back in his chair with his arms folded across his chest.

I broke the silence, "Thanks for seeing me so quickly."

He nodded, but said nothing.

I wasted no time. I went right for the jugular. "I just wanted to discuss our situation. It seems to be getting kind of ugly."

I saw the muscles of his jaw tighten. He said nothing. His expression was blank. It was like we were in a high-stakes poker game. This was going to be difficult.

Then, by the grace of God, my mind flooded with the things that I had done wrong. I began to speak my thoughts, "I wanted to apologize for the way that I have handled the discussions surrounding your VAD patient. I have made countless unfair and incorrect assumptions. As a direct result, I have unfairly vented my anger in your direction on several occasions. I have fostered a malignant climate that is not conducive to the communication that is so very necessary in these contentious situations. The miscommunication that has resulted is 100% my fault."

I was on a roll. The words were just rolling out. Best of all, I knew that I was not the author of my words. Jesus was speaking, not me. This was Jesus in my heart. I knew I personally had no ability to so openly apologize to an enemy.

This may sound a little weird, but I was invigorated by the candid and humble nature of my words. Wow. I was sitting there actually doing something of which I knew I was incapable.

I laid it all out on the table. "I want you to know that I recognize that in almost every situation, I have been pouring gasoline on the fire instead of putting it out. I want you to know that I am truly sorry for the way that I have acted."

I wanted him to know that I assumed full responsibility for the whole mess. By God's grace, I left nothing on that field of battle. I did not hedge on anything. I told him that I was truly sorry for hurting him—and, most amazingly, I truly was.

I held nothing back. I surrendered completely. I jumped off the precipice. I took a daring, fully unsupported, no-safety-net jump into empty dark space, relying only on the arms of Jesus to catch me. I asked nothing in return from Dr. Butkis—except for his forgiveness. I was completely disarmed and as vulnerable as I could be.

So the king gave the order, and they brought Daniel and threw him into the lions' den. The

*king said to Daniel, "May your God, whom you
serve continually, rescue you!" (Daniel 6:16,
NIV)*

I was alone in the lion's den with no weapons, no
armor, and no escape plan. But as bad as things were at that
moment, they were about to get worse. Just at my most
vulnerable moment, boom! Right in the middle of my
confession, the office door swings open and in walks Dr.
Butkis's boss, Dr. King—suddenly and completely
unannounced! He was a powerful man, a very imposing
figure.

Oh, great, another lion joins the feast.

Dr. King had obviously been told of the confrontation
in Dr. Butkis's office and had come in response. Like I said,
the office staff was put into a frenzy by my brash foray into
enemy territory.

Dr. King walked boldly into the office and took a seat
near Dr. Butkis. Needless to say, he was loaded for bear. It
was immediately obvious that he was looking to pick a fight.
He loved a good fight. He was the alpha-male at this hospital
for good reason. The pack's territory had been invaded. The
pack had been threatened. I could tell that he was just
looking for an excuse to verbally pound me to a pulp. I could
tell from the look on his face that he was hungry and just
waiting for the right word from me to trigger the assault. It
startled me, but somehow I felt immediately strengthened by
God and managed to continue.

*"When you are brought before synagogues,
rulers and authorities, do not worry about how
you will defend yourselves or what you will say,
**for the Holy Spirit will teach you at that time
what you should say.**" (Luke 12:11-12, NIV;
emphasis added)*

As I look back on that moment, I cannot help but be reminded of the perfection of the timing of God's grace. Instead of cowering in silent fear, I turned directly toward Dr. King. By God's strength alone I went on the attack. I rapidly repeated the main confession points to Dr. King, apologizing to Dr. Butkis in front of him and then apologizing to him also. I made sure that he knew that I was there on my own volition and that I had only one purpose to my visit. I wanted to end this fight by removing one of the combatants—me! I wanted to surrender.

So, I surrendered to him too.

Needless to say, they were both caught completely off guard by my confession. They had obviously never suffered through such a brazen and ruthless attack. I had them both on the ropes by the audacious nature of my assault. They were speechless—literally speechless. They both just sat there staring at me with their mouths open. In my mind's eye, I can still see every detail of the scene in that office—just as if it happened today.

I sensed weakness. I smelled fear. I tasted blood in the water. The warrior inside of me reminded me of precisely what I should do when the battle swayed so definitively in my favor.

I attacked.

I attacked again and this time I was ruthless. I hit them with the old one-two punch. "I want you both to know that I am completely committed to making sure that this conflict never happens again. I promise to be open to your communication at any time and I am asking you to forgive me and give me the benefit of doubt in future situations."

The smell of victory filled my nostrils and I continued, "I need you to be tolerant of me if my first response is a poor one—I'm human after all! I need you to allow me to correct any mistakes I make. I am asking nothing of you except your forgiveness. I am telling you that I am sorry and I am asking you to let me prove it to you."

This time it was I who made the commitment entirely one-sided. I had learned from my encounter with Dr. Bull. It would be I who would voluntarily give everything and ask nothing in return.

You could have heard a pin drop. They both just sat there. They had looks of astonishment on their faces. Their mouths were closed now (after having picked their jaws up off the floor).

My God sent his angel, and he shut the mouths
of the lions. (Daniel 6:22, NIV)

Then, unbelievably, Dr. Butkis softened his whole demeanor, slumped down in his chair in a relaxed posture, and immediately admitted some of his contributions to the situation. His boss seemed to relax and a brief discussion followed. Then, abruptly, his boss stood up and left. I figured he was so completely taken off guard by the situation that he didn't have a clue how to react, so he just got up and left. Bosses can do that. Dr. Butkis and I talked a bit more then I excused myself and left.

Battle over. Victory won. Somehow, I knew in my heart everything would be okay. I knew I would be okay. I knew I did not have to fear. I knew that even though I had just disarmed myself in front of my enemies and exposed my fragile pride to them, I had nothing to fear. I knew God would protect me. I knew Jesus had my back. I knew Almighty God, Himself, would be my *rear guard*. I knew that the Right Hand of Almighty God had been raised above me in battle. I walked away knowing that by God's grace I had done well that day and that the victory was mine in the strength of my King, Jesus. Somehow I knew I had just been given claim—by the grace of Jesus—to a tiny piece of the awesome victory that was won by Jesus on Calvary 2000 years ago. I praised God for His endless mercy every step of my walk through the connecting corridors back to my hospital. I praised Jesus for the strength that had been mine by His great grace.

It still utterly amazes me that the grace found in the acknowledgment of the power of the cross of Christ is available to each of us in our daily lives. God loves to be tested in its regard—and how He came through in this battle! Instead of traveling down a road to shear disaster—for surely it would have escalated as it always has in the past—I got to witness the rescue of Almighty God in the midst of my every day life. The fire of the conflict was snuffed out. Dr. Butkis and I continued in a cordial and professional relationship. Further still, so also did I continue in a pleasant relationship with his powerful boss, Dr. King.

And, sure enough, a donor heart became available and the patient, his family, and I all survived the 10-hour ordeal of that all-night cardiac transplant operation.

CHAPTER THIRTEEN

Sanctification Battle

Before moving on to more battle vignettes from the Valley of the Shadow of Death, several questions surrounding these initial confrontations are worthy of further discussion. Despite describing only a few of many of my inter-relational encounters, a recurrent pattern has become readily apparent. This pattern is foundational in any practical strategic battle plan for real-life application of the teachings of the Bible. Acknowledgment of this pattern is critical because it involves the battles that are sent our way every single day of our life.

God orchestrates these battles into our lives for the express purpose of achieving His will in our salvation and sanctification. Ultimately, every single thing that happens in the life of a believer has the singular purpose of making us into the likeness of Jesus Christ. The mechanism of this perfection is through the knowledge of God that is found only in actually stepping onto the battlefield with Jesus at our side. In regard to our daily battles, Jesus is the consummate warrior. His is the first foot to step onto our battlefield and His is the last to step off. When we walk in the way prescribed by God in His Holy Word, God not only goes into battle with us, He goes to battle before us and is our rear guard. This is His express promise.

But you will not leave in haste or go in flight;
for the LORD will go before you, the God of
Israel will be your rear guard. (Isaiah 52:12,
NIV)

Although the Bible clearly reveals the will of God in regard to our approach to our daily interactions, it remains just *information* until we put it into action. It is put into action in only one manner: real world inter-relational battle. This is why the daily relational encounters described in this book are an unavoidable part of the life that God has planned for each one of us. By God's very specific plan, we simply cannot avoid them. They are the mechanism by which God reveals Himself to us. Only when we have actually stepped in faith into the fury of relational battle—with a steadfast heart committed to doing battle God's way—do we actually get to see God in action.

When we see God acting powerfully on our behalf, it sets something off inside of us. It is an almost magical, heart-captivating feeling of adventure, intrigue, exhilaration, and passionate love all combined into one unbelievable rush. God's response to the simple act of trusting Him speaks to our heart like nothing else. It shows us a glimmer, a hint of that mysterious and captivating relationship for which we were created. It speaks volumes regarding our eternity. It gives us a visual, auditory, olfactory, and palpable demonstration of what it is like to walk with God in the manner in which He has prescribed. It is a tiny whiff of what Jesus did every day of His life on earth. It is the cry of our hearts—and it is our eternity. It is precisely that for which we have been created.

In the midst of these relational interactions, we must remind ourselves that it is God who sends battle our way. Each and every battle was designed by the infinitely wise mind of God before an atom of the creation came into existence. Each one, no matter the timing or circumstances, we can be assured, is exactly that which we need at precisely that moment in our life. It is perfect. It is never too much and it is never too little. It is battle with a purpose and we cannot avoid the obvious fact that it is God who is sending it right at us for His very specific and righteous purpose. None of these battles are frivolous. None are unnecessary. None are too much for us to handle. None warrant disdain, disrespect, or disinterest on our part, for each offers an encounter with God.

Although each of our relational battles is unique, they all have a similar pattern. In each we are confronted with a choice. Although it sometimes seems more complex than this, there are really only two alternatives from which we can choose. Despite the seeming simplicity of this choice, let there be no question in our minds, this choice *is* the battle. This choice determines entirely how this battle will go down—and this choice is 100% ours to make. This is nothing less than our God-ordained free will intersecting in a tangible fashion with God's orchestrated plan for our life. The fact that God knew our response before He created the world is irrelevant in regard to our actual choice. We still absolutely have the ability, right at the moment of decision, to choose either way. We can go into battle the way that the world prescribes—utilizing the weapons of the world—or we can go into battle the way that God prescribes. We can enjoin the fight with the perspective of the world or with the eternal perspective of God.

Satan is, of course, right there in the middle of our decision. He is tries to convince us that God doesn't really care, that He doesn't really love us, and that He won't be there when the fury hits the fan in the midst of the fray. That is Satan's only weapon—deceit. He is a liar.

> *You belong to your father, the devil, and you*
> *want to carry out your father's desire. He was a*
> *murderer from the beginning, not holding to the*
> *truth, for there is no truth in him. When he lies,*

he speaks his native language, for he is a liar
and the father of lies. (John 8:44, NIV)

Satan wants us to do things his way. He will tell us anything—truthful or not (usually not)—that will convince us that his way is the best.

At precisely that critical moment of decision, however, so also is the Holy Spirit whispering into our ear. He is telling us of the love God has for us and that God's heart for us is good. He is telling us that God's plan for our life is solely motivated by His everlasting love for us. He is reminding us that God has always been there—especially during those times when we could not feel His presence. He is telling us to trust God and to do it God's way. Thus, with each of these battles, it is Eve in the Garden of Eden all over again. Satan is telling us that God's heart for us is not good. The Holy Spirit is reminding us that Satan and the world are liars and are making promises that they simply cannot keep.

The Holy Spirit also tells us that the antidote to Satan's lies is the Bible. We need the pure truth of God to counter the pure deceit of Satan. Only the written word of God can serve that vital function of helping us to accurately discern between truth and deceit, between God's battle plan and the treachery of the world. Jesus used the word of God to counter Satan and so should we. Knowledge of the mind of God is found there. Only in the knowledge of God do we discern the proper course for the daily events of our life. Reading the word of God therefore is the vital first component of this sanctification process.

Reading the Bible is the prep work for the second component of our sanctification: actual battle. We learn God's will in His Word and then we put it into effect in the daily battles that God orchestrates into our lives. This is the pattern of every life of every believer. This palpable real-time implementation of God's word in our daily life is, somehow, vital to our eternity. It is the process by which God prepares us for that which lies ahead of us in eternity. It is the process by which God slowly chips away at the world's paradigm and substitutes His own eternal perspective. It is precisely the process by which God slowly makes us more and more into the likeness of His Son, Jesus.

Even though this is all by God's design, we may not recognize or acknowledge this pattern. We may recognize and acknowledge it, but refuse to use this knowledge to shape our daily life. But, no matter what our approach, it doesn't change reality. It doesn't change truth. The fact that we do not choose to use this information in our life decisions does not change the fact that this information is vital to these very same decisions.

In other words, we may or may not want to read the Bible every day. We may or may not recognize it as the only source of truth. We may or may not recognize the written word of God as vital to forming the correct perspective with which to face our daily battles. We may not learn from our daily battles because we do not have the information found in the Bible. We may be destined to repeat our errors over and over because of our lack of knowledge and our lack of recognition that these are decisions placed in our life by God for His specific purpose. Nonetheless, our choosing to not acknowledge the importance of the Bible in dealing with the God-ordained daily battles of our life does not somehow reduce its importance. There is nothing *relative* about the absolute nature of the truth found in the Bible. It has been made available to us as a vital component of our sanctification. To move forward without it is to move into vital and furious battle with blindfold, earplugs, and handcuffs in place.

This is why reading the Bible—preferably at the beginning of each day—is so critically important. When we read the Bible in the morning, we allow the word of God to send us into the battles of the day armed with the very knowledge of God. This way, we are armed with the weapons of God even before our enemies can initiate their battle plan. The word of God enables the Holy Spirit to direct our every battle maneuver. It is the primary weapon that He uses in our life. It allows the *knowledge* of God to be right there with us in the middle of the fray. Through it, God Himself speaks the truth to us. He is there to repeatedly tell us that if we will do battle His way—by finding a way to love our enemies—He will go before us into that battle. The Holy Spirit assures us that we are free to love without fear because God Himself has our back: *There is no fear in love* (1John 4:18a, NIV).

Further, the Holy Spirit reminds us that the promise goes even further than this. His promise is pure joy, no matter what happens, because it assures us that *it is going to end well for us*. Not every such ending is easily discernible (from our worldly perspective) as *ending well* for us—for we do not think eternally like God. Nonetheless, from God's eternal perspective, we can be assured that every single battle that God sends toward us will indeed end well for us.

With God promising to accompany us into battle, why is it so hard for us to do things His way? Why do we struggle so much with this? What is so hard about simply choosing God's way? After all, in the middle of the fight we have the truth of the Bible in our hearts and the Holy Spirit right there as our real-time battle Commander! The problem is obvious. We have all been there. No matter the assurances we carry into relational battle, it is still battle. It is still ugly. It is still a melee. It is still accompanied by body blows and sword-inflicted wounds. It still hurts. There is nothing simple or easy about it. And yet, we can be assured, that God's grace in the middle of the fight will always be enough. In the middle of the fury, in the middle of the hurt, we must stick with God's battle plan. It ends well for us.

This is the fight we must fight. We have been raised in the ways of the world since our birth and thus believe that the ways of the world are the *real* reality and, therefore, the only *logical* way to deal with the battles that we face. It is precisely these feelings that we must overcome. This is that critical first step of faith. In following God's battle plan, we are called to go against what we just *know* to be true, what we believe is *logical*. Faith is never easy. But, with perseverance through the battles, that logic of the world is replaced with the logic of God as our minds undergo the sanctifying renewal that is promised.

Do not conform any longer to the pattern of this world, but be transformed by the renewing of your mind. Then you will be able to test and approve what God's will is—his good, pleasing and perfect will. (Romans 12:2, NIV)

Sure that first step of faith is tough. After all, it never *makes sense*! But, there is good news. That good news relates specifically to the second major battle of my academic career, the battle with Dr. Bull. That good news is that once we take that first overcoming step of faith, the *next* such step of faith gets easier. It is easier because we have seen God in action. This is the second vital feedback function of our sanctification process. We obtain the knowledge of God's will in the Bible—then we encounter battle. The second time around we know God is there because we have been to battle with Him before. We have seen Him act in our lives and we have seen it with our own eyes. We have seen God act faithfully just as He says He will in the battle manual. We know there is a supernatural punch, a divine lightning bolt, a stealthy 2,000 lb. bomb at the end of the step of faith that far outweighs anything that we ever could have come up with on our own. And what a feeling we experience as we see God go to work. It is more than just being rescued from a difficult situation. There is something deep-heart about it. There is a voice way down deep that says "Now *that* is what it's all about!"

Then, the very next time we are faced with a similar challenge—the challenge of forgiving the unforgivable, having mercy where there is none deserved, loving the unlovable, and surrendering to our worst enemy—the Holy Spirit again reminds us of our previous encounters. Suddenly the "logic" of the world seems a bit more illogical as we remember how God rescued us in the past. With the battle-acquired knowledge of what we can expect from God, all of the sudden it seems *logical* to do it God's way. It makes sense. The sanctifying process is powerfully underway. We practically run to do things God's way because our heart reminds our mind and we begin to think like Jesus. We remember the thrill of going to war with God. We remember the thrill of watching God go to work and the thrill of knowing that we have tangible evidence that everything the Bible says is really true. These are miracles on the scale of those described in the Bible. These are extreme faith builders.

The whole of God's Word testifies to the faithfulness of God. It testifies to the fact that if we call upon His Name and put our faith in Him as our Lord, God, Redeemer, and

Savior, that He is always trustworthy to deliver us. Only one problem, here—the deliverance may not be what we expect. Further still, as we have discussed, there is no promise that it will not be accompanied by suffering. But—and we have God's assurance here—it is always accompanied by abundant grace and it is always in our eternal best interest in accordance with His divine plan for our lives. Always. If we can count on anything in this life, we can count on this. We don't have to worry—we just have to obey. By God's eternal perspective (not necessarily by the world's standard) the outcome will be nothing short of perfect. Not just okay, perfect!

Our God of perfect provision has indeed provided many special passages in the Bible that reassure us that He will be there in full force when we trust Him and do the unthinkable, trust the untrustworthy, forgive the unforgivable, and love the unlovable. God must have known what a basket case I was going to be in this regard because He really spells it out clearly in several passages. My favorite, without a doubt, is from the book of Exodus. The Lord is speaking to the Israelites as they are preparing to receive His law and proceed toward the Promised Land:

> *"See, I am sending an angel ahead of you to guard you along the way and to bring you to the place I have prepared. Pay attention to him and listen to what he says. Do not rebel against him; he will not forgive your rebellion, since my Name is in him. If you listen carefully to what he says and do all that I say, I will be an enemy to your enemies and will oppose those who oppose you. (Exodus 23:20-22, NIV)*

This knowledge of God's tactical battle plan for dealing with the difficult times in our lives redefines the word *warrior*, which I seem to claim as a natural birthright. This new definition resonates within me. It strikes a chord that absolutely lights me up. It tells me that I am to make war by loving and to win by surrendering—and I know in my heart that this is the purest of truth. This truth is exactly that for which I was made. This truth feels so very right because this is how I am wired. I was made to bring Glory to God by loving—by letting Him love through me. This loving is war the way that God wants us to fight it. Our God is a God of love. We are His creation. We are wired to love and when we hit it, He is always close by. We feel His touch and the power of the cross of Christ. It feels so right because it is in our DNA. We know we are on the right track and we go in search of more.

> *Taste and see that the LORD is good; blessed is the man who takes refuge in him. (Psalm 34:8, NIV)*

> *Know therefore that the LORD your God is God; he is the faithful God, keeping his **covenant of love** to a thousand generations of those who love him and keep his commands. (Deuteronomy 7:9, NIV; emphasis added)*

We thus have a choice in every battle situation: to believe and to follow and to submit by loving our neighbor and enemy; or to rebel and follow our own devices—those of the world and its prince, Satan. We can fight the battles alone or we can let Almighty God go before us in battle to subdue our enemies before our very eyes.

> *"But my people would not listen to me; Israel would not submit to me. So I gave them over to their stubborn hearts to follow their own devices. If my people would but listen to me, if Israel would follow my ways, how quickly*

would I subdue their enemies and turn my hand against their foes! Those who hate the LORD would cringe before him, and their punishment would last forever. But you would be fed with the finest of wheat; with honey from the rock I would satisfy you." (Psalm 81:11-16, NIV)

In summary then, by God's ordination, relational battle is the process of our sanctification. Reading the Bible gives us the foundational information regarding precisely what is God's will and what is not. Then, in the setting of interpersonal battle, God orchestrates relational decision-points into our lives—each with a God-choice and a non-God choice. When we choose the non-God choice we receive negative feedback in the form of God's discipline. When we choose God's will, we—one way or the other—get to see God act mightily in our life. Either way, we learn that God means what He says and that His reality trumps the world's "reality" every time.

We then begin to substitute God's perspective for the worldly perspective (that has been ingrained in us from the time of our birth) in the many relational decision-points that God orchestrates in our life. This substitution occurs more and more often in more and more areas of our relational life as we see God go to work. This feedback cycle begins to affect the way that we see things. It allows us to see things as God sees them. It begins to change our worldly perspective into an eternal perspective. It begins to transform us by the renewal of our mind.

We begin to substitute God's viewpoint for our old way of viewing things—not necessarily because it is the right thing to do, but because it is the *logical* thing to do. God's perspective begins to show us at each relational decision-point that the God-choice is the logical choice. In other words, we begin to realize that God's way is, in fact, the best, most efficient, easiest, and least painful choice at every decision-point. We substitute God's perspective for the world's perspective and this is manifest in our life as we begin to make godly, instead of worldly, choices at more and more of our relational decision-points. This means that we choose to love, we choose to serve, we choose to forgive, we choose to not judge, we choose to have compassion, we choose to have mercy, and we choose to surrender—all because we realize that God means what He says and will faithfully go into battle with us every time that we do. When we realize that God loves us too much to let us get away with worldly choices, the truth of His written Word intersects with our day-to-day life and His way is no longer a step of faith, it is a step of logic.

Along with the realization of the logic of God, we cannot help but simultaneously realize that Satan has been lying all along. His way—the world's way—never delivers on the promises that he makes. His way, in the long run (and often in the short run) is always the worst, always the least efficient, always the hardest, and, in fact, always the most painful choice that we can make at the relational decision-points in our life. We realize that we want no part of hating, judging, demanding, scheming, plotting, striving, and unforgiveness. Not only are these choices against God's will, they also never do anything but make the situation—and our lives—worse.

When we have finally substituted God's paradigm, God's perspective for that of the world, it will all be by God's plan, God's grace, and solely by the work of the cross of Jesus Christ. Ultimately, God's eternal perspective will be that which we persevere to use in every relational situation because it is the logical choice. This is the renewal of our mind that is our promised sanctification, the guaranteed transformation. Our hearts were transformed when we believed. The transformation of our mind, however, is the purpose of the battle that follows. Both transformations are critical. With each, we are being transformed into the likeness of Jesus—because only in His likeness can we achieve our deepest heart desire to subserviently, sacrificially love God just as He has loved us. And in this, we prepare for the spectacular eternity God has planned for us.

CHAPTER FOURTEEN

If Someone Takes Your Cloak...

I wish that the only difficult parts of my job had to do with operating on the human heart. Unfortunately, this is assuredly not the case. Another example of sanctification trials outside of the operating room once again occurred early in my career. And, once again, I almost blew it. Once again, I, by my naturally nefarious, rebellious, and pugnacious nature, almost snatched defeat from the jaws of victory.

A new faculty member had just joined our staff. We'll call him Dr. Famous. The members of our cardiothoracic surgical division knew him well before we hired him. He did his cardiothoracic surgical fellowship at our institution. We were, therefore, able to observe his behavior for two full years. We knew well that Dr. Famous did not suffer from a lack of ego—and reasoned that this qualified him to fit right in with the rest of us!

What set Dr. Famous apart when he joined our division was the fact that he saw no need to be subtle about his intentions. All of us are confidently ambitious—we wouldn't be at this institution if we weren't. Ambition and confidence are considered favorable attributes in academic cardiothoracic surgery. In general, however, most of us recognize an unwritten rule that places politeness, camaraderie, and group solidarity above individual self-promotion. Discretion, therefore, is required in regard to publically vocalizing one's intentions. Dr. Famous didn't see it that way. He definitely had a few things to learn about being discreet. Within a month of joining our group, he caught all of us off guard by making an outright declaration—in a division meeting with all of his new partners present—that he "would be the next great world-renowned cardiac surgeon"!

That may not sound like a threat to you. Nonetheless, every member of the division recognized that the practical ramifications of this statement would impact every one of them—and probably not in a desirable manner. So, whether Dr. Famous meant this as a threat or not, it was perceived to be exactly that by most every cardiac surgeon present at that meeting—and many of them told me precisely this.

As we have previously discussed, this is not surprising. After all, we are a very competitive lot. In some respect, we were all competing to be what Dr. Famous had declared himself to be—we just had the discretion to not flaunt it in front of our fellow division members. The fact that he had done precisely that, despite having literally just joined our group, irked more than a few of his new partners.

Regardless of his true intentions, that comment set the tone for Dr. Famous' introduction into the fellowship of our cardiac surgical group. Whether each of us really believed it then or not, we all professed a unifying belief: cardiac surgery at our hospital was a team sport and we all wore the same colored uniforms. Optimal patient care depended upon our adherence to this belief. It was not about the individual; it was about the team. This common esprit-de-corps is vitally important, especially at a large academic, university-based, medical center like ours. It must be accepted by all that when the interests of the individual square off against the interests of the team, we work together—at least publically—to achieve the common goals of the team.

Needless to say, Dr. Famous' comment was the talk of the hallways for weeks. He learned what we all took for granted: if you want to rock a group of academic heart surgeons back on their heels, tell them that you are going to surpass all of them as an academic cardiac surgeon. In practical terms, we all knew precisely what his comment was meant to convey. To meet his goals, he would have to do the lion's share of the cardiac surgical cases done at our institution. He was already well connected here—he really was an otherwise pleasant and charmingly gregarious individual with excellent interpersonal skills—and I knew he would have no trouble getting surgical referrals. He carried himself well and looked and talked every bit the part of *the next great world-renowned cardiac surgeon*. The *old guys* in the division soon brushed it off. Nonetheless, to all of the young bucks in the division—including me—the very clear and present danger was perceived from the moment those words rolled off his lips. It was apparent to all of us young rascals that Dr. Famous just didn't quite *get it*.

Was Dr. Famous really a threat? Was the threat real or just perceived? It doesn't really matter, does it? The world has just one response to Dr. Famous and it was also mine on that day: defenses up and on full alert! A threat had been perceived. My worldly wiring glowed red hot with defensive strategic communication from my brain. I don't know about you, but I have been a warrior so long that my defense systems are automatically triggered at even the first strokes of an aggressor's pen—and that without conscious effort. The world owns most of us from our very early life and these automatic responses are very often ingrained in our personalities.

Normally, I would have continued at *DEFCON 1* indefinitely following Dr. Famous' statement. But, as we have discussed, I'd responded that way previously and it had not gone well. Believe me, I had noticed. God was starting to work in my heart. By the time of Dr. Famous' taunting challenge, I was consistently spending serious daily time in the Bible and in prayer. I knew that God's written Word clearly does not support our aggressive opposition of the so-called "evil enemies" that God sends into our life. It was clearly not God's will that I go to war with Dr. Famous in the subtle and not-so-subtle ways that I had so readily employed in the past.

So, from the very beginning, I took what was for me a very bold step. I resolved in my heart not only to not fight with Dr. Famous, but also to actively seek ways to affirm him. I repeatedly asked the Lord to help me because I knew only too well how weak I was against the temptation before me. Previously, when people picked a fight with me, they usually got the fight they sought. I was more than happy to oblige. So, this was new ground for me. I tried very hard to not oppose Dr. Famous publicly and resolved to always greet him with a smile. I tried to think of the good things about him—and there were many. This was the easy part. He really was a good guy. I resolved to not plot against him or allow myself to take him apart in the mental gymnasium of my mind—an art that I had honed to a fine skill over the years. I resolved to be his friend and to trust the Lord to defend me. I tried to clean up my heart in this regard and laid my fear and anger at the foot of the cross of Christ.

For the most part I behaved. By the grace of God, I actually appeared to demonstrate some degree of control over my thoughts and actions in his regard. This was a huge change. Let me repeat, I was not the force behind this change. This was grace, pure grace. God is so faithful to answer our prayers when they are in line with His will. Praise God for His work of sanctification. Praise God that this work has nothing to do with my strength. Praise God that His offer to have Jesus live in my heart (and in yours) is for real.

I did have my weak moments. On days when I was sitting with nothing to do and Dr. Famous was very busy in the operating room, I must admit that I faltered. In financial review sessions where his clinical productivity rapidly began to eclipse mine, I struggled. Opportunities to roll my eyes in response to my partners' comments about Dr. Famous were sometimes too much for me to resist. Nonetheless, God poured His sanctifying grace into my heart and, for the most part, I trusted Him. I took the claims of the world—that I should aggressively go right after this guy—right to the foot of the cross. I begged Jesus for His strength because I knew my strength would fail. Dr. Famous' response was affirming. He clearly made an effort to not oppose me and to even treat me a bit like a mentor despite the fact that he was already a better surgeon than I.

All through the early days of this battle, the Lord was tugging on my sleeve. Instead of warring, I was trusting. My future was in God's hands and I knew that my *enemy* wasn't going to control anything that God didn't want him to control. But, the Lord is relentless. He wanted to take me further still. The sanctification process goes on and on and on. *Perseverance* seems to be such a vital component of sanctification. God wanted more from me. It was as if He was whispering, *There's something more. You can go further in this battle. You can draw closer to me.*

Ah, the relentless pursuit of the Holy Spirit—I knew He was hot on my trail. Right through the middle of this threatening confrontation with Dr. Famous, familiar scripture that I had read so many times before began to take on new Spirit-driven meaning. I began to linger over words I had previously just flown past. In particular, the words of Jesus from the gospel of Luke were so very convicting.

And if someone wants to sue you and take your tunic, let him have your cloak as well. (Matthew 5:40, NIV)

Whoa! Now wait a minute. I've already agreed to try to love this guy and be his friend. He has continued to dominate me in the clinical practice of cardiac surgery. I have humbled myself. He has humbled me. His very presence, attitude, and actions threaten me. Surely this is enough.

To be very honest with you, I really felt that my initial response to the presence of Dr. Famous seemed more than adequate. Nonetheless, in the depths of my morning Bible study, a soft voice in my heart seemed to keep whispering that I needed to take my obedience one step further. I reluctantly agreed.

Fine, Jesus, I trust you to take care of this guy. I trust you and not the world for my future, my career as a cardiac surgeon, and the wellbeing of my family. So what do you want from me? What more do I have to do?

God's answer to my question was not long in coming. Dr. Famous was actively pursuing his stated goal of advancing in the academic ranks of cardiothoracic surgery at our institution. Doing a lion's share of the cardiac surgical cases was critical, but alone it was not enough to get Dr. Famous where he wanted to go. He needed *academic* credibility. He needed the triple threat of academic cardiothoracic surgery. He needed to operate like a champ (he was doing that), be a great educator of the next generation of surgeons (he was an outstanding teacher), and *he needed to do important research.* The only thing he lacked was the final achievement, research credibility.

Years before this turn of events, I had advanced in academic rank to full professor of surgery. This can admittedly be a bit of a chore at our university medical center. I had, by God's grace, fully understood the importance of sustaining an active clinical cardiac surgical practice—something at which I was more than holding my own. I had also understood the importance of publishing clinical results—advancing the field of *clinical* cardiothoracic surgery. I wrote plenty of clinical papers describing our surgical results. I even performed and published descriptions of cardiothoracic surgical procedures that had never been performed before. I wrote *position* papers on cardiothoracic surgical controversies. Then I had scored the cardiothoracic surgical academic *hat trick* when my laboratory research culminated in NIH funding. Truly God was pouring His blessing into my life.

This triple combination of academic cardiac surgical activities is what supposedly separates the so-called *academic* cardiac surgeon from all the other cardiac surgeons who are out there in the private practice of cardiac surgery. This combination is critically necessary for national credibility in our subspecialty.

That being said, at our university medical center, *being academic* means only one thing. Let there be no question about this. It means that we must advance the science of heart surgery and cardiovascular physiology by doing *basic science* research. This, as defined by our university, is what makes us "us," and them "them," and doing advanced and important basic science research is not really optional.

Our particular university goes one gigantic step further in delineating the pathway by which one is deemed worthy of academic advancement to a tenured professorship. Their definition of a significant and successful research effort worthy of academic advancement revolves around a single metric. Although not written in any university document, the only real metric is the acquisition of *peer-reviewed* funding from the National Institutes of Health (NIH) by the successful submission of research grants.

NIH grants are secured only by writing research proposals that are innovative enough to be judged as fundable by an NIH *study section* of experts (*peer-review*). The NIH is very stingy with our tax dollars. At most, only one grant out of every 10 that are submitted actually receives NIH funding. The unstated rationale of this metric is that if you secure NIH dollars, then you have obviously been judged—by your national research peers—to be very competitive in your particular area of research.

Thus, the university message to Dr. Famous and the rest of us could not be clearer: NIH dollars = academic advancement. Not negotiable. No NIH dollars = no professorship. Dr. Famous needed and desperately wanted to advance to the rank of full professor of surgery. This was a critical, mandatory, and inflexible step in his life quest to be a world-renowned academic cardiac surgeon.

Dr. Famous had a problem. To be competitive in seeking NIH funding in cardiovascular physiology, you have to come up with innovative ideas that will have a big impact upon either the basic science understanding of heart disease or the clinical treatment of cardiac patients. In the world of cardiac surgery, this is usually accomplished by exploring basic physiology-based methods to do things better in a cardiovascular surgical sense. In other words, you must come up with ideas that no one else has come up with (a definition of innovation) that have the potential to profoundly impact cardiac surgical patient care.

After you come up with an innovative and significant idea, you must then design the research study, assemble the appropriate research team, and gather preliminary data. This preliminary data must not only support your hypothesis, but also supply evidence that you actually have the capability to carry out the study that you are proposing they give you millions of dollars to perform. Then you have to write the grant, submit it, and convince the peer-review study section to approve it. The process is uniformly guaranteed to be a whole lot of work—and at least 9 times out of 10, destined to failure at the national level. But this is what we do and Dr. Famous knew that this is exactly what the university demanded of him.

As I have discussed, the Lord had clearly blessed me in regard to research. Early in my career, the leaders of our division supported my efforts and, by God's very abundant grace (if you knew me you would know how abundant it has been), I had been repeatedly successful in obtaining NIH funding. As a direct result of God's intervention in my research efforts, I advanced rapidly from assistant professor to associate professor with tenure and then to full professor of surgery.

Despite his dominance in the area of clinical cardiac surgery, I therefore had something that Dr. Famous didn't: academic credibility at our university. He knew that if he was to obtain his goal of being *the next great world-renowned cardiac surgeon*, it was mandatory that he advance to associate and then full professor. You can't be an academic leader of our subspecialty at an assistant professor level. Dr. Famous knew well the rigors of facing the very tough tenure committee at our university. They granted promotions only after very tight scrutiny of academic qualifications, rigorous adherence to tenure guidelines, and satisfaction of the unwritten metric of NIH grant support. Dr. Famous had seen plenty of other promising academic surgeons fail to scale this critical summit.

As time progressed, Dr. Famous struggled with a few of his own innovative, but short-lived attempts at research. All of his projects seemed to flounder on the craggy reefs of relevance, lacking in either innovation or significance. Unfortunately, his efforts went nowhere in regard to the much-coveted NIH funding. Hallway talk was already beginning to surface that Dr. Famous was not going to make it because he had no chance of advancing academically—specifically because he had no NIH grant.

No way! You've got to be kidding!

My initial response to the Holy Spirit's prompting was disappointing.

You want me to assist him in obtaining the only thing that I have over him—academic credibility?

Things were not going well. My success in this area had always been my *ace in the hole*. I knew that if it ever came to a showdown, this was going to be one thing I had going for me. And now the Lord wanted me to help my "enemy" get an NIH grant? I had just read the words of Jesus from the gospel of Luke regarding the treatment of our enemies and they were so very convicting.

> *"But I tell you who hear me: Love your enemies, **do good to those who hate you**, bless those who curse you, pray for those who mistreat you. If someone strikes you on one cheek, turn to him the other also. If someone takes your cloak, do not stop him from taking*

your tunic. **Give to everyone who asks you,** *and if anyone takes what belongs to you, do not demand it back. (Luke 6:27-30,* NIV; *emphasis added)*

This is different!

My resistance to the idea persisted. I was not going to give in easily.

Dr. Famous is no ordinary enemy! He is already a better surgeon than I am. This just can't apply here in my life—not in my life because my circumstances are special!

Special. Isn't that always our response when the word of God convicts us of the applicability of His difficult truths in our own lives? We are so quick to point out that *our* lives are different and that His rules don't apply.

These truths may have been applicable to the individuals in the Bible, but things are different now. Besides, who wants to be a "super" Christian anyway?

The Holy Spirit was unrelenting. He would not leave me alone. I began to think about the specific words Jesus used in this passage from the gospel of Luke. He's talking about someone stealing our coat. That presumably means that it is cold outside—otherwise we wouldn't have our coat with us. Maybe it is *really* cold outside. That guy in the parable clearly means us no good and, in fact, obviously means us harm. By stealing our coat, he is placing his own wellbeing far above ours. We could catch pneumonia and die!

And what is our Savior's response to this? I'm standing there shivering in the cold and our Redeemer asks me to give him my shirt too! That presumes the enemy is still standing there in front of me. From my worldly perspective, I might propose a different response. Sure, I guess I don't have to haul off and clobber the guy (in response to that mean little voice in my head—after all he is a thief!). So, the first place I go is to *compromise*. I figure that maybe I can reason with the guy who just took my coat.

Nope.

Not only does Jesus not offer us the option of forcibly getting our coat back, He also never even mentions the option of just *reasoning* with the guy. No compromise. Even reasoning, which certainly would be the very best of which I would normally be capable in this situation, is not good enough to get us where Jesus wants to take us. What Jesus asks us to do is simply unbelievable by any worldly standard. It defies all worldly logic. Jesus asks us to also give him our shirt. Jesus is asking for nothing less than total surrender.

This request requires that we *really* trust God. After all, the hard, tangible, physical evidence of the world around us testifies loudly and logically against that choice.

After all, it's cold! I'm freezing here!

God's will in this situation, as clearly defined by the words of Jesus Christ, requires us to trust our Savior to take care of us in the cold. We must trust Him to warm it up, get us another coat, protect us from pneumonia—*something*! And God most assuredly doesn't promise that we won't suffer. That promise is glaringly missing.

Oh, great, this is going to get ugly.

We may turn blue in the cold. It may be incredibly uncomfortable. In that case, what we may get is a very palpable chance to *know* Jesus in His suffering. This would certainly qualify: directly following the word of God to help someone else, and suffering as a result. This is the heart of God's subservient, sacrificial love. This is the heart of total surrender. God wants to pull us closer. These difficult situations are always precisely this—God is offering us an opportunity to know Him better. Are we going to make the choice that will allow this to happen? Or, are we instead going to once again believe the world's lies?

I hear the sound of gunfire. I hear the bullets as they whiz by my head. This opportunity in this set of circumstances with this individual will occur only once in all eternity. When this opportunity passes, it will be gone forever. I will spend eternity with the knowledge that I did or did not choose to move toward the gunfire.

I prayed hard about my situation, about the difficult decision-point that God had clearly placed in my life. This was a very disruptive moment, as my walk with the Lord clearly and tangibly intersected with my professional career—two things that I had unfortunately worked very hard to keep separate. The tension between the demands of the world and those of my Savior was palpable. Nonetheless, from the moment the Lord audaciously invaded my heart with the idea of helping Dr. Famous obtain an NIH grant, I knew it was right. I knew that this was another Holy Spirit-arranged situation that was nothing less than an opportunity to bring glory to God by my subservient and sacrificial obedience. It was indeed a once-in-eternity chance to participate in an unambiguous demonstration of my professed belief in the sovereignty, faithfulness, and love of God.

No doubt—and this through no effort of my own—God passed very close to me that day. Once again, this was God's grace in its purest form. This was nothing less than a brush-against-the-shoulder, ruffle-the-collar, mess-up-the-hair, Holy Spirit fly-by.

Needless to say, it lit me up.

God's answers to deep-heart desires always do. We can't help this. From the moment that the idea was placed in my heart, I knew that it was from God. I knew it was the right thing to do and I knew that it was what I had to do. I had to give away my ace in the hole to the very guy who could use it against me. I had to hand over my best stuff to my number one competitor. By worldly standards, I was being asked to surrender my only advantage. If I followed through with this request, it would leave me holding absolutely nothing in my hand. It would leave me trusting my future in this academic cardiothoracic surgical division to God alone.

Whoa!

The age-old adage that *something is never really yours until you are able to turn it over—100%—to God* rang through my head that day. I knew that anything that I could not give up in deference to a clear request from God was, by definition, an idol. In the very act of attempting to preserve my academic standing by ignoring the Biblically-defined will of God, I would be elevating this idol of mine to a hierarchical position *above* God. God guarantees that if we do not release things to Him, He will take them away. He cannot do anything less. He is our sovereign Father and He loves us desperately. He cannot let us pursue destructive behavior without a response. Further still, by the very definition of His righteousness and holiness, He will not be mocked.

Do not be deceived: God cannot be mocked. A man reaps what he sows. (Galatians 6:7, NIV)

Our heart, by God's design, has only one focus inscribed in its deepest chamber. Things that compete with our heart's central focus on God cannot be allowed to stand uncontested by a God who truly loves us. Thus, by the specific plan of God, things that we value on earth gain *eternal* value only in that moment in which we give them back to the generous God who gave them to us in the first place.

Although I regularly receive all the credit for it, I have no doubts regarding the true source of *my* success in obtaining NIH research funding. God trained me, put me in the right place with the right tools, gave me the ideas, fleshed them out for me, wrote the grant applications, and clearly favored me in the hearts of the members of the NIH peer-review study sections. There is no question about this. My success would not have happened otherwise. God is 100% responsible for that which I am so readily willing to claim as my very own. In regard to academic research success, God has clearly given me all that I have. And now, He was simply asking me to give it back.

I had no idea what Dr. Famous' response would be to an offer to help him write an NIH grant based upon the research program that my lab had established over the preceding 10 years. Nonetheless, I knew that God was clearly blessing this plan and I proceeded to lay out my proposed assistance in a meeting with Dr. Famous shortly thereafter. My "enemy" responded with true gratitude and together we went to work. The Lord blessed Dr. Famous with some very good ideas that utilized the technology that my laboratory had developed. He had a bright mind and really was a phenomenally innovative guy.

We submitted the grant. It was funded on the first try without even a revision. Up until that point, I had personally never had a grant funded on the first try without revision. Dr. Famous was immediately put up for promotion and became an associate professor with tenure—in line to be a full professor in the required 2-year interval.

So what was Dr. Famous' response to all this? He quickly became my strongest ally. He went to bat for me repeatedly when I was in trouble. Instead of becoming competitive enemies, we became good friends. And God has continued to support me and exalt me in my research. What a great lesson—it made me eager to go there again. I grew in my resolve that my ever-present, always faithful Savior was just waiting for me to take a step of faith at each of the decision-points He placed in my life.

My favorite part of this encounter was the not-so-subtle reminder—once again—that everything that I have achieved has been 100% by the grace of God. When something that you are or have is clearly recognized as a gift—as something that you did not *earn*—it gets very hard to rationalize not sharing it with others. There is no logic to hoarding the gifts that God gives us. They are to be shared by us, just as they had been shared with us. This all boils down to *logic* and *fairness*. The critical first step is in the recognition that they are gifts—that we were not as responsible for their presence in our lives as we so readily assume. When God made this transformational fact very obvious to me—a fact that is revealed on nearly every page of the Bible—the consequences were obvious. There really was nothing emotional about my decision to help Dr. Famous. It was just the fair, just, loving, and logical thing to do.

It is so much easier for us when we have adopted an eternal perspective and instituted God's logic as the driving force behind our decisions. We are creatures of logic. When something doesn't *make sense*, we rarely want to do it. Satan knows this. He spends a lot of time trying to convince us that his way is the easiest, least painful, most equitable, most efficient, only logical, and thus the *most sensible* way to approach a problem that God has brought into our life. Satan knows that this *logic* algorithm is what drives our thoughts and our decisions. God counters Satan's so-called logic by revealing His eternal logic in the written word of God. God's logic then becomes entrenched as *our* logic when He supports its use in our daily life.

Dr. Famous was obviously a very special part of my sanctification process. I saw God's word in action. I was an eyewitness to the palpable triumph of God's logic. By the intervention of the Holy Spirit in my life, I was able to apply the truth I read in the Bible to my daily life. I felt the power of God's truth as the guiding light in my life. As a direct result of this incident, I reoriented my life compass just a degree closer to the True North that is found in Jesus Christ.

By the way, God further blessed Dr. Famous. He had chosen the right response to God's overtures in his life. He was offered an excellent promotion to a position of leadership at one of the most famous heart surgery centers in the world. There, he continued to demonstrate a humble and loving heart. He even became a prominent leader in one of our most prestigious cardiac surgical national organizations. He has indeed become that which he told all of us he would become—*the next great world-renowned cardiac surgeon.*

CHAPTER FIFTEEN

Jesus Plus *Nothing*

This book is about Jesus Christ, wholly, exclusively, and all-inclusively. It cannot be about anything else because my life as a heart surgeon, just like your life, is about nothing more, nothing less, and nothing other than Jesus Christ. He planned it, orchestrated it, implemented it, and perfected its every nuance. It can't help but be by Him, through Him, under Him, for Him, held together by Him, and all about Him.

> *In the beginning was the Word, and the Word was with God, and the Word was God. He was with God in the beginning. Through him all things were made; without him nothing was made that has been made. In him was life, and that life was the light of men. The light shines in the darkness, but the darkness has not understood it. (John 1:1-5, NIV)*

It always has been, is, and always will be Jesus *plus nothing.*

Despite the fact that in every moment of our life we are relentless in our attempts to make our life *all about us*, it is nonetheless still all about Jesus. Whether we ever acknowledge it in this life or not, the very first reality that we will face when we finally step into eternity is that every single moment of our life—and of every life—was about only one thing: Jesus Christ.

Can it be any other way?

And yet when the fullness of the cross of Christ is considered, it is readily apparent that the mighty, omnipotent, omniscient Son of God—the Master of the Universe—cherishes us so dearly that it was His choice to make it all about *us*. Does the magnitude of all that which was done on the cross of Calvary have any other explanation?

As documented by multiple eyewitness accounts, Jesus claimed to be the Son of God. A discussion regarding His status, His importance in our life and in the world in general—as the only Son of God—simply cannot, therefore, be a casual conversation.

In fact, because He claimed to be the only Son of God, He is either absolutely nothing—a joke, a creep, a psycho, a liar, a great big zero—or He is absolutely everything. There can be no middle ground in this, the most critical of life discussions. If Jesus is truly, as He clearly claims, the only Son of God, His impact in our day-to-day life cannot be anything less than all pervasive through every moment, through every facet of our life.

Indeed, every single day we can praise God for the magnificent complexity of the situations, dilemmas, and conflicts in which we find ourselves—and likewise also praise Him for the utter simplicity of the solution to every one of them. This logical and obligatory all-pervasiveness of Jesus in our life means that in every difficulty, in every storm, in every frenzy, in every heated battle, and in every darkened night, we can know—there is no hidden mystery here—exactly to whom we can and must turn.

Jesus is always there and He is always the answer.

Even in the difficulties we face this very day, we can be assured that Jesus is all we need for this and every situation.

In addition to His day-to-day impact in our life, we can also be assured of His importance in the single most important aspect of this life: our eternal salvation. It is Jesus plus nothing for our salvation—the most eternally important mission and purpose of our life. In regard to our salvation, the verdict is clear: even with a full life of toil—even if we are the nicest person in the whole world—we have zero impact on our salvation and can add absolutely nothing to what Jesus has already done.

And in this regard—in the matter of our salvation—belief "in God" alone is incomplete—and in that incompleteness, utterly fatal.

Fatal.

No one who denies the Son has the Father; whoever acknowledges the Son has the Father also. (1John 2:23, NIV)

Without belief in Jesus, all is lost. With Jesus we get everything. Without Jesus we get nothing. The Bible is clear in its revelation that we can have the most sincere belief "in God" without belief in Jesus—and in that state we are utterly and hopelessly lost.

The impact of Jesus in our life is so pervasive that we can be assured whenever we find ourselves in trouble it is because we took our eyes off of Jesus—and put them on ourselves. In fact, in this life we should never worry about ourselves at all. We should never concern ourselves with our lives, our accomplishments, our happiness, our fulfillment—or even our heavenly rewards. We should concern ourselves with bringing glory to Jesus by the expression of His subservient, sacrificial love through us toward those individuals He brings into our life—and let Him worry about everything else (including our heavenly rewards).

There is nothing that we can do to impact the love that Jesus already has for us—we cannot make it increase and we cannot make it decrease. Instead, we can relax—there is no competition here—if we are in Jesus Christ. It is not about us, it is about Jesus Christ. Actually, it is wonderfully comforting—almost freeing—to know that it is not about us and what we have to do, but rather about Jesus, His infinite love for us, and what He has already done on our behalf.

It is also Jesus plus nothing for our sanctification—the second most eternally important mission and purpose of our life—our transformation into the very likeness of Jesus Christ.

> *Let us fix our eyes on **Jesus**, the **author** and **perfecter of our faith**, who for the joy set before him endured the cross, scorning its shame, and sat down at the right hand of the throne of God. (Hebrews 12:2, NIV; emphasis added)*

It is Jesus *plus nothing* that solves every situation in which we could ever find ourselves. These situations comprise and are the fullness of the sanctification process. All such situations were known, planned, and created by God, the Master of the creation of the universe, such that every moment of our sanctification is in fact about Jesus. Jesus is thus the answer to every question. He is the Savior in every battle. He is the way out of every trap. He is the shelter in every storm. He is the water in every drought. He is the bread in every famine. He is the light in every moment of absolute darkness. He is the only truth in the sea of untruth in which we are hopelessly submerged. He is the only satiation of every deep craving of our heart. He is the only *True North* by which to chart the course of our life. His is the only voice that answers the deep cry of our heart. His is that hand that reaches down and grabs our hand as we sink for the last time into the dark lagoon of our self-deception. He is our redemption, our only salvation, our only rescue.

Grace is all that we must learn in this life and Jesus is the only Mediator of grace. In the acknowledgment of the grace of the cross of Christ is found the utter abandonment of all that we pursue to make ourselves righteous. Acknowledging the power of God's grace in our life is the most *freeing* thing that we will ever do. Grace. It means that we have absolutely nothing to do with our salvation and sanctification—and it is the very best news we will ever receive.

Jesus is not *part* of the solution to anything—He is the whole solution to everything. Jesus plus nothing satisfies our hungry heart.

Jesus is the entirety of our eternity and in our eternity is our hope and in our hope is endless joy. Jesus is our only hope, our only joy. Indeed, we will romp with Jesus through the adventures of eternity dressed immaculately in the pure white righteousness of His perfect life, perfect death, and glorious resurrection. It will be as if we had never committed a single rebellious offense against the perfect holiness of the Uncreated, Mighty, and Most Holy God—and all this utterly and only by the work of Jesus Christ. For whenever the Father looks at us, He will see us *through* Jesus! *Only* through Jesus—always and everywhere and only...and that for all eternity!

We can therefore relax if we are in Jesus.

He calls this His *rest*.

Jesus is our interface, our connection, our mediator, our only link to the eternal, uncreated, infinite God. He is that seemingly impossible link between the temporary and the Eternal, the created and the Uncreated, the finite and the Infinite, the unrighteous and the Most Holy.

Jesus is our life. Jesus is our eternity. He is our eternal life and in that eternal life, He is our hope—and in that hope, our infinite joy. We are simply and utterly unable to even imagine the all-consuming joy of the eternity that God has planned for us in Jesus Christ.

Do you think that I have overstated the case for Jesus Christ? Overstatement is, very simply, impossible. It is outside of the mental, emotional, and spiritual capacity of any man or woman to exceed reality in his or her description of the glory ascribed to Jesus Christ, the Uncreated Son of God.

> *He is the **image** of the invisible God, the **first**born over **all** creation. For **by** him **all** things were created: things in heaven and on earth, visible and invisible, whether thrones or powers or rulers or authorities; **all** things were created **by** him and **for** him. He is **before all** things, and **in** him **all** things hold together. And he is the **head** of the body, the church; he is the **beginning** and the **first**born from among the dead, so that in **everything** he might have the **supremacy**. For God was pleased to have **all** his fullness dwell **in** him, and **through** him to reconcile to himself **all** things, whether things on earth or things in heaven, by making peace through his blood, shed on the cross. (Colossians 1:15-20, NIV; emphasis added)*

All that we can "know" is, by definition, *created*. We are, therefore, incapable of knowing about that which is described as Uncreated. Jesus is Uncreated. We know the created tip of the iceberg. We are incapable of comprehending that which lies beneath the waters edge. We have never and can never look beyond the boundary that separates created from Uncreated. We know that which Jesus has revealed about Himself, but really know very little at all.

But what we *can* know for sure is that it is Jesus *plus nothing*.

Yesterday, today and for all eternity in every setting, every time, and always.

It cannot be anything else.

CHAPTER SIXTEEN

Perseverance

In my life as a heart surgeon, there has been no harder sanctification lesson than that of perseverance. The emphasis placed upon perseverance in the word of God, combined with its undeniable importance in our lives, clearly indicates its preeminence on God's sanctification priority list. That which makes persevering so relevant is the clear fact—demonstrated nearly every day of our life—that our good responses to God's daily tests do not consistently eliminate either the associated suffering or further repetition of the test. This fact therefore requires us to *persevere* through the suffering or through God's repeated testing—or both.

This is a problem for most of us. We believe that if we can just make the right call the first time that we face a tough life lesson, it should be fixed forever. Because of our natural resistance to embracing the concept of *delayed* gratification, we think that if we are able to just do things right when challenged with a difficult relational situation, we should never have to face that difficult trial again.

For example, when God challenges us with loving a worldly enemy, we believe that if we can just love them once in the Name of Jesus Christ, then the Lord should take them right out of the picture—right then! In other words, if we get a passing grade on God's test, we should be allowed to move on. When we make a godly choice at one of the decision-points that God places in our life, it should be exactly like we just *aced* the final exam—we get to graduate and move on to the next grade.

The fact that pleasant consequences are not necessarily tied in a direct temporal fashion to our godly decisions is difficult for most of us. Our human nature, the world we live in, our American society in particular, and most certainly the world of cardiac surgery truly demand that they be. Nonetheless, like it or not, this is just not the way things usually work. We can be assured that God has designed this system of sanctification precisely as it needs to be designed to get the results that He desires. Our seemingly mandatory training in perseverance was not a mistake. God wants the product of His creation to be sons and daughters of God who are appropriately and perfectly equipped to join the subservient, sacrificially loving eternal fellowship of the three Persons of the Triune Godhead. We can be assured that this eternal result mandates the process of sanctification that we are experiencing, because we serve an infinitely perfect, and therefore infinitely efficient God. If it weren't necessary, we would not be going through it. Building endurance in our faith, therefore, must somehow be critical to God's perfect eternal outcome. Our lives are a direct testimony to the fact that God chooses to teach us the vital eternal lesson of perseverance by repeating difficult lessons. Apparently, the only way to build that critical mass of perseverance with which we are to enter eternity *is to actually persevere.*

> *Consider it pure joy, my brothers, whenever you face trials of many kinds, because you know that the testing of your faith develops perseverance. Perseverance must finish its work so that you may be mature and complete, not lacking anything. (James 1:2-4, NIV)*
>
> *For this very reason, make every effort to add to your faith goodness; and to goodness, knowledge; and to knowledge, self-control; and*

to self-control, perseverance; and to perseverance, godliness; and to godliness, brotherly kindness; and to brotherly kindness, love. For if you possess these qualities in increasing measure, they will keep you from being ineffective and unproductive in your knowledge of our Lord Jesus Christ. (2Peter 1:5-8, NIV)

Therefore, since we have been justified through faith, we have peace with God through our Lord Jesus Christ, through whom we have gained access by faith into this grace in which we now stand. And we rejoice in the hope of the glory of God. Not only so, but we also rejoice in our sufferings, because we know that suffering produces perseverance; perseverance, character; and character, hope. And hope does not disappoint us, because God has poured out his love into our hearts by the Holy Spirit, whom he has given us. (Romans 5:1-5, NIV)

A recent foray of mine into the Valley of the Shadow of Death provides a great illustration of the extremes to which God will subject us in our training in the *art* of perseverance. I've had a longstanding interest in a particular area of cardiovascular physiology research. We've touched on this before. God blessed me with success in this research early in my career. Great God-given ideas generated great God-given experimental plans, which generated great God-given publications and great God-given NIH grant applications. I hope I've made my point: I readily acknowledge that all is by God's unending grace. As I look back, the powerful influence of God's hand is readily apparent in every single aspect of my research career.

Several years ago a young cardiologist at our institution—we'll call him Dr. Einstein—was in need of a startup research project. Being a cardiologist, he was in the department of medicine (not surgery) at our medical school. The rules regarding academic advancement nonetheless extend across all departments and he knew the importance of NIH funding in his academic career. We had worked together taking care of patients with cardiac disease in the clinical setting and had developed a reasonable professional relationship. So, when his need for NIH funding became critical, he met with me and asked for my help. My lab personnel and I truly bent over backwards in assisting him in the development of his project—and the subsequent submission of a successfully funded NIH grant application.

As I've mentioned, NIH grant applications are incredibly important at our university medical center. Needless to say, his status was elevated considerably and he was rapidly academically promoted with tenure. I sought no thanks or tribute, as I recognized then that all of our success was by God's hand alone. Nonetheless, I have come to expect an atmosphere of camaraderie, teamwork, and humility in all of my research collaborations. That is just the way we do things. It is the way that we treat our collaborators and it is what we expect in return. In this regard, Dr. Einstein had a very interesting response to his success in obtaining NIH research funding. My lab workers and I never saw it coming.

Instead of becoming a member of the team and contributing to the team effort, Dr. Einstein blossomed into Dr. Arrogant. It was like a Dr. Jekyll and Mr. Hyde transformation had occurred. Out of the blue, Dr. Einstein became the most arrogant guy that my laboratory had encountered in all of our research collaborations. He chose a response, a path, which was 180 degrees in the opposite direction, for instance, of that chosen by Dr. Famous in a very similar set of circumstances. Despite the fact that he had no research experience in our area of expertise prior to coming to our lab, Dr. Einstein suddenly proclaimed himself an *authority*.

I was okay with that. Our goal with our young investigators, after all, is for them to stretch their wings and ultimately develop an independent research effort of their own. It was the voracity with which Dr. Einstein approached this independence that surprised us. This change in attitude was most apparent at inter-departmental research meetings. He began to speak of the technology we had developed over the previous decade as his own. He even began to take credit for laboratory work that we had completed *before* he began his collaboration with us.

To say that we were caught off guard by this profound and sudden change would be an understatement. The change was so intrusive and obstructive to our laboratory effort that several members of my team met privately with me to ask me to do something about it. And yet, how awesome is it to have the Creator of the universe resident in your heart? What an awesome God. He helped me look the other way and just go on with my work—God's awesome grace, indeed. I encouraged my team to do the same. I directed my laboratory workers to help Dr. Einstein in any way they could. I held back nothing; I contested nothing. By my Savior's grace alone, I tried to subserviently and sacrificially love Dr. Einstein.

Even as I was patting myself on the back for passing what I considered to be the *final* exam in regard to Dr.

Einstein, God was just beginning His lessons on perseverance. At one of our subsequent lab meetings, Dr. Einstein made us aware of his plan to develop a new collaboration with another professor from another department. We listened with interest. How surprised we were when we were told the identity of the target of Dr. Einstein's collaboration—a senior professor with whom I had collaborated for over 10 years! Dr. Einstein was not only using our hard-earned technology in his new collaboration, but he had also chosen my closest research ally. My collaboration with this particular basic scientist on the main university campus was the most important academic relationship that I had developed during my career to date.

Once again, I thought this was a bit excessive—Dr. Einstein was clearly stepping on my well-travelled turf. Nonetheless, by the grace of God, I said nothing. I was determined to love this guy. Miraculously, Jesus had hold of the reins of my heart and would not let go when I tried to grab them back. My fellow lab workers rolled their eyes at Dr. Einstein's comments, but nonetheless agreed to follow my commands to help him. By God's unending grace—and I really mean that, for my prideful human heart wanted to take things in the exact opposite direction—I threw my support behind the association that Dr. Einstein was trying to develop with my longtime collaborator. I persevered in this support, even though it was obvious to everyone that Dr. Einstein was trying to displace me from a relationship that I had been nurturing for over a decade. Surely, Jesus was resident in and in control of my heart then. Normally I would have defended my hard fought efforts—for truly I had the fruits of a lot of hard work on the line.

Okay, I thought. *Test passed.*

I continued to feel pretty good about my support of Dr. Einstein's new collaborative efforts. I knew that this was God's will and I hung in there. I comforted myself by remembering that these fruits of my previous work had all been gifts from a generous God and that He was simply checking to see if I would treat them like idols. God wanted to know if they were more important to me than He was. I felt that I had correctly answered this question by my support of Dr. Einstein. Unfortunately, as I was once again patting myself on the back, I was also heading straight into even more lessons on perseverance. God was just about to turn up the heat even further.

The heat, in fact, became literally palpable as the real point of Dr. Einstein's new collaborative effort suddenly came to light. One afternoon in a laboratory meeting, he informed us that he was working on a *commercial* software product. We listened intently as he revealed that this commercial software product would be almost entirely based upon the work that I had been doing with that collaborative professor for over a decade! My coworkers and I had already recognized that the software that we had been developing to perform the data analysis needed for this particular line of research had considerable potential to become a commercial product sometime in the future. The commercial software product that he was proposing would obviously be in direct competition with the software that we had developed. It was clear from the discussion that followed that Dr. Einstein did not think much of our software. He had just entered this particular field of research and was already sure that he could develop better software than ours—all, of course, still based upon the research my laboratory had done and the collaboration I had developed.

Despite my sanctification progress to that point, *this* got my attention. Now we were talking dollars. It was obvious to even the most naïve of us that Dr. Einstein was positioning himself to reap the financial harvest of the collaborative work that had been going on for years before he arrived on the scene. Once again, although I was getting more than just a little bit nervous—and Satan was using every opportunity to point out how all this was to my detriment—I held on and trusted God that He would go before me even in this new battle.

This was a very difficult time. I understood that God wanted me to love my enemies. I honestly felt that I was dragging myself out of my self-centered cellar and I was enjoying the progress God was making in turning me into someone that I could actually like. And then, all of the sudden, here came a very real challenge that rocked me to my foundations. This was real world plotting and scheming. There were serious financial considerations. This was where the rubber met the road in testing the truth of my statement of faith in Jesus Christ. This was where everything that I professed to stand for was really put to the test.

I knew exactly what God wanted. The question was whether I could trust Him enough to actually do it.

Everything inside of me said to cut and run—to go back to the old way of handling these provocations and problems. I wanted to grab tightly to the steering wheel that I had previously handed over to Jesus and yank it right out of His hands. Still, by His grace and the strength of His cross, I resisted the worldly instincts that still held powerful sway over the *logic* of my mind. Many of my lab co-investigators expressed their complete disbelief in my strategy to remain silent as this went on around me. They knew me well and knew of my previous worldly warrior tactics. Many of them were also accomplished worldly warriors, and Dr. Einstein clearly also represented a threat to them. The threat was unmistakable and it was readily within my power and theirs to smash this threat soundly.

After all, they knew what I knew. If we had withdrawn our support at that moment, Dr. Einstein's efforts would have collapsed. He simply did not have the research wherewithal to carry it off. Nonetheless, my fellow lab workers followed my lead and assisted Dr. Einstein in his efforts. I'm sure they were wondering what had happened to their *warrior* chief.

Despite their misgivings, I was nevertheless bound and determined to hang in there. I had been repeatedly asking Jesus to take me *one step further* in my knowledge of Him. Well, my prayers were being answered. This really felt like God was doing exactly that—taking me one step further—and I was determined to go with Him. It was a battle of faith—more specifically a battle in perseverance in faith. As I said, it was well within my earthly power and ability to simply take *my stuff* back and end the invasion into my research arena that was being led by Dr. Einstein.

Nonetheless, I knew that attacking Dr. Einstein with the weapons of the world just wasn't right. Was I going to give my Savior's command to love the people that He brought into my life lip service only? It is easy to talk big, but when faced with a real world scenario that really threatened me *where it really mattered*, was I going to run back to my old habits? Needless to say, I spent a lot of time on my face at the foot of my Savior's cross—asking Him to take complete command of my weakening heart and the battle that engulfed it.

As all of the gory effects of Dr. Einstein's final assault gradually sank in, his true intent became very clear to all of us. We were, therefore, not entirely caught of guard by his next move. God obviously thought it was time to turn up the heat a little more. After Dr. Einstein had spent more time on the software issue, he suddenly decided to shelve his software development efforts. Instead, he decided that not only should he completely take over the research project itself, but also that he should take over the development and management of *our* software! He informed us he would be completing the entire project—*our* entire project.

The fact that the entire project and software were 95% completed already—by our efforts—was lost on him. The fact that we had all previously acknowledged that it was heading toward a possible commercial development project also didn't matter to him. As far as I could tell, he had gone completely rogue. Our university academic community has specific guidelines and laws forbidding the exact activity with which Dr. Einstein was now boldly proceeding. He was attempting to wrench both the control of and credit for this project away from its originators.

Further, this was an amazingly flagrant and bold assault on my leadership of the pack. The alpha male of the laboratory was being challenged to open combat. It had gone beyond taunting. This was a fight. My efforts at appeasement apparently had not registered with him. My act of love had been interpreted as an act of weakness. Rather than being appreciative, he had clearly been emboldened by my lack of response to his earlier incursions into my territory and now brashly took his attack to an altogether new level. The gloves were, as they say, *on the ice*.

As the details continued to gradually come to light, it was readily apparent that Dr. Einstein had been quite busy behind the scenes for quite some time. He already had it all worked out. He had—without telling anyone in my lab—already hired a computer programmer to complete the project. Then, at a lab meeting, he suddenly proposed that we literally hand over to him and his programmer the entirety of our software code so that they could complete the project. He wanted us to just hand over ten years of development work so that he could complete and commercialize it. You could have heard a pin drop in that conference room. My programmer looked at me with the eyes of an abandoned orphan. The rest of the people in the room turned and looked at me with similar facial expressions of utter disbelief that Einstein would so directly cross the line like this. He seemed utterly oblivious to their concerns.

Luckily, there was someone else in that conference room with me that morning. Jesus was present in my heart and stood with me, right by my side. I can guarantee His presence, because I know my dark heart. Under my own steam, I never would have done what I did. Right there in that conference room, the perseverance made available only by the grace of the cross of Christ made its presence palpably manifest in my life. At precisely the right time in precisely the right place under precisely the right set of circumstances, Jesus did exactly what He promised He would do. He controlled the very depths of my heart. He was really there! He would forgive and He would love where I could not. When the bold assault embodied by Dr. Einstein's proposal hit us like a tidal wave, Jesus stepped right in to save the day.

I can guarantee that it was not me speaking in that conference room that day—for I know what I would have done and what I would have said. I would have shredded the guy. *What was he thinking?* And, I can objectively assure you, by every worldly standard, by all worldly logic, and by every academic university metric, I had every right to do exactly that. I would have shown no quarter in my complete destruction of this arrogant young upstart.

But, my precious Lord chose instead to *love* Dr. Einstein. Jesus spoke up for me—He knew that I never would have been able to get these words past my lips on my own. Right there in front of everyone, He promised Dr. Einstein anything he needed to complete the project. He commanded my computer programmer to give Einstein all of the software code and ordered my lab personnel to help Einstein's programmer in whatever way they could.

Now you really could have heard a pin drop.

I glanced around the room at the rest of my lab team like I was an off-site observer. It was like I was having an out-of-body experience because I was no longer part of the conversation. Jesus was doing the talking now. I had a ringside seat to the Master of the Universe doing what He does better than anyone—subserviently and sacrificially forgiving, rescuing, and loving.

I will be honest with you. That was a day in my life like no other. I was enthralled with the leadership of my heart provided by Jesus, while simultaneously being terrified at what had just happened. I was absolutely sure of the words my mouth had just formed, and simultaneously questioning every syllable. I bowed in humble servitude at pure unadulterated truth, while simultaneously screaming "Liar!" at the top of my lungs. I had just leaped off a precipice and had not yet felt the strong arms of my Savior gently breaking my fall.

I walked out of that meeting emotionally disheveled. Nevertheless, I knew in my heart that I had just seen the awesome power of God displayed in my life. My awesome Savior, my Rock and the very *Fortress that I run into* had just taken command and acted where I was powerless to act. That day I knew what it meant to have my Savior inhabit the very secret places of my heart. He was at the controls in that conference room on that terrific day of very great battle.

As I walked down the hallway to my office, the word that most fit my emotional state was *terrified.* Nonetheless, thoughts of *What the heck did you just do?* were gradually replaced with that warm feeling of the Holy Spirit flyby that I had just experienced. I knew that I had just brushed up against something that could only be described as *eternal.* I knew that I had just experienced Jesus in a palpable, audible, visible manner. I knew that I had just watched a *Mighty Warrior* step between the old way that I used to run my life and the new me that was found in Christ—and thereby did something of which I was completely incapable. This is the stuff of which heroes are made, and my Hero was Jesus. This was an incredible feeling—very literally like nothing else in the world. And to say that I loved it simply does not do it credit.

As you can imagine, the arrogant boldness of Dr. Einstein's flagrant attack was not lost on my laboratory co-investigators. They later insisted that I sit down with Einstein and try to reason with him. But, once again, this made no sense to me. That was the *old* way of doing things. I knew how it would end. I had been there many times before.

Instead, I had experienced my first tastes of a *new* way. I had felt the power of Jesus. *This was utter surrender.* It had to be. And in that surrender was the promise of *total* victory. There was no way that they could convince me to go back to my old way of doing battle. Besides, Dr. Einstein was obviously not seeing things the same way we were. In my humble experience, you can reason with guys like that until you're blue in the face, but they will never truly *get* it.

Nope. Einstein had stolen my coat. Jesus had given him my shirt also. Einstein had then asked me for my undershirt and Jesus had just handed that to him too. I was shivering in the cold. I felt so very alone except for the Presence of my Savior—but I knew He was all I needed. God's grace abounded in an infinite and endless fashion. I stood back and watched as my guys proceeded to hand over the software. We continued to work on it just as we always had, but now Dr. Einstein had a copy of the code and was directing his programmer through the project. It seemed as if he was bound and determined to seize total control of my 10-year old software development project, very literally at the last minute.

Nonetheless, I knew then that something had changed. A light was shining in the previously dark places of my heart. I felt as if a weight had been lifted off of my shoulders. The feeling was very similar to how I felt when I made the decision to go into Dr. Butkis's office and humble myself. I just knew in the deepest reaches of my heart that it was right—very right. I knew that it was what God wanted and I had this incredible feeling of anticipation. I felt like I did when I was 5 years old standing outside of my parent's bedroom at 6 AM Christmas morning. It was as close as I think I have come to what C.S. Lewis so elegantly and simply defined as *joy*. It was a special time of true holy anticipation in which I was trusting wholly in God. And best of all, I knew that I could expect His awesome Presence in the outcome. I reasoned that God might well be sending His *hornet* (Exodus 23:28, NIV) before me onto this pre-ordained battlefield. The anticipation of His appearance was palpable.

In the meanwhile, I went about business as usual—at least as well as I could, considering the circumstances. The initial Holy Spirit *rush* after the lab meeting left me feeling off balance for quite sometime. And, as one would expect, Satan came back strong and counterattacked at the most opportune time and place.

There will be no rescue. Where is your God now that you need Him? Has He abandoned you?

Satan tried to convince me that I was alone and that I still had time to fix this problem. I was subjected to Satan's near continual attacks. This was some seriously ferocious spiritual warfare. Sometimes the attacks came in my own thoughts. Sometimes my coworkers delivered them. In fact, my coworkers—in no uncertain terms—repeatedly urged me to stomp Einstein into the proverbial academic dirt. But, even through the anxiety that their words provoked, Jesus supported me. The chosen course of action felt very, very right.

And then the Lord struck.

It was as sudden and decisive as it was awesome. As quickly as the threat had risen, it was gone. The new programmer quit suddenly without warning and Dr. Einstein's whole plan simply fell apart. Our rescue smacked of nothing less than the Lord's deliverance of Jehoshaphat from the armies of the Moabites and Ammonites (2Chronicles 20) and of Hezekiah from the massive army of the Assyrian king, Sennacherib (2Chronicles 32). It was over. And Dr. Einstein faded from contact with my laboratory and busied himself elsewhere—literally never to trouble me again.

Everything went promptly back to normal. It was as if nothing had happened. It was like the streets of Jerusalem after the Assyrian army trudged back to Nineveh with its tail tucked between its legs. What a God. I praised Him for giving me the strength to hold on. I rejoiced that night with my wife and children as I told them the whole story (my wife already knew what was going on and was supporting me prayerfully in my effort). I think my kids were very proud of their daddy. I also think they got to witness firsthand the awesome power of God that was also available to them in the skirmishes of their day-to-day lives. Together in our devotional that night, we read 2Chronicles 32 and praised the Holy Name of Jesus Christ. We praised His perfect faithfulness. We praised the perfect completeness of His provision. We praised Him for His perfect plan. We praised Him that He let us in on His plan and let us have front row, 50-yard line seats to watch the spectacle of the Mighty God in action. We praised Him for His perseverance and His gift of perseverance. We praised Him for His love that, indeed, endures forever.

> *And the LORD sent an angel, who annihilated all the fighting men and the leaders and officers in the camp of the Assyrian king. So he withdrew to his own land in disgrace. And when he went into the temple of his god, some of his sons cut him down with the sword. (2Chronicles 32:21, NIV)*

CHAPTER SEVENTEEN

Bright Light

It was a dark and stormy night. I was a senior surgical resident in my 5th year of post-medical school training. I was stationed at the flagship tertiary care hospital of the West Coast university medical center where I completed my general surgical training. That fateful evening, I was serving my term as the senior workhorse surgical resident on the Trauma and Emergency Surgery Service in the Department of Surgery. In addition to being at the hospital from 5:00 AM until 8:00 PM *every* day, every third night I also took in-house, all-night call. One of my responsibilities during this time was to be the initial buffer for anyone who arrived in our large trauma emergency room needing general surgical attention.

My nights on call on the Trauma and Emergency Surgery Service were always busy. We were the landing-zone for a sizable amount of significant blunt and penetrating trauma, the latter ranging from simple knife wounds to bullet wounds sustained from automatic weapon fire during gang-related turf battles. We also saw our fair share of the massive trauma dealt out by high-speed automobile accidents. As a result, we did a lot of nighttime surgery. We also did a fair bit of follow-up surgery during the daylight hours.

As is the case for all busy trauma services, the main drive of all involved is to keep the service as lean, mean, and mobile as possible. There is near universal agreement that the more efficient the trauma surgery service remains, the better the patient care rendered to these critically ill patients. Their injuries were often multiple and complex, and many of these patients were just as sick as they could be. They required a wide range of surgical decisions ranging from emergency management of massive hemorrhage to the complex management of complicated pancreatic injuries. Efficiency in patient management sustained the ability to intervene in a timely fashion, which was critical to optimal patient care. Because were so very busy, it was a physically, mentally, and emotionally challenging service for everyone involved.

Because of the demanding nature of their surgical issues, the complex trauma patients were clearly best served by keeping the less critical *chaff* off the service. The chaff was comprised of those patients who could be dealt with by a less acute, less busy service. Some of these chaff patients, despite not being acutely ill, were quite *needy* and could generate a lot of resident work. They clogged the gears of an efficiently running trauma surgical service and it was our firm conviction that they simply did not belong there. They were the biggest impediment to a surgical trauma service remaining lean, mean, and mobile and, therefore, the biggest threat to the high quality care that we strove to deliver to our hospital's burgeoning trauma patient population.

So, when these less critically ill patients were encountered in the emergency room in need of a quick look by a surgeon or a minimal emergency room surgical procedure—such as drainage of a subcutaneous abscess—the plan was clear. The minor surgical procedure was performed, the paperwork was done, the surgical service signed off, and the patients were sent on their merry way to the medical service to have all of their other problems treated. Needless to say, our medical colleagues sometimes deeply resented our attitude—despite the fact that when confronted with the every day reality of our trauma surgical service, they also would uniformly agree that these patients did not belong there.

Having been thoroughly indoctrinated in this trauma surgical mindset toward the beloved chaff patients, I was an efficient surgical machine in the emergency room. I was a pro at rapidly dispatching the needed surgical attention in the emergency room, signing off, and sending the chaff to the medical service before anyone knew what hit them. I was a force to be reckoned with on any emergency room consults and had a reputation of being an unassailable *wall*, keeping these patients from the hallowed halls of the trauma surgical service.

I don't want to seem insensitive to these patients—as my reference to them as *chaff* would clearly insinuate—but we truly had limited surgical manpower resources and were responsible for some heinously ill multiple trauma patients. These critically ill patients were our primary responsibility and no other service was equipped to handle them. They truly deserved our undivided attention. I acknowledged that the medical and surgical services each felt that the chaff belonged on the other's service. Regardless of the feelings of our medical colleagues, however, this battle had been fought on timeless emergency room battlefields of yore—and these patients went to the medical service. I was devoutly committed to not being the surgeon responsible for a change in this historic precedent established by the surgical heroes of the past.

Unbeknownst to me, this age-old precedent, set by countless previous emergency room skirmishes, was about to be challenged in the wee hours of that dark and stormy night. I readily accepted the responsibilities of my position as the first line of defense against the proverbial chaff *dumps*—as our medical colleagues referred to them—that might be sent our way. My commission from my chief resident on the surgical service at that time was simple and well understood by all of the involved combatants. I remember it as if it were yesterday. He had stared directly at me with cold, gray, steely eyes as he drove home the point. "You are a stone wall! You are indestructible and impenetrable! You are a wall that cannot be scaled! Patients who require emergency room drainage of superficial pus are never, I repeat, never to be admitted to the trauma surgical service! Are we straight?"

I nodded in agreement as I grunted my usual foot-soldier response, "No problem."

The message was clear and it had been delivered with emphasis. I was to perform any necessary minor procedures rapidly and efficiently. If the patients required admission for antibiotics or other care, they were to go to the medical services. Period. This was simply not negotiable.

Out of the gloom of that dark night came a very pleasant young drug addict with a problem. She had been injecting drugs into the veins of her forearm. She had developed a small abscess just beneath the skin at one of her many injection sites. She was the precise patient about whom my chief resident had given me his stern warning. This was *superficial pus* that needed to be drained.

Patients like her unfortunately comprised a large portion of my late-night emergency room work. The management of her medical problem involved a very minor surgical procedure under local anesthesia. The plan was straightforward, simple, and routine. The surgical resident on call would drain the abscess in the emergency room and the patient would be admitted to the medical service to receive antibiotics until the infection was clearly controlled. She would then be discharged on a course of outpatient oral antibiotics.

Unbeknownst to me on that fateful night, the young senior medical resident (my counterpart and worthy opponent from the Department of Medicine) manning the general medical services of the emergency room had a different plan. She had initially seen this patient and for some reason—maybe she was bored or something—she had decided that this particular patient on this particular night would be the perfect patient with which to challenge the age-old paradigm regarding how these patients were managed. She decided that this patient, counter to all established precedent, should be admitted to the *surgical* service. Little did I know that she, like a warrior of old, had picked up the gauntlet that was perpetually cast at the feet of the medical residents by their surgical resident colleagues. She had made herself the standard bearer for the oppressed medical residents of the world.

By all reports, she had a gleam in her eye when she inquired of the ER head nurse regarding who might be the trauma surgical resident on call that night. "Who's up for consults on the surgical service tonight?"

Before the head nurse could answer, she somewhat haughtily responded, "I have a *popper* in room 3 that needs some pus drained from a collection in her forearm. I am thinking that tonight that patient gets admitted to the *surgical* service."

The head nurse sensed the potential for emergency room drama. "Good luck with that, kiddo. The surgeons will *never* let that happen!"

"Well maybe we're long overdue for a change around here," the resident responded as she spun lightly on her heels and headed back down the hallway.

As she walked away, her voice trailed off as she quietly completed her thought out loud, "Maybe its time for the surgeons to start taking their fair share of these patients."

She hadn't actually said it, but her intent was clear to everyone: *There's a new sheriff in town and things are going to be different this time.*

Although the head nurse's eyes must have rolled back in her head at the brash young resident's response, secretly I am sure she was delighted. The medical resident had taken the bait. As the head nurse had hoped, her initial negative response had thrown liquid oxygen onto the fiery plot that was brewing in this young resident's mind.

Let the drama begin.

The head nurse grinned from ear to ear as she told her the identity of the surgical resident on call. "He's a brick wall," she yelled as the resident disappeared around the corner. "You'll never get past him!" There may have been just a bit of taunting in her voice.

Game on.

It is unclear whether any actual bets between the head nurse and the medical resident were tendered. Reportedly there were, but there is considerable disparity between the accounts of the disputing parties. I suppose that really isn't the point. Knowing her as well as I now do, however, I am sure that this preposterously emboldened medical resident simply flipped her long black hair back across her shoulders and sallied back to the patient's room with an unmistakable air of utter confidence in her strategy.

Her plan was simple. She would become forever famous among the emergency room staff by taking on the *system.* She would challenge the prevailing culture. She would ambush her surgical opponent in a head-on emergency room firefight of near Biblical proportions—and she would rout him like the rogue mercenary that he was. She would outwit this guy, this surgical resident that they had dared to call *a brick wall*. Before the night was over, the patient would be admitted to the surgical service. She had a masterful plan. She would attack him at his point of maximum weakness. On behalf of the Department of Medicine and her medical colleagues, she would—in one swift attack—win back the power of established precedent.

I knew nothing, of course, about the trap being set for me. To me, the call to consult on a patient in the emergency room who had a subcutaneous forearm abscess was just like the countless others I had already dealt with over many years as a surgical resident. It was in fact so *routine* that from the moment I got the call my mind simply went into the automatic mode. This would be simple. I would cruise down to the ER, say hello to the patient, take a brief history, do a quick exam, write a note in the chart, give the patient her antibiotics, get a consent to do the procedure, prep and drape her arm, administer a local anesthetic, incise her forearm pocket of pus, pack it full of gauze, and, with the appropriate amount of intimidation in my voice, tell the accompanying medical resident that "No!" the patient would not be admitted to the surgical service for antibiotics. I would be out of there in 10 minutes, tops.

Little did I know that the ambush had already been set. This medical resident was crafty. She new my vulnerabilities—I still don't know how—and struck swiftly and deftly. In fact, it was over before I knew what hit me. She was so smooth that I wasn't even aware that I had been in a fight until the next morning (more about that later).

Regardless, when I walked into the ER examining room, a smiling patient—whose right arm was laid out on the table next to her—greeted me. Her entire arm had been sterilely prepped and draped. It was completely ready for the incision and drainage of the small abscess. The patient had already been consented. The chart note with history and exam—which I confirmed myself—was already written and in the patient's chart. The antibiotics had already been given. There was a pair of sterile gloves laid out for me along with a scalpel and some surgical sponges already on the sterile field. The local anesthesia was drawn up in a small syringe, ready to be administered. All I had to do was confirm the chart note by taking a history and doing a brief physical exam—although that which was already written in the chart was far better than any that I would have written—put on the gloves, and drain the abscess.

I gathered in and processed every detail of the scene that was set before me. All of the work was *already* done. Everything was perfect. I had never seen anything like this before. This was awesome! Someone had finally gotten it right! To this point of the process, I had not paid any attention to my opponent. I was just elated that all of the work was done. She, the medical resident and perpetrator of this emboldened attack, was standing quietly with her arms crossed in the corner of the small exam room in her long bright white coat. I had not even noticed—like I said, it was 3:00 AM and I was in the *automatic* mode. Nonetheless, I was caught off guard and somewhat overwhelmed by the fact that somebody had actually gone out of her way to do all of the *scut* work—my scut work—required for the care of this patient. This was simply unheard of—so I turned to compliment my, as of yet unacknowledged, "opponent."

I must admit that I was somewhat taken aback by the vision before me. I was exhausted. I had already been working for almost 24 straight hours. Admittedly, I was very possibly hallucinating from the exhaustion. Nonetheless, nothing could have prepared me for that which greeted my tired eyes. I simply had no idea that the vision awaiting me that dark night had been prepared specifically for me from before time began. There standing in the corner of that small ER exam room was…an angel. She was gorgeous. In my mind's eye, I can still picture her standing there today. Her slender beautiful face, narrow dark eyes, classic jaw lines, and sharp cheekbones were contrasted against her long bright white physician's coat and framed by her long, thick, dark hair. She had her arms folded across her chest and had a cute little grin on her face.

Admittedly I worked in a huge medical center, *but how had I missed this girl?*

And in that moment when our eyes first met, she knew she had won. I was standing there with my guard down, a huge grin on my face, and bewilderment in my eyes. I might as well have had *naiveté* written across my forehead with a black marking pen. My very worthy opponent was experienced enough in emergency room tactics to know that the battle was already over. She knew that like a fly fluttering aimlessly into a spider's web, I had gone to the emergency room that night thinking that everything was going to be *routine*. She had sprung her trap and it was over before I ever even knew that I was in a fight. I could barely keep my eyes off of her as I drained the abscess. Little did I know what I now know—that God had written that face on my heart, her face and her face alone—before the creation of the world. One life, one wife—and this bright white angel in the midst of the Valley of the Shadow of Death was to be mine.

By the time the topic of which service the patient should be admitted to finally arrived, I was practically falling all over myself. She didn't even have to ask! I *volunteered* to admit the patient to the surgical service. In this most critical of emergency room battles, I had been utterly routed. My plight was not lost on our little ER patient. She had easily figured out what was going on. I think she knew that she had just witnessed one of those *moments* between man and woman. I still remember that as I turned to tell her which floor she would be admitted to, she had this great big grin on her face. I got to look at that knowing grin for the next three days.

Needless to say, things did not go well for me the next day when I had to explain why this *medical* patient was on the trauma surgical service. I had already forgotten about her admission several hours later on rounds that same morning. I was trailing along as the rear guard at the tail end of our rapidly moving 6-member surgical team when they turned into her room on our ward. My memory was unpleasantly jarred back to reality when I heard the chief resident yell out in what can only be described as a shrill shriek emanating from the bowels of hell itself: "Who admitted this patient to *my* service?"

I tried to make up some sort of excuse, but it was pointless. There was no excuse. This was a sign of weakness and my chief resident scowled at me as he informed me, "I will not be rounding on *your* patient anymore. *You* are her doctor and *you* will take care of her."

I sheepishly responded that, of course, I would be happy to comply. Once again, *my* patient was sitting there with that big grin on her face. She thought it was hilarious. She was the only other person in the room who actually knew what had really happened and she reminded me of that fact with her cute little smile and an approving nod of her head. Without further comment, my chief resident and the trailing team of surgical residents and interns were out of the room and down the hallway. I tucked my tail between my legs and followed the team to the next patient room.

My patient did well and went home 3 days later on oral antibiotics with her wound healing well. I was, of course, the target of considerable chiding from the other members of the surgical team for many days thereafter. They were not used to such lapses in surgical team etiquette and protocol from a seasoned warrior who was well recognized for his battlefield pugnacity.

Meanwhile, I kept my eyes open for my emergency room angel, but it was indeed a huge medical center and I did not see her again for several months. I had been too overwhelmed by the moment to get her name in the emergency room. I found it scribbled next to her note in the chart, but I did not recognize it. I didn't know who she was, but I figured that I would undoubtedly run into her again soon.

I didn't.

I began to think that maybe I had just encountered a real angel or that she was just a beautiful apparition conjured up by the chronic sleep deprivation that plagued all surgical residents at big academic medical centers. Nonetheless, I kept my eyes open. There were lots of beautiful women at that huge university medical center—but I knew from the very beginning that this one was different. I didn't know then why this woman had so quickly enraptured my heart. I had given my life to Christ by then, but was an incredibly immature Christian. I had no idea that God had been the one who had set me up that night and that He had planned it all before time began. I was smitten bad and it was all God's doing.

As impressed as I was by this first meeting, my second encounter with my ER apparition was even more notable than the first. Several months later I found myself sitting in the medical center's *Surgical Infection Control Intensive Care Unit* writing a note on one of my patients. This ICU was reserved for surgical patients with very severe infections. For the wellbeing of other ICU patients—to keep from spreading infection—we kept these critically ill and infected patients in their own surgical ICU. This ICU routinely had some of the sickest surgical patients in the hospital. The surgical trauma service always had one or two patients in this particular ICU because of the propensity of severely injured patients, especially those with penetrating trauma, to develop severe infections.

The ICU patient I was caring for that day was quite a character. He had been in a horrific accident and had initially been treated for his surgical injuries at a nearby smaller hospital. He developed a horrible complication—a pancreatic abscess—and was quite ill for quite sometime. He was airlifted to us for further surgical care after he bled massively from his pancreatic bed. He had been in our ICU for over a month. He had recovered from the initial trauma and we were dealing with the complications stemming from his pancreatic abscess, which had been surgically drained multiple times. Every time we re-explored his abdomen, we left large caliber plastic tubular drains in the pancreatic bed. This was *business as usual* for pancreatic abscesses. I still remember that this unfortunate gentleman had so many plastic tubes sticking out of his abdomen that he looked like a human pincushion.

One of the expected complications of being so critically ill for so long in the confines of a windowless ICU was the development of ICU psychosis.

This guy had a major case of this so-called *ICU-itis*. In the parlance of one of my fellow surgical residents who had grown up in the south, this gentleman was "crazier than a peach orchard borer."

When it comes to ICU psychosis, there is *good* crazy and there is *bad* crazy. This guy was definitely *good* crazy. He was never mean or violent. In fact, he was hilarious. He always had this totally wild-eyed look on his face and would often make some funny comment when the team made rounds on him in the ICU. Even though he was a bit loose on his appreciation of reality, his comments were always witty and surprisingly intuitive and observant.

His bed in the ICU was separated by simple hanging curtains from the two beds on either side of him. These curtains were suspended from the ceiling on rollers so that they could be retracted completely out of the way. Most notably, these curtains only came down from the ceiling to a level that was about waist-high on the nurses and physicians who worked in the ICU. This height was very functional, giving the patients some degree of privacy, while also allowing the nursing staff to have near immediate visualization of all of the patients, should problems arise.

Unfortunately, while I was sitting in the ICU that day, the patient in the bed immediately adjacent to my patient suffered a cardiac arrest—like I said, they were a sick bunch of patients. Even though the arresting patient was not under my direct care, I immediately jumped in to help run the code protocol until that patient's surgical resident and the hospital *code team* arrived. Once they arrived, I took a backseat to them since they had the primary responsibility in that patient's care. You guessed it. The resident physician in charge of the hospital code team was none other than my ER angel.

Luckily, the ICU patient who had suffered a cardiac arrest demonstrated a very favorable response to our initial efforts. The members of the code team completed the follow-up stabilization therapy and routine post-code evaluation before they moved on. This time, however, I wasn't about to leave the ICU after turning over the patient's care to the code team. I had the perfect excuse to *stalk* this beautiful young lady who had skillfully avoided me for months. I stealthily went back to writing my note at the ICU desk. I kept a vigilant eye on her as she skillfully ran the code team in front of me. Once again, she looked beautiful with her long dark hair and classic facial features. She looked slender and gorgeous in her long white coat. She also ran a perfectly efficient code protocol. I was sizably impressed to say the least.

As all of this was going on, I happened to glance over at my patient in the adjacent bed. He also was similarly impressed with the commotion in the next bed, but in a slightly different manner than I. He glanced at me and caught my eye, then looked back toward the curtain separating him from the commotion in the bed next to him. He looked back at me, smiled a great big toothy and mischievous smile, and then again looked back at the commotion to his immediate left. All of the sudden it became crystal clear what he was looking at and what he was about to do. My ER angel was standing on the other side of the curtain facing the other patient's bed, where she was diligently involved in his post-arrest medical management. My patient's eyes were locked on her shapely hindquarters. They were outlined by her white coat and visible just beneath the hanging curtain. Before I could intervene—and I am not sure I would have even if I could have—he grabbed a great big handful of that which had so thoroughly captivated his gaze.

Needless to say, he caught her completely off guard. I am sure that being grabbed in such a manner was absolutely the last thing on this earth that she expected at that moment. I didn't know it then, but she had played NCAA Division 1A women's basketball at her undergraduate university and had an impressive vertical leap. I got to see every inch of that vertical leap at that enchanting moment. When she hit the earth again, she rapidly swung the curtain around and looked at her assailant who was sitting there with his big, wild-eyed grin. She immediately knew precisely what was going on. She looked back at me—as did her assailant. I am sure that my eyes were as wide as his. She had a great big smile on her face, knowing that she had been the victim of a little surgical ICU psychosis. Everyone started laughing—including me.

Needless to say, I could not wait to quiz the patient the next day. I had recounted the entire episode to my surgical team—it was one of those special moments in the life of a resident that just had to be shared with my coworkers. When we approached the patient's bed on rounds that next morning, I could not resist a little whimsical interrogation. "Anything special happen yesterday?" I queried.

At first he just looked at me with that crazy grin. He didn't appear to remember. I prompted him by asking if a big commotion had occurred around the adjacent patient's bed the day before. His eyes suddenly lit up in immediate acknowledgment and his mischievous smile returned to his face as he summed it all up with one simple statement, "I saw it and I went for it!"

Everyone burst into laughter at his candor. He grinned from ear to ear. He knew he was the star of the show. We all recognized that he was probably a little less crazy than we gave him credit for—but nonetheless entirely uninhibited.

As they say, the rest is history. I got her full name before I left the ICU that day and this time I wrote it down. Several days later I asked one of my fellow senior surgical residents about her. He apparently knew her quite well and his response was an immediate, "Oh, no. No, she would not be good for you."

I was taken aback by the immediacy of his answer. It turned out that he had asked her out several times and had been frustrated in his attempts to get a date with this beauty. I would not let his negative response stand in my way, however, and I soon had a date with her myself.

I was in love. I didn't know it then because I just didn't *get it* back then, but God had chosen this woman and all of her admirable traits and attributes (and also her quirks and faults) to be the perfect *foil* against which I would be shaped into that person that God wanted me to be. As I often still tell her, before time began, God looked at every single woman that would ever be born and chose the perfect one for me. Every other woman in the entire creation, past, present, and future was found *wanting* in this regard. She was the *only* one for me. I have no doubt whatsoever of the veracity of that statement. She is my one and only and somehow I knew it from the very beginning on that dark and stormy night in the emergency room.

My ER angel and wife finished her training to become board certified in intensive care medicine as I was finishing my cardiothoracic surgical training. When I was recruited to my current academic cardiothoracic surgical position (after two years as an assistant professor at another academic institution) the chief of our division soon found out that my wife was a fully trained, board-certified intensive care specialist. Partly because he was a nice guy and wanted to make me happy, but mostly because he was a really intelligent, visionary, and wise leader who had an incredible grasp of where our subspecialty was heading, my division chief moved quickly to hire my wife. He made her the medical director of the entire cardiothoracic surgical intensive care unit at our large tertiary care hospital. It was very literally an ideal job for a young professional subspecialist who was also in the process of starting a family. She rolled in at 7 AM and left at 3 PM, Monday through Friday. Although she was available for phone consultation at night and on weekends, there were no direct, in-house *on call* responsibilities.

Our cardiothoracic ICU was run under the old (and ideal) model where the cardiac surgeons each took the calls on their own patients. That was very much the way that all of us wanted it. We operated on our patients, we had a vested interest in their wellbeing, and we took all critical calls. The surgical residents and cardiothoracic fellows, of course, took the brunt of the routine calls. Nonetheless, if something bad was happening to our patients, we were very much involved. This is how we wanted it, for sure.

This left my wife doing the job that most cardiac surgeons want an intensive care consultant to do. We can handle all of the surgical problems and also the overwhelming majority of the small *medical* problems that arise in the post-operative course of cardiac surgical patients. On the other hand, we all very much appreciate help in the management of patients with more complicated medical issues. This, of course, was where my wife excelled. She basically spent her day handling the complex medical issues that challenged our patients in the cardiothoracic ICU.

She is a pro in this regard. She has a quick and brilliant mind and is a master of intensive care. The 13 years that she managed the cardiothoracic ICU were the best years of my career. She was kind and forgiving and encouraging to all of the cardiothoracic surgeons, even when we behaved badly, and there is no doubt that her critical care expertise saved countless lives in our ICU. This was well recognized and acknowledged by all of my partners. There are always lots of opinions on how to handle complex medical issues. She always made sure that the patient's best interest was what drove the discussion, assured that the patients received evidence-based care, and did it all without ruffling the feathers of the surgeons. Surely I am biased, but I think she is a master intensive care specialist.

She also, obviously, assisted me in the care of my patients. In this regard, she was absolutely the best. She had nothing to prove to me—I already knew that her mind could run circles around mine without even breathing hard—and we worked incredibly well together. I am so blessed to have married the smartest doctor I have every known. Between the two of us, I really believe that my patients received the very best care available. There are not too many couples that can claim to have shared equal professional responsibilities outside of the home like we can. Outside of the saving mercy of the cross of Jesus Christ, she is still the best thing that has ever happened to me—and remains the brightest of bright lights in the heart of the Valley of the Shadow of Death.

CHAPTER EIGHTEEN

Transition

A foundational truth separates this life from the next: in this life, all good things must come to an end. In the later stages of my career, I gradually came to the realization—as all heart surgeons must—that the pertinent question then was not *whether* my cardiac surgical career would end, but rather *when* and *how*. This is a matter of great importance to most cardiac surgeons. As we have touched upon, our cardiac surgical careers often become our most overpowering idols. Cardiac surgery, by its very nature, dominates our lives. So, when it comes time to lay down the proverbial scalpel, it cannot help but be a time of major transition in the life of every cardiac surgeon.

Some cardiac surgeons handle this transition—out of the only world that they have ever really known—quite well. Sometimes, however, the end of an otherwise illustrious career deteriorates into a disastrous tailspin. A major contributor to this catastrophic ending is the indisputable fact that the favorable financial wellbeing and elevated social status of most cardiac surgeons are both entirely dependent upon actually continuing the practice of cardiac surgery. Further still, the preponderance of the cardiac surgeon's ego support structure is also based in this unforgiving and difficult world, despite the fact that every cardiac surgeon would argue to the contrary. Regardless of their protests, the truth is still quite clear and the result is easily predictable: most cardiac surgeons try hard to hold on far too long. This leads to a career ending that at best can be described as out-of-control, but far too often is downright calamitous.

Holding on to one's career too long in the world of cardiac surgery is similar to holding on too long in most other professional careers. Instead of going out at the top of your game, several factors contribute to a predictable downward slide. The normal aging of the body creeps in despite that fact that most cardiac surgeons act like they are somehow above all that *aging nonsense*. Regardless of these claims of immortality, the body weakens over time and the stamina needed to hang in there in top form during those 6-10 hour disaster cases is considerably compromised. The result is often predictable: more *avoidance* behavior. Older cardiac surgeons often try to avoid cases that have a strong chance of turning into a marathon. Unfortunately, long operative cases are not always predictable. As we have discussed, in the world of cardiac surgery you don't always know when the pathway upon which you begin your "routine" sunny day ends deep in the dark recesses of the Valley of the Shadow of Death. Very literally, any routine 3-hour case can turn into a messy all-day disaster.

In addition to the weakening of the body, there is also an indisputable weakening of the mind. As you age, like it or not, you become more forgetful and your mind responds less quickly to sudden emergencies. These are just facts of life. For physicians, the recognized consequences of forgetfulness include the tendency to become fixed and rigid in the application of therapeutic algorithms. When these therapeutic algorithms change as new techniques are added, older cardiac surgeons tend to adopt these changes less readily.

Just as is the case regarding physical stamina, the older surgeon's response to his or her mind being less *quick* in emergency situations is—you guessed it—more avoidance behavior. They try to structure their practice, especially in regard to the emergency call schedule, to avoid those emergency situations altogether. This just makes the problem worse. In the world of cardiac surgery, *practice makes perfect*. The more you avoid the emergency situations, the less well you handle them when they do occur—and in the world of cardiac surgery they will continue to occur no matter how hard you try to avoid them.

All of us, at one time or another during our cardiac surgical career, get to witness the old cardiac surgeon who just holds on too long. It is so sad to see. These surgeons need to give it up and transition to something else—but they just can't do it. They have become so dependent upon the ego support offered by cardiac surgery that they just can't imagine centering their lives upon anything other than cardiac surgery. Deep down they cannot help but know they are holding on too long, but they hold on nonetheless. To do this, they become especially adept at the fabrication of complex rationalizations for why the rules of aging don't apply to their particular situation.

Unfortunately, the people who suffer the most are their patients. The hard reality is that cardiac surgery is a surgical subspecialty that is characterized and defined by the indisputable need for both mental acuity and physical stamina. When these attributes naturally wane as we age, the result is predictable. There are way too many times in the cardiac surgical operating room—truly the Valley of the Shadow of Death—when mental acuity and physical stamina are the only things that carry the day. When these attributes are not at the appropriate level, patients suffer and patients die. Despite the fact that these patients and their families believe they are getting top-notch cardiac surgery, they are not. Every single day across the world, patients suffer complications and even death because of the old-age errors of their old-age cardiac surgeons.

I have watched this unpleasant scenario play out many times in my career—including several notable cases in which cardiac surgeons continued to operate well into their late 70's. I cannot speak for them, but hurting my patients because I was unable or unwilling to recognize the fact that my skills were not what they needed to be is not why I went into medicine and certainly not why I became a cardiac surgeon. I have often pondered the possibility of intervening in these aging surgeon situations—and even attempted it once. Needless to say, I met incredible resistance—and truly astonishing rationalization. An honest appraisal of the results of my efforts in that attempt is not favorable. I am pretty sure that I made the situation worse. It was almost as if the surgeon overreacted to my gentle nudges by intensifying his efforts.

Needless to say, I knew that I did not want to end my career by holding on too long. Can you imagine anything worse? Hurting patients because of my need to bolster my sagging self-esteem? I cannot think of a more horrible end to a career otherwise dedicated to saving lives! I did not know how my career would end—how I would make that transition to another life—but devising a scheme that allowed me to prospectively define my transition was a focus of much thought during the later stages of my career.

I have already described part of the process by which God intervened in my life to provide that which, in my younger years, I could not even imagine needing—an exit strategy from the rigorous daily practice of cardiac surgery. As I have outlined, for me that daily practice included dealing with a large number of the complex cardiac surgical cases that are routinely referred into university-based academic medical centers, as well as the difficult cases that predominate in the world of heart failure, heart transplantation, and mechanical ventricular assistance. The only thing that I knew for sure regarding my exit strategy transition was that it was not going to be easy.

In that regard, I cannot even begin to describe the palpable impact of the abundant grace of God during this transition period. Unbeknownst to me, a solution to that which I had given so much thought had apparently already been very well thought out, even before time began. God had a plan. During my career, without my knowledge or intervention, He clearly set out to supply me with precisely the training and attributes that I would need for Him to orchestrate my gradual—and remarkably atraumatic— transition out of the rigorous practice of cardiac surgery.

To my amazement, God's plan for my transition was nothing short of gently nudging me into what I can only describe as a *dream job*. Although often inconvenient and characterized by long hours, the need in my new job for the razor sharp mental proficiency and physical stamina that had been critical during my cardiac surgical youth would be remarkably reduced. Expertise in the world of cardiac transplantation—that which I had not sought, but God had so amply supplied—furnished the gentle transition step in the area of *thoracic donor organ procurements*.

The procurement of thoracic organs (hearts and lungs) for transplantation requires the application of only very basic cardiac surgical techniques. Although there are occasionally unanticipated and precipitously catastrophic problems in the process of thoracic organ procurement, these cases are much less demanding than the 02:00 AM redo sternotomy, VAD-extraction, heart transplants to which I had become accustomed. Those complex cases take a toll on even the young and strong—and I was now neither of these. Such marathon cases as these, which I was doing on a routine basis and to which one can never really become totally acclimated, made thoracic organ procurement look pretty attractive.

In fact, once I got the technical routine down, leading the cardiothoracic fellows through the procurement procedure was really a lot of fun for me. Thoracic organ procurement is part of the invaluable training that is offered to cardiothoracic fellows at large tertiary referral heart failure hospitals such as ours. The fellows, with few exceptions, are generally quite eager to participate. Not only is learning the procurement procedure an important part of their training as cardiothoracic surgeons, but they also got to see, just by the nature of the procurement operations, thoracic anatomy that they don't routinely get to see. Learning the relationships of the various structures that inhabit the thoracic cavity from as many angles as possible is invaluable to a surgeon who must deal with middle of the night emergencies such as a gunshot or stab injuries to the vital organs of the chest. The procurement procedure requires that we dissect out the entire aortic arch, the major venous structures of the chest, and the trachea and main stem bronchi. The attentive trainee gains an invaluable thoracic anatomical familiarity that is found nowhere else in their training.

The only downside of this position as an organ procurement surgeon is that it requires me to be on call for thoracic organ procurement 24 hours a day, seven days a week. This can be a bit inconvenient, especially in regard to making plans. It can also result in some seriously long hours, many of which are at night and on weekends. Nonetheless, inconvenience is a state of mind and long hours have never been a problem for me. More importantly, the operations require less stamina because they are inherently shorter and less stressful. The need for quick reaction to unanticipated disaster is present, but markedly reduced. Although the actual donor organ procurement procedures can still have their own brand of stress and disaster, they still clearly represent a far less taxing load for my aging mind and body. My new position also generates a very large and consistent revenue stream. As I transitioned into this new position, I was happier and the Chairman of the Department of Surgery, whose interest in my career change was primarily financial, was delighted. As in any job, when the boss is happy, life is easier.

Although the surgical procedures involved in thoracic organ procurement themselves were usually relatively uneventful from a technical standpoint, there is, nonetheless, always the issue of dealing with the many and diverse personalities of the surgeons who gather for these multi-organ procurement procedures. These surgeons come from many different transplantation centers across the country. Of interest, the primary interpersonal problems encountered between the different transplant teams involved in these procurement procedures are not centered so much upon psychosocial issues as one might expect. Instead, the problems arise from one physiological fact with huge technical implications: reconstruction of an adequate blood supply source is vital to all solid organ transplantation. More specifically, each of the many different organ implantation procedures primarily involves suturing connections between the blood vessels that are vital to maintaining the donor organ's blood supply in its new recipient environment.

Thus, at least two, and sometimes more, blood vessel anastomoses (connections) must be created to reestablish the transplanted organ's blood supply. This involves at least one arterial connection and one venous connection for each organ. For each of these vascular connections, there is therefore a *cuff* of donor vascular tissue that, during the implant procedure, must be sutured to a similarly shaped recipient vascular cuff. It is in the division and preservation of these donor vascular cuffs that surgeon interpersonal problems most often arise. The various organs that may be going to many different recipient patients in many different locations across the country must *share* the donor arteries, veins, and cardiac chambers that make up these cuffs. Since the interests of many patients can be on the line at any particular donor procurement procedure, many different surgical personalities can all have a voice in the donor operating room. In fact, I have been involved in organ procurement procedures that resulted in as many as 8 solid organs going to 8 different recipients from a single donor.

Although the problem of shared vascular cuffs can be a significant issue with many abdominal organs also, the perfect example of this potentially contentious issue is found in the chest. The heart and the lungs are connected to each other by the blood vessels that course through each organ. For example, the pulmonary artery forms the *outflow* tract from the right ventricle of the *heart* and the *inflow* pathway of blood into the *lungs*. Thus, to make the connections of the new donor heart to the recipient's lungs, there must be a donor pulmonary artery cuff that is sewn to a similar recipient pulmonary artery cuff. And likewise, when the donor lungs are sewn into the lung recipient, a similar cuff of donor pulmonary artery must be sewn to the recipient pulmonary artery to make the vital blood supply connection between the organs. A similar issue is found in the donor left atrium, which must supply adequate atrial cuffs for both the heart and the lung transplant left atrial anastomoses.

The primary problem arises in the fact that the bigger the cuff of vascular tissue, the easier and safer is the respective anastomosis that must be completed in the implant procedures. Skimpy vascular cuffs can predispose to suturing errors that can be catastrophic for the respective recipient. The facts in this regard are clear: suturing errors are one of the most important technical reasons for early organ failure in both heart and lung transplantation. As someone who has sewn countless vascular anastomoses for both donor hearts and donor lungs, I am particularly sensitive to the issue of supplying adequately sized vascular cuffs for the implant surgeons. Most of the procurement surgeons that I have encountered feel the same way.

This may not seem like such a big deal to you. After all, transplant surgeons are big boys and girls and they can get along, right? Wrong. It is absolutely amazing to me how many times this donor vascular cuff issue has been the source of contention, controversy, and outright ire between the two thoracic procurement teams who stand opposing each other like warriors at the donor operating room table. The problem really rests in the perspective with which each of these teams enters the donor OR. If you have done enough organ procurements, you have dealt with the occasional surgeon who purposefully *shorts* your cuff to enhance their own. This is the guy or gal who believes that there can be only *one* winner in the cuff battle—and therefore there must also be a *loser*. Since, in his mind, there *must* be a loser, his goal is clear: to make sure that his *opponent*—the surgeon standing opposite him at the OR table—is the loser. The perspective with which he enters the donor OR is that this *must* be a fight and that he is not going to be the loser of that fight. When that is the pervasive perspective, all it takes is one condescending voice inflection or one poorly chosen word to quickly turn this into a major league firefight. If allowed to escalate, posturing, shouting, and even threatening language all follow. I have actually heard of several instances where blows were exchanged. Unbelievable.

When I first started doing thoracic organ procurements, I really had to prepare myself mentally for these encounters. It is so easy to succumb to the temptation to fight when the person standing across from you believes that *taunting* is normal OR behavior. This is especially difficult when he or she is two decades your junior and is a rookie in the game of thoracic organ procurement. Luckily, there is usually some time involved in getting to the donor hospital and so there is time for the Holy Spirit to remind me to pray. I very literally cannot remember the last donor procurement procedure in which I did not prep in serious prayer. It is a battle and I need Jesus there with me, in my heart, and making the calls for me. I need to let go of the reins *before* I find myself in the middle of the fight.

What Jesus has taught me in the hundreds of procurements that I have performed is the same lesson that He has taught me in every life situation: *He will never let me down.* Donor procurement is just like anything else. If we can just muster the faith in every tenuous situation to just do things His way—by His grace—we will be delightfully reminded that He is *always* there with us. He will help us settle the nerves of the anxious rookie. He will temper their hearts. He will drop a delightful air of cooperation over the operating room—if we can just get out of the way and volitionally choose to let Him go to work.

My goal in every procurement procedure, therefore, is to go into that operating room with the goal of just loving every single member of the various involved procurement teams.

A new command I give you: Love one another.
As I have loved you, so you must love one
another. (John 13:34, NIV)

His command is to *love one another* and this is exactly what He wants me to do in these situations. By God's grace alone, I have gotten very good at it. Calming words assuring the young rookie that my goal is to make sure that *he or she* gets a perfect atrial cuff are often all it takes to disarm the most contentious of situations. It is amazing how often the room is just thick with tension until Jesus disarms it. By His amazing grace, He has repeatedly acted in my heart to let *my* words be the mediator of *His* peace in the donor operating rooms.

And how this changes everything. Believe me, I have more than enough personal knowledge of how easy it is to listen to Satan's lies. He would have me believe that the surgeons from the other team are just looking to take advantage of me. Instead, I must remind myself that they are just as anxious as I am and that a careless word can be like a spark in an open can of gasoline.

By nothing less than the direct intervention of the Holy Spirit, I have learned that the solution to every contentious situation—including the most rambunctious donor OR—is quite straightforward. As the previous chapters attest, the primary principle of the cross of Christ—subservient, sacrificial love manifest in utter surrender—has the potential to impact every single situation in which we find ourselves. Before I head into a donor OR, I just need a gentle reminder that everything changes when one party surrenders.

When I begin the case by assuring the other thoracic procurement surgeon that the wellbeing of *their* recipient is my primary concern, the battle is over. You may not believe it, but I mean it every time I say it. I know that most of you might argue that *my* recipient should be my primary concern—and precisely in that statement is found the power of the cross of Christ. The wellbeing of my recipient is the part that I give to Jesus. The wellbeing of my recipient is where I put my trust in the power of that which was done for me on the cross of Calvary. I put my faith in Jesus—and He has *never* let me down. When I look out for the other surgeon's recipient, Almighty God looks out for mine. He can be trusted to be perfectly faithful to all of His promises and He has promised to never abandon us when we do things His way. In other words, the best way for me to look after the wellbeing of my recipient is to look after the wellbeing of the other surgeon's recipient—and let Jesus look after mine. That is the way God works. God's way of proceeding always seems to be the exact opposite of the world's.

I must admit that I just love it when God empowers me to surrender. Every single time that I have, by God's grace, been able to do things His way, God has moved mightily to settle even the edgiest operating room. Even when the OR is ripe for crisis, the tension just melts away. It can have a profound effect upon the nurses, anesthesia staff, and other OR staff who have all too often seen these situations spin rapidly out of control. They are always terrified that a mildly contentious situation might turn into a very real fight. When God begins to do His remarkable healing work, it feels like everyone in the operating room just heaves a great big sigh of relief. These fights are no fun for anyone, including the innocent bystanders—and when they flare, they put all of our recipients in danger.

The concept that there does not have to be a winner and a loser is foreign to most donor procurement operating rooms. The possibility that everyone—including and especially all of the organ recipients themselves—can go home *winners* is preposterous...*until someone surrenders.* It utterly changes the atmosphere of the operating room when a little bit of love is sent across the table instead of the first salvo of contentious gunfire. When one surgeon surrenders, God's presence becomes palpable. It is nothing less than this tangible presence of God that makes the opposing surgeon lose his desire to take advantage of the surrendering surgeon. Surely this is Jesus going before me into battle. He is in the business of changing hearts. This, like everything else in our life, is all about the subservient, sacrificial love of Jesus Christ on the cross of Calvary.

When I get out of the way and let Jesus run my heart, it absolutely amazes me what loving words come out of my mouth! When I let Jesus do the talking, when I agree to do things His way, He is always faithful to go before me into the fight. Sure, there has been the occasional surgeon who has still tried to take advantage of me after I have surrendered to them. But no harm has ever come from their attempts to take advantage of my humbled heart. They may think they have gotten away with something, but they *never* have. This is what I mean by Jesus being my *rear guard* when I leave the battlefield. If I am faithful to surrender, He is faithful to never let them win. I have never taken back a heart or a lung that could not be sewn in. *Jesus has never let one of my recipients suffer because of a poor sewing cuff.* Jesus goes onto the battlefield before me and He is my rear guard.

In addition to these changes, God also brought about another one of His very special miracles in my life. As God transitioned me into my exit strategy from the world of cardiac surgery, He mercifully brought me into a favorable position in the hearts of my fellow cardiothoracic surgeons.

This clearly could have gone either way. But, God was faithful to send a Spirit of favor toward me into the hearts of the people at my hospital. I would be the first to admit that it was underserved. I had done nothing to merit the kindness that found its way into the hearts of my partners.

God's grace went even further than that. To the nursing, anesthesia, resident, and ancillary staff, I suddenly—and quite unexpectedly—became this *sage* old cardiac surgical warrior. Instead of becoming a *nobody*— which clearly had been a big source of anxiety for my humungous ego—suddenly I became *the professor*. I knew I was an imposter for sure, but the people I worked with suddenly took on this almost reverent attitude toward me. Maybe their respect had been there before and I had just not recognized it. Unlikely. Maybe they had the respect but the occasion just never arose for them to express it. I doubt it. Instead, I recognized this for what it was, a forgiving, merciful, compassionate God once again faithfully delivering abundant grace to the unworthy. The Bible is replete with clear examples of God influencing the hearts of those who interact with His children. Clearly He worked His very special magic in my work environment. This was such a very great blessing for me at this stage of my career. I readily recognized it as such and praised God daily for His presence in my life.

Surely it is true that I have been at this institution a long time. Nonetheless, my new position of esteem was clearly much more than could be explained by my longevity at this hospital. My opinion was sought much more than would have been warranted by just my status as an "old guy" experienced heart surgeon. For example, when I made the transition to my new job description, I knew I would have some extra clinical time so I immediately sought to become a surgical mentor to two of our junior faculty members. I wanted to supplement my clinical income to the division by assisting them on difficult cases, especially when there was not a resident trainee available to *first assist* them. They both loved it. It was a win/win situation for all of us. I kept my skills up and they enjoyed an experienced first assistant, as well as a senior surgeon to help them make tough decisions if anything out of the ordinary occurred.

God really went before me into this particular battle. My career *redirection* could have been a gigantic career-ending disaster for me. Instead God blessed those junior faculty members with a great heart for me and they welcomed me into their operating rooms with open arms. Once again, this could have gone either way. As we have discussed, big egos are not exactly in short supply among heart surgeons—even (and especially) junior level heart surgeons. As junior faculty, they could have felt threatened by my presence. To some degree I am sure that this occurred. Nonetheless, both were superb surgeons and they clearly must have felt assured enough of their abilities to not feel threatened. Either that or they were willing to accept whatever small ego hit my presence might invoke in order to get senior-level surgical assistance.

I did have a pretty good reputation of getting myself (and others) out of big time trouble. This fact may have weighed heavily in my favor when they contemplated their response to my offer to help. That which I correctly recognized as the compassionate grace of God rescuing my patients from my mistakes, they saw as skill, experience, and clinical wisdom. Regardless of the reason, I think my junior colleagues just appreciated the fact that I would be there to offer solid surgical assistance and years of experience in case of an untoward disaster. I made very sure that they knew I was there only to help and that I would never question their decisions unless I truly believed that the patient's wellbeing was directly and seriously threatened.

I also made a commitment to myself to be affirming whenever possible and to criticize only in the very rare circumstance where a change was truly warranted. I desired the heart of Jesus in this regard: that my response to a surgical error on the part of my junior colleagues would have only restoration and affirmation—and never punishment—as its motivating force. I wanted them to feel safe having me in their operating rooms. I wanted them to feel that they could consult me on any problem without fear of repercussion and in utter safety and confidence. I wanted them to feel safe enough to openly discuss their biggest errors. Everyone makes mistakes. The key is to learn all that can be learned from them. Making sure they experienced a constructive maximal learning experience from every error was my job.

By God's grace I was fairly successful at keeping this commitment. One way or the other, whenever they were doing a very difficult case, or whenever there was no resident assistance available, both junior faculty not only accepted my offer, but consistently sought me out to join them in the operating room. God's assistance during this difficult period of my life was obvious and deliberate.

But even beyond this surgical assisting on routine cases and consulting on tough operative situations, God did even more to promote me among the people with whom I worked every day. I was amazed how flagrant God's grace became during this transition time in my career. In fact, I simply could not believe the extremes to which God would go to promote my reputation at the hospital. Repeatedly He orchestrated catastrophic circumstances in the operating room, intensive care unit, and even the surgical wards. All hell would break loose with great threat to human life. He would bring almost bizarre circumstances to bear in the treatment course of some of our patients. The spectrum ranged from great clinical mysteries to outright catastrophic exsanguinations to severe cardiovascular collapse and profound hemodynamic compromise.

As I began to take stock of these repeated episodes, a recurring pattern became readily apparent. A catastrophic situation threatening one of our cardiac surgical patients would develop. The involved surgeons, house staff, and nurses would be gathered en masse to try to save the patient's life. As if the catastrophic nature of the situation was not enough, the clinical circumstances would often be shrouded in great mystery and confusion regarding precisely what the problem was and what should be done next. And then—there in the middle of the melee—I would be emergently paged. Over and over again, I found myself praying like crazy for God's special wisdom and guidance as I moved quickly to the scene of the disaster. As I have described, the world of cardiac surgery is the world of death and dying and unfortunately these circumstances were all too common. Truly, even in my new "scaled-back" surgical role, I could not escape the Valley of the Shadow of Death.

As this repeating pattern became more apparent, my prayers for wisdom and guidance on the way to the scene of the fight turned into prayers of praise for God's goodness. I somehow just *knew* that God was just about to glorify me in the eyes of those around me by working through me to save the patient's life. That may sound arrogant, but it really isn't. I take no credit for what happened. I am just describing what I personally witnessed over and over again on our patient wards and in our operating rooms. I was as surprised at the results as anyone! My life at the hospital was starting to resemble the lead actor hero role in a cheap action movie. I would be running to these emergencies with my eyes wide open to see the great victory that God would bring about. It quickly got to the point that I already knew—before I even got to the scene of the battle—that God was going to give me the wisdom needed to solve the dilemma and to save the patient's life. It was weird, but I just *knew*. And over and over again, that is precisely what happened.

It is a natural human tendency to move away from scenarios in which there is a high possibility of great anxiety, strife, battle, suffering, risk, hard work, and death. But, just as I had known during the early stages of my medical career, I also knew then—I am sure by the prompting of the Holy Spirit—that God had placed me precisely in these situations at precisely the right time with precisely the right capabilities. I knew that my job in these emergency situations was to arrive on scene with the right attitude, to unhesitatingly step directly into the battle, and to use my gifts to help the on-scene physicians try to remedy the deadly situation. In each circumstance, I must admit, I would find myself slipping toward considerable anxiety. I guess we all worry about screwing things up and looking stupid. When the gunfire of an ambush catches us off guard, our first inclination is to dive for cover or run in the opposite direction. I guess we all naturally hesitate to move toward the gunfire.

Nonetheless, each time the anxiety would sweep over me, God would bless me with the overriding thought that I was in fact born precisely to step into the battle to fight for those who did not have the capability to fight for themselves. God replaced my anxiety with great confidence and affirmation in these precarious situations. He convinced me that my whole life, including all of the tough cardiac surgical fights that He had put me through, had been in preparation for exactly that moment, in that location, in that exact set of circumstances. I was thus enabled to plunge into the battle in full faith that if I stepped into harm's way and fought for the disenfranchised, Jesus would be there with me. God would go before me, and He would have my back. The power of the cross of Christ would be there in full force. I just kept telling myself that Jesus was in charge, He was all-powerful, and He loved me.

And so instead of taking the comfortable route and moving in the opposite direction of these disasters, I moved eagerly toward these spiritual fights. Despite my own fears and reservations—and by God's grace alone—I stepped in faith into the battle on behalf of my colleagues and their patients. When the sounds of battle echoed down the steep walls of the Valley of the Shadow of Death, by the grace of God, I moved toward the gunfire. It was so amazing. I have no idea why God chose to bless me in this way. I have always figured that it is just His overflowing abundant mercy, compassion, grace, and love that push Him in this direction.

Regardless of His unknown motivation, all that I can say for sure was that God's repeated orchestration of these situations only served to embellish my warrior reputation. When I would go cruising down the hallway of the main cardiac operating room suite, even the cleaning personnel would stop what they were doing and yell out, "There he goes—called in to save the day again!" Or they would ask, "What disaster are you going in to fix?" or echo down the hallway after me "Looks like they called in the *big gun*."

Truly I was—and continue to be—humbled by the kindness of God's heart.

CHAPTER NINETEEN

Warriors, Back-to-Back

As my reputation as a gunfighter, "fearless" warrior, and rescue *artiste* began to grow, the junior faculty continued to become even more and more comfortable with my assistance. When disasters loomed, my pager number was often the first one they dialed. I continued to be called into their operating rooms to consult on tough decisions on a daily basis, even when I was not first-assisting them. In addition, one of the more senior surgeons had also always been relatively comfortable calling me in for second opinions. He had been doing this for many years and nothing changed after my transition to my new position in the division. In fact, as I assumed my new role, he made it a regular occurrence. Needless to say, I was delighted. I felt incredibly blessed. It was episodically stressful, but I knew in my heart that this was my calling, and I was right in the middle of it. I knew that God had very precisely gifted me to fight these fights.

With all of this going on, there was one notable exception to my open-armed reception as a surgical assistant, consultant on tough therapeutic decisions, and redeemer of lost cardiac surgical causes. One of my senior and most internationally recognized colleagues, Dr. Faust, either never needed senior advice, or at the very least never reached a similar level of comfort in asking for my assistance. He simply never asked for my advice on a case—that is until about four years into my job change. I remember that day as if it were yesterday.

That morning had started out quite routinely. I was first assisting one of the junior faculty cardiac surgeons on an elective case. Even though bad news normally circulates quickly through our OR suites, we had not yet heard any rumblings of trouble that morning. Suddenly, a circulating nurse from one of the other cardiac operating rooms burst into our operating room. She was breathless. Her speech was pressured, not loud, but so pressured that it immediately flooded our operating room with a tidal wave of palpable anxiety.

"Dr. Faust is having trouble in OR 615! He can't figure out what is wrong and wants to know if you can come over and take a look!" She could barely get two sentences out because of her breathlessness. We were in OR 614, so I knew she wasn't short of breath from a *long* walk from OR 615. Suddenly it hit me. She was breathless from anxiety. No, it was more than just anxiety. She was frightened!

This was not a good sign. Something bad was happening next-door.

"You need to come right now," she followed up. There was a defined tone of desperation in her voice as she delivered her last comment as more of a demand than request. Dr. Faust was in trouble.

I froze for a second. For me, it was a bit of an awkward and weird moment in that operating room. The junior faculty member looked at me with a wondering and inquisitive look. He knew that this was simply unheard of. He knew that Dr. Dante had *never* called for anyone's help— that would have been interpreted as a sign of weakness and he never allowed himself that luxury. He never asked for help. No. Something unusually bad was happening in his operating room.

I scrubbed out. In the depths of my heart, I immediately began to pray. Prayer has become a reflex in these situations. I prayed every single step of the many steps it took to move me rapidly from my operating room to the hallway and next-door to Dr. Faust's room.

As weird as this may seem, I had known this day was coming. God had been progressively elevating the tenor and intensity of the situations into which He had been throwing me lately. Somehow, I knew I was headed toward bigger and more dangerous things. The pace and accelerating intensity of these episodes made it feel as if we were building up to something really big.

And I was confident. The previous 40-50 similar episodes over the previous 3-4 years taught me that when God threw me into these circumstances, I could be assured that He would be there with me. He had repeatedly pounded that lesson into my brain and I had finally learned it. I knew that if I just relied upon Him, He always gave me the wisdom that I needed to solve the clinical dilemma. I had learned to make my mind receptive to the clues that God would supply, to focus on His deliverance, and to ask Him in the middle of it all to raise me above the fray.

So, once again I asked God to go to war with me. With every step I took, I asked Him to solve the problem *even before I got there*. I asked for Jesus to stand back-to-back with me in the middle of the fury of this great battle.

And amazingly, as I walked toward the other operating room, I *praised* God. It was just like 2Chronicles 20 with Jehoshaphat and the *vast army* that lay before Jerusalem. I praised God because His promise is that His grace is always enough—and He is perfectly faithful to His promises. I praised God for always having been there with me—every single time—such that I could know without any doubt that He would be there yet again in the middle of this fight. I praised God for orchestrating these circumstances and asked that His Name be raised in glory in the outcome.

When I walked through the door of Dr. Faust's operating room, I knew immediately that this foray into the Valley was going to be different. Even though this was the world of cardiac surgery and all operations are matters of life and death, this was something else altogether, something exceedingly more. Dr. Faust's demanding personality had raised the emotional overlay of this situation to a fevered pitch. The feeling of utter frustration that permeated the room, as if every possible remedy had already been tried and had failed, immediately overwhelmed me. Defeat was thick in the air. The room and everyone in it had that air of hopelessness—as if nothing I could say or do would make any difference anyway.

I must be honest. My confidence fluttered weakly inside my heart. Despite my earlier confidence, I admit to being overwhelmed by the sudden fury into which I had just walked. This was palpable spiritual warfare. This was, somehow, *dark*. It felt like I had walked in just in time for a disastrous ending. It was as if I were in a barrel that had just reached the edge of Niagara Falls. The barrel was going over the falls and I was now in it. It was too late to stop it. The whole scene had an overwhelming air of tragic inevitability.

By God's grace, though, I walked confidently right into the middle of the operating room, into the middle of the fight.

I felt every pair of eyes in the room—except Dr. Dante's—immediately turn toward *me*. There was absolute silence from every mouth associated with those pairs of eyes. Only Dr. Faust was speaking. His voice was elevated—as always. But there was something more. Usually his voice exuded power and authority. He was a steamroller for sure. When he got into an anxiety-provoking situation like this, he would just put the pedal to the metal and flatten everything in sight. His voice would grow very loud and he would simply overwhelm the opposition. It was how he got things done. This was very effective for him. I could tell that he was still trying to maintain that authority, but his voice repeatedly cracked and the end of every sentence seemed to just trail off.

I knew that voice.

It had been mine too many times before. I knew what desperation sounded like. Dr. Faust was truly desperate. His patient was dying on the operating table before him and he didn't know how to fix the problem. I was confronted by a sinking ship caught up in a flurry of deck activity in response to the desperate commands of its captain. I had known this would be a fight and it did not disappoint.

I cannot express in words what a horrible feeling Dr. Dante was experiencing at that moment. I confess that I really do know it all too well. I have been there way too many times before to not recognize it immediately. All too often, the cardiac surgical procedure had started out quite well only to have a small complication spin into a seemingly unrecoverable death spiral. One moment you are on the offense with everything moving along as planned. Your battle plan is still intact and you are attacking. Then, just a moment later, things have changed. In the next moment you are on the ropes. You are pure defense with things spinning rapidly out of control. I knew immediately that Dr. Faust's procedure had followed precisely such a trajectory.

Even the most complex cardiac surgical procedure can be broken down into an intricate series of many smaller surgical moves. These small moves must all proceed in an orderly fashion. There is a small amount of leeway in many of the tasks in regard to their order, their timing, and the perfection required in their completion. Nonetheless, for the most part each of these small steps must be performed in the correct order and completed perfectly prior to proceeding to the next. Luckily, these small steps are, in and of themselves, fairly easy. When taken as a whole, the operation may appear to be incredibly complex and difficult—and it is—but each of the small moves that comprise this operation are relatively straightforward. As easy as they may be in their performance, however, so also can these small moves be equally unforgiving if they are not performed flawlessly.

Every cardiac surgeon knows this.

If you mess up one of these small steps, it is best to stop right there and spend the time necessary to make it perfect. Moving on to the next step before the last operative move is perfected results in a propensity to mess up that next one also. These steps are often interrelated and therefore directly dependent upon each other. This means that at the drop of a hat, at a single miscue on a single step, things can begin to rapidly cascade in the wrong direction like an avalanche picking up speed, momentum, and mass as it slides down a mountainside.

Most cardiac surgeons know better than to proceed further when the *small step* rule has been violated. Admittedly, there are plenty of circumstances in which you simply must move on. But, for the most part, you go back and fix the problem before you move on. There is only one problem with this paradigm. Sometimes you mess up one of the small moves *and you don't know it*. All of the sudden you begin to see the wheels coming off the cart and you have no idea why it is happening. Such was the case with Dr. Faust's patient. As I said, I have been there before. You are making all the usual moves, and suddenly—almost out of the blue—the patient and their hemodynamics (blood pressure, heart rate, cardiac output) do not respond the way they should. Before you know it, you and your patient are in a world of hurt.

As their careers advance, most cardiac surgeons develop a sixth sense with which they can detect this impending disaster—almost like a high-resolution sensor array that automatically absorbs and processes all of the tactical battlefield information during a cardiac surgical procedure. Somehow, one just *knows* immediately when something is not right. Experienced cardiac surgeons know these patterns well, having been subjected to them and learned their associated catastrophic consequences in many similar scenarios over years of cardiac surgical practice. Those catastrophic consequences are the drivers that burn this sensitivity into your very being. You know when it is just a speed bump, you know when it is important, and you know when disaster is pending. This innate early warning system is what allows you to kick immediately into the attack mode and to move quickly to fix the problem before it escalates.

And yet before you can fix the problem, you must identify it. You have to know which step in the cascade of hundreds of completed steps generated the problem and you must go back and fix it immediately before things get out of control. *Out of control* can happen *so* very quickly in the world of cardiac surgery.

And just to add to an already heightened sense of anxiety, when your cardiac surgeon sensors go off, you are not the only one who knows—everyone in the operating room can sense the change. The various members of the OR team are bright, attentive, and intuitive; they quickly learn to read their cardiac surgeon. They know almost immediately when things are not right. This is a horrific feeling for everyone involved in the patient's care. It is especially miserable being the cardiac surgeon who looks up in the middle of the mess just in time to catch everyone in the room looking directly at you. Their eyes tell you that *they know*. As the cardiac surgeon, you are the captain of this ship. When things go wrong, very literally every eye in the room is on you. The oppressive weight of their expectations can be palpable. They want to be reassured that not only do you know what the problem is, but also that you can fix it.

After all, the OR staff have all been there many times before. They know the consequences of failing to fix the problem. Human life is at stake. Human life is at immediate risk of being abruptly terminated. This is not plastic surgery. We are not doing a breast augmentation. This is not orthopedic surgery. We are not fixing a torn anterior cruciate ligament. A *problem* in the world of cardiac surgery does not result in asymmetry of the nipples or a limited range of motion in the knee joint. A problem in a cardiac surgical procedure means that your patient's very life, their very existence on earth, is immediately threatened. So, when things start to go wrong, memories of the dark consequences of *heart surgery gone bad* begin to flash though the minds of every member of the operating room team. It is hard to describe how the pressure can build if you are the focal point of the mess, the lightning rod in the fiery thunderstorm. It is as if your brain is being rushed by a thousand formless shouting voices.

Luckily, the countless similar scenarios you have faced over the years have burnt the warning signs of impending disaster into your brain. You are ready. At the first hint of a problem, your brain goes through its problem-specific checklist immediately and automatically.

Initially, you reach for all of the usual fixes for all of the usual problems. These are the things that you have learned are most likely responsible for the specific problem that you are experiencing. You bang through those options quickly and automatically. Your mind is like a machine in this regard—it is a machine or you would not be there. Cardiac surgeons who do not automate this part of their medical brain do not stay cardiac surgeons for long. The years of cardiac catastrophes weed out the weak. If your mind is not quick, agile, and correct, you are not standing there. If the first solution does not work, you move immediately to the second and to the third. Something will work. It always does—almost always.

This was one of those *almost always* situations. The problem that Dr. Faust was experiencing had many possible causes and therefore many possible solutions. By the time that I arrived on the scene, he had been through them all. Literally. He is an incredibly bright surgeon. He would not be in a senior position at one of the premier cardiac surgical units in the world if he were not. He is compulsive, quick, detail-oriented, and very thorough. He is internationally considered to be a technically superb, experienced, and brilliant heart surgeon. He had already thought of and remediated possibilities that would not have even crossed my mind. He had meticulously gone through every one of the possibilities and had enacted the *fix* for each of the problems. He was a machine. He was a powerful cardiac surgical machine and on that day, he had done everything perfectly.

But this time he did not have a clue regarding the real problem. There was something more going on here and he had no explanation, no solution. This was not business as usual for Dr. Faust. He had just encountered the Living God.

I have no idea why God does these things. I have no explanation. My first guess is that there were *lessons* being doled out to every individual in that operating room that day. Everyone is at a different stage in his or her life. Everyone comes to the operating room with a different perspective, operating under a different paradigm. Everyone has different expectations, attitudes, skills, mindsets, and temperaments. And yet I knew by the perfect wisdom of God that the life of every person staring at Dr. Faust would have been incomplete without precisely that set of circumstances at that moment in that operating room. God is perfectly efficient and we are assured that God pays close attention to every detail of our every day.

> *I praise you because I am fearfully and wonderfully made; your works are wonderful, I know that full well. My frame was not hidden from you when I was made in the secret place. When I was woven together in the depths of the earth, your eyes saw my unformed body. **All the days ordained for me were written in your book before one of them came to be.** (Psalm 139:14-16, NIV; emphasis added)*

We can be confident that nothing enters our life that didn't need to be there and nothing is excluded that does need to be there—our God and His plan are both perfect. It is no different for Dr. Faust. At that moment, he was under attack and his attacker was the consummate Warrior. God knows all and is all-powerful and He had a point to make that day—and, no matter how it manifested itself in the lives of everyone present, it was to be to God's glory. This was a perfect attack aimed at the one weak link in the impressive armor of this senior cardiac surgical warrior—who was now frantically trying to save his patient's life. By the time that I walked into the operating room, things had progressed from desperately frantic to the utter paralysis that follows unrequited panic. Other than Dr. Faust stressfully and expressively thinking out loud, you could have heard a pin drop.

When he saw me, Dr. Dante immediately began to explain the problem. After all, I was there at his specific request. He started from the beginning, giving me a rapid recount of the patient's significant history and cardiac-related findings. He moved rapidly through what had transpired in the hour before my arrival. He had never spoken to me like this.

He explained that this was to have been a "routine" replacement of the patient's diseased aortic valve. The aortic valve, once again, is the outflow valve of the main pumping chamber of the heart, the left ventricle. Its job, very basically, is the same job of all cardiac valves—to allow the blood being pumped through the heart to flow in only one direction. Without one-way valves, a pulsatile fluid pump will not work efficiently. The aortic valve's *job description*, therefore, is to be zero resistance to blood being ejected out of the left ventricle, but, at the same time, to be 100% resistant to blood leaking backwards from the aorta to the left ventricle.

The aortic valve allows the left ventricle—the main pumping chamber of the heart—to eject blood into the biggest blood vessel of the body, the ascending aorta. As we discussed in Mrs. Filander's case, the aorta is like a large garden hose and its first section is called the ascending aorta. The ascending aorta is the conduit through which the blood first flows when it is ejected from the left ventricle. From there it goes to the rest of the aorta and its many side branches that supply blood to the various vital organs of the body.

Dr. Faust explained that everything had been proceeding normally up until the moment that he had applied the aortic cross-clamp. In order to operate inside of the heart—mandatory if your goal is to replace one of the internal valves of the heart—you must have bloodless access to the valve. Two basic steps are required to obtain access to the valve and a bloodless operative field. As we have previously reviewed, the first step is to use the cardiopulmonary bypass machine to take over the work of the heart and the lungs so that the heart can be stopped for its internal surgery. According to Dr. Faust, this first step of placing the patient on cardiopulmonary bypass had proceeded without complication.

The second step is to separate the operative area, which in this case was the proximal ascending aorta, from the blood flow to the body that is being returned from the cardiopulmonary bypass machine. As previously described, the plastic tubular cannula that returns the blood flow from the cardiopulmonary bypass machine to the patient's body is routinely placed in the *distal* ascending aorta. To gain access for the surgical replacement of the aortic valve, an oblique incision is made in the *proximal* ascending aorta near its connection to the left ventricle. The aortic valve is easily visualized through this small incision since it sits at the junction of the left ventricle and ascending aorta. It doesn't take a rocket scientist to realize that a serious problem exists in making an incision in the proximal aorta, since the cannula from the cardiopulmonary bypass machine is continually returning a large volume of blood to the body in that very same ascending aorta, just an inch or two downstream from the planned incision. When the incision is made in the ascending aorta to gain access to the aortic valve, something must be done to separate the operative field from the pressurized blood stream or blood from the aortic cannula would obviously shoot across the room.

The solution is simple. It is utilized in hundreds of thousands of cardiac operations every year. The surgeon simply places a metal *cross-clamp* across the ascending aorta. Since the ascending aorta is malleable and easily compressible by a metal clamp, this technique mechanically separates the high-pressure blood flow returning in the distal ascending aorta from the proximal ascending aorta where the aortic valve replacement operation will take place. This clamp-mediated blocking of blood flow into the proximal ascending aorta, while it gives the surgeon a dry operative field in which visualization of every aspect of the aortic valve replacement is readily obtained, leads to one other small problem. The coronary arteries, which feed the muscle of the heart its blood supply, are small branches off of the proximal ascending aorta, just adjacent to the aortic valve. When the cross-clamp is applied, therefore, the blood supply to the heart muscle is cut off for the duration of the valve replacement.

Cutting off the blood supply to the heart, even for just a few minutes, can have serious consequences. For example, the sudden occlusion of a coronary artery is precisely the primary mechanism of myocardial infarction, otherwise known as a *heart attack*. The extreme sensitivity of the heart to sudden cessation of its blood supply is not surprising. After all, the heart has very high metabolic demands. It never stops for a rest. It must continually pump pressurized blood under the wide variance of demanding conditions to which the body is subjected. This myocardial *ischemia* (cutting off of the blood flow to the heart muscle) was a major problem in the early days of heart surgery. The extremely high mortality that was experienced in the early days of heart surgery was primarily due to heart failure that resulted from the contractile injury caused by unprotected myocardial ischemia.

Only decades of research carried out by cardiac physiologists—many of them also cardiac surgeons—have supplied a methodology to protect the heart muscle during the mandatory myocardial ischemia that must take place during most cardiac surgical procedures. If the blood supply must be temporarily interrupted, then the technique most often employed to protect the heart muscle is to *reduce* its metabolic demands. It is the simple law of supply and demand. If the metabolic *demands* of the heart are radically reduced, then it is far less likely to be significantly injured by the cessation of its nutrient blood *supply*.

Since the blood pumping demands of the body are already being met entirely by the cardiopulmonary bypass machine, the contraction of the heart muscle can be forcibly terminated to reduce metabolic demands to a fraction of their normal levels. This reduction in metabolic demand is most commonly obtained by administering a solution called *cardioplegia* into the proximal ascending aorta (and therefore into the coronary arteries) immediately after the cross-clamp is applied and before the incision is made in the ascending aorta. This cardioplegia solution most often employs a high potassium concentration. This high potassium concentration causes the heart muscle to cease contraction and remain in a relaxed (or diastolic) state. Cardioplegia is most often also administered at a cold temperature to cool the myocardium and further reduce its metabolic demands. Once again, this solution results in the heart being put into a sort of *suspended animation* during its reparative surgery.

Dr. Faust reviewed that, indeed, the first steps of the operation seemed to have proceeded uneventfully. The two plastic cannulas that serve to channel the blood to the heart-lung machine and then back to the patient were in place. This *cannulation* portion of the procedure had apparently proceeded without problem. The cannula had been placed in the right atrium to capture all of the blood returning from the veins of the body. It appeared to be doing its job of channeling the blood out of the heart into the reservoir on the heart-lung machine. As per routine, Dr. Faust had placed the second *inflow* cannula in the distal ascending aorta. By his account, all had proceeded uneventfully. The heart-lung machine had been turned on and the patient was being supported on cardiopulmonary bypass. Dr. Faust repeatedly assured me that this placement of all the tubes and cannulas had proceeded without event. Further, the *perfusionist* operating the heart-lung machine added that the membrane oxygenator and all other aspects of cardiopulmonary bypass apparatus appeared to be working "perfectly normally."

It was at the very next step of the operation that everything seemed to fall apart. Every time that Dr. Faust attempted to put the cross-clamp on the distal ascending aorta, utter chaos would break loose. Normally, after the cross-clamp is placed, the cardioplegia infusion, as previously described, is initiated through the cannula into the proximal ascending aorta, which gently distends as the coronary arteries are being perfused. The cessation of the contraction of the heart is almost always immediate. The heart normally decompresses. This occurs because another plastic cannula, which serves to vent the heart, has been passed into the left ventricle to decompress it when its contraction stops. This decompression also normally results in decompression of the left atrium, pulmonary artery, right ventricle and right atrium. In other words, the heart stops and shrinks down as it is emptied of the majority of its internal blood.

Unfortunately, this is precisely the opposite of what actually occurred every time that Dr. Faust applied the cross-clamp. Instead of stopping, the heart continued to vigorously contract. Instead of decompressing, literally every single chamber of the heart became massively distended—*massively* distended. By now Dr. Faust had placed the cross-clamp many times as he worked through the various solutions to the problem, only to have to immediately remove it because the heart would blow up like a balloon. As I mentioned, he had already done all of the right moves. He had even placed an extra vent into the pulmonary artery to further decompress the heart and had assured that his left ventricular vent was working well. He had done everything right and still nothing had worked.

Dr. Faust immediately reapplied the aortic clamp and started the cardioplegia infusion to show me what had been happening and I must admit it was pretty scary. Within only a very few moments, the heart became massively distended. The perfusionist was at a loss as Dr. Faust yelled at him to stop the cardioplegia infusion. All of the vents, the venous drainage, and the aortic perfusion seemed perfect from the perfusionist's perspective. I could tell from the look on everyone's face that this had been going on for quite some time. Dr. Faust had time and again repeatedly replaced the cross clamp only to have to remove it each time. With each repetition of the massive deformation of the heart and the yelling that followed, the angst in the room had skyrocketed even higher. Dreadful fear gripped everyone. Countless eyes met mine as I glanced around the room. Their message conveying extreme anxiety would have been clear a mile away. The operative procedure could not go forward and it could not go backward. It was totally immobilized. And in that immobilization, it was entirely out of control. This was a death spiral and everyone knew how it would end if something wasn't done quickly.

I could tell that the OR personnel were so traumatized by what they had experienced that no one even wanted Dr. Faust to place the aortic cross-clamp again. They were obviously terrified of what would follow. I could not tell how many times Dr. Faust had repeated this sequence only to have it fail. It was obvious from the extreme apprehension in the room, which occurred whenever he reached for the cross-clamp, that he had done it many, many times. I was sure that the panic in the room had elevated each time as Dr. Faust's voice had gotten louder and louder. He had started out yelling and built to a crescendo, but now his voice was quiet and desperate. You didn't have to be a great surveyor of the human condition to adequately assess the situation. It was desperate unto death. I had known that this might be the case even before I walked into the room, because, as I said, I had *never* before been called into Dr. Faust's operating room.

The reason for the extreme nature of the situation was obvious. Dr. Faust very literally could not proceed beyond this step of the operation. The operation cannot be performed without placing the cross-clamp and every time the clamp was placed, the results were not just inconvenient—they were catastrophic. To have come to the operating room and progressed to this point, only to be unable to complete the operation was simply unheard of. For the patient, the consequences of such an outcome were grave and everyone knew it. In the last decade, I cannot recall walking into a more desperate operating room.

The solution to this disaster is easy and logical in retrospect, but in the midst of the bludgeoning battle in that operating room, it was anything but easy and logical. It had clearly stumped one of the most experienced and gifted heart surgeons that I had ever known, not to mention the rest of the operative team that shared in his torment at that vital moment.

And yet in an instant the Holy Spirit supplied me with the answer. In that instant, I knew why I had had to suffer through so many similarly trying and devastating moments in the operating room during my career. In that instant the necessity of all of that anxiety became crystal clear. It was like the suffering of Joseph in Egypt that ultimately allowed him to save his family and the infant nation of Israel. It all made sense only when viewed in the context of God's magnificent plan.

Our God, the King-of-last-minute-rescues, struck in that operating room with the finality that was typical of His Old Testament rescues. In literally an instant, I diagnosed the problem that was threatening to kill Dr. Faust's patient. This knowledge occurred far too quickly to have originated in any logical thought process. There was no thinking involved. The answer was just there. So, I promptly, quietly, and humbly—for I had been here too many times to not be filled with compassion for my colleague—prepared to tell Dr. Faust precisely what was wrong. The precise mechanism by which the problem had occurred had been supplied to me and so also I would describe it in detail for Dr. Faust.

In the instant that the answer was delivered to me, however, another problem immediately surfaced: I knew I had to be very careful in how I delivered this message. I took a deep breath and edged closer to the drape at the head of the table that separated me from the sterile operating field. I peered cautiously over the top of the drape at the frantic scene. Dr. Faust had just removed the cross clamp from the aorta. I could see the aftermath of the massive cardiac distention. I could feel the hopeless anguish that had flooded this normally confident surgeon.

I quietly began, "There is only one scenario that I can think of that would result in this exact set of events. I had a similar situation happen to me once before." That was a bit of a stretch, but I needed to eliminate any chance of a condescending overtone.

I continued, "When I put the aortic cannula in, it flipped backwards and pointed into the ascending aorta toward the aortic valve instead of pointing downstream into the aortic arch."

"No way!" Dr. Faust yelled. The immediacy of his response caught me off guard. It hit me at about 100 decibels and rocked me back on my heels. "No way!" he repeated. "No chance—I have always cannulated this way! I am sure the aortic cannula is fine!"

I was on thin ice here. I cautiously responded, "That is the only scenario that I can think of that would give you a massively distended heart when you place the aortic cross clamp. All of the pump flow from the cardiopulmonary bypass machine gets forced into the occluded ascending aorta, overwhelms the leaky aortic valve, and results in massive cardiac distention."

I decided to go for it. With my next statement, I might as well have leaped off a tall building. In a hushed tone, I responded, "I would just have the perfusionist turn the pump flow down and feel for the cannula tip in the proximal ascending aorta."

I had just gone out on a long limb with my suggestion. If I was wrong, I knew I was toast. I was suggesting that the problem resided in something Dr. Faust had done to his patient. As surgeons, we naturally hope that when something goes horribly wrong that it has nothing to do with anything *we* have done. Nothing makes a bad outcome worse than finding out that it resulted from something we did. After all, we are surgeons—surgical technique is what we are all about. To find out that the worst situation Dr. Faust had encountered in years was entirely his fault would make the whole situation immeasurably worse. If I was wrong, I had just wrongly suggested that there may have been a technical misstep. Not good. I was freefalling in open space hoping desperately for a rescue. I was praying that Dr. Faust would just give it a try instead of yelling at me. I knew I was right. Along with the solution, the Holy Spirit had filled me with bold confidence.

I prepared for the next onslaught. My mind was going 90 miles an hour now. I searched diligently through every word I had spoken and every possible reply with which Dr. Faust might respond. I went through the physiology again. I knew Dr. Faust liked to use a long straight aortic cannula in these situations. They seem to have a mind of their own sometimes and would often go in unexpected directions. If that cannula was pointing back toward the heart, this meant that every time he put the aortic cross-clamp across the distal ascending aorta he was also placing the clamp across the aortic cannula. The cross-clamp had soft padded jaws, while the cannula was made of a firm, wire-wound plastic—so the cross-clamp could not completely occlude the cannula. If I was correct, that meant that the entire output of the cardiopulmonary bypass pump was being directed back against the aortic valve—and this with a cross-clamp essentially occluding the distal ascending aorta!

This meant that all of that blood being pumped into the body by the powerful cardiopulmonary bypass pump had nowhere to go except into the heart. The left ventricle was being blown up like a balloon because the aortic valve (which was both blocked and leaky—that was why it was being replaced) was not able to stop the full force of the blood being pumped directly at it by the cannula tip. As I mentioned, Dr. Faust had even placed a venting cannula in the pulmonary artery—in addition to he one in the left ventricle—in an attempt to remedy the left ventricular distention. Neither had worked. The vents were simply being overwhelmed by the massive output of the cardiopulmonary bypass pump—over 5 liters per minute—being diverted *into* the heart by the aortic return cannula.

"No way!" I can still hear Dr. Faust's immediate response to my suggestion echoing in the operating room.

He continued, "No, I am sure the cannula is fine. I did it the way I always do it," he replied as he stared down at the aorta. His fingers were nonetheless busy feeling for the cannula.

His next remark was music to my ears. It was directed to the perfusionist who was running the cardiopulmonary bypass pump. "Okay, down on the pump flow."

This was what I was waiting for—the message had been delivered. Dr. Faust was telling the perfusionist to drop the pump flow in order to decrease the pressure in the aorta so that he could feel precisely where the cannula tip was positioned.

Every eye was on Dr. Faust. No one else dared speak. Every ear was turned toward Dr. Faust and tuned to his next words, "Oh, you're right! I can't believe it! It has flipped the wrong direction!"

His three short sentences slipped out quickly. There was no thought involved. With that single simple acknowledgment, Dr. Faust immediately switched off his conversation mode and went to work, methodically barking out the rapid series of commands that were necessary to allow his now rapidly working hands to remedy the situation. Not only had our conversation ended, he no longer even knew I was in the room. He was totally focused like a warrior in the fight of his life. He had an aortic valve replacement to do. I immediately knew exactly what I needed to do at that moment.

I needed to get out of there.

I needed to exit quietly and go back to the other operating room. As I have said, there is no gloating or boasting in heart surgery. Surely nowhere in the entire universe is the age-old adage, "There but for the grace of God go I," more applicable. If applause is what you seek, the world of heart surgery is not for you. I had been in similarly desperate situations many times myself. What I had just fixed was not by my hand and I knew it. Maybe in any other setting there would be accolades due the guy who had pulled back on the stick just in time to keep the downward spiraling plane from becoming a catastrophic smoking hole in the ground—but not here and not now and certainly not me.

Every single person in the room had just gone from fearful, anxious terror—for that is what results in a cardiac operation when the surgeon has tried everything only to reach a point of utter helplessness—to breathing a giant sigh of relief. And yet I knew that it could have been—and has indeed been—me in that very same desperate situation. The right move for me was to slink quietly out of the room. And that is exactly what I did.

Every eye in that operating room silently followed me as I moved quietly and quickly from my position above the anesthesia screen, back behind the scrub table, and out the door. I wish that every heart associated with every one of the eyes that tracked my progress out of the operating room was privy to precisely what I was doing in those brief moments.

It was so awesome.

I, by God's grace, had gone right to the hidden deep recesses of my mind. Sure, my eyes automatically directed my legs to propel me along the familiar path out of the operating room. But I was somewhere else at that moment. I had gone to the most holy place of my heart. I had gone to that place where I meet with Jesus. I had gone where I go when very special praise is due.

I don't go there often enough.

In that dark chamber where the mighty warrior cherubim guard the mercy seat of my heart, I was very literally singing at the top of my lungs to the Most Holy God. I was praising Jesus. It was exhilarating.

How God had just blessed me. How He had singlehandedly made a hero out of me. How He had set up this situation—before time began—and directed me into it, all just to lift me up! My King had just glorified and celebrated his humble prince in the eyes of his cardiac surgical coworkers. Every step I took toward the door of that operating room was broken into a thousand different intervals. In the timeless midst of every one, I praised God. In my heart I was singing. In my heart I was shouting! In my heart I was repeating the Name that is above all names,

Jesus! In my heart I very literally had my hands raised to heaven. In that brief walk out of the operating room, I experienced pure joy.

Me, of all people—in all of my besetting sin—had been so gloriously exalted! I had somehow known that God was going to honor me that day. And how He had faithfully carried through on His promise to always be there with me in the thick of the fight. After all, it was He who had so faithfully prepared me for this fight. He had carefully scripted so many previous operating room scenarios just so I could learn the sometimes-scary lessons of cannula placement—all for this moment! And I wanted every angel in heaven, every saint in Abraham's bosom, to know that I not only knew and acknowledged what God had just done, but also that I praised Jesus as the Rock, the Shelter, and the Tower into which I had just run!

Once again God had elevated me in the eyes of all of my coworkers in the division of cardiothoracic surgery. I had no answer to the question of, "Why me?" It was most certainly not because I had done anything special. It was purely and simply grace. It was just exclusively and awesomely the grace of God. It was just the compassionate mercy of Jesus, my Savior.

Sure, I had been made to look brilliant and the patient recovered, but the real winner that day was Dr. Faust. He had reached a point where he, for the wellbeing of his patient, was willing to admit that he needed help and that I might be the one to supply that help. As a senior cardiac surgeon at one of the biggest and best-known hospitals in the world, it can be very hard to admit that you need another cardiac surgeon's help. I give Dr. Faust all the credit for placing the needs of his patient above his own. He didn't know it then, and if you asked him now I am sure he would never agree, but he had a very good day that day. He delivered on the promise that we make to every patient. This promise is innate to the consent process and it is simple: that Dr. Faust would put *nothing* above his patient's wellbeing.

I returned to my junior colleague's operating room to continue helping there. He had no idea what had happened. I said nothing other than responding, "He figured it out," when queried about Dr. Faust's disaster in the other room. There was no way that I was going to take credit for anything. My junior colleague also did not hear me praising God at the top of my voice through every single event of the rest of that very good day.

CHAPTER TWENTY

Move Toward The Gunfire

God is sovereign and God is good.
You either believe this, or you don't.
If you do believe this, fear is inexcusable.
If you are facing a disaster,
it is because God has brought it into your life.
There is nowhere else that you are supposed to be.
There is nothing else that you are supposed to be doing.
You are exactly where you are supposed to be,
doing exactly what you are supposed to be doing.
Before time began, God decided
that this is how you would spend this day.
If God did not want this to be happening to you now,
it would not be happening to you now.
Turn toward the battle.
Engage the fight.
When you hear the thunder of an ambush erupt around you,
move toward the gunfire.
In eternity you will face similar adventures.
Jesus will be beside you then and there will be no fear—
only excitement, only fun.
He is there now also.
There is now no reason for fear—
only excitement, only fun.
Have fun!
Enjoy this adventure.
Believe in your heart that Jesus will be there with you
every single moment in the thick of the battle.
Do not fear sudden disaster.
Jesus will get you through it.

He always has.
Do not fear fatigue.
Jesus will give you strength.
He always has.
Crying out to Jesus is the answer
in every desperate moment.
His grace will always be enough.
In the middle of the battle, your number one job
is to love God
by loving ALL of the people He sends into your life.
This takes faith.
You either believe all this, or you don't.
Make the call right now.
This is a once in eternity chance.
This chance to glorify God will never come again.
So don't blow this.
And have fun,
*for **God** is with you as you*
move toward the gunfire.

CHAPTER TWENTY-ONE

True Worship

I am a black and white, right and wrong, cut-and-dry, in-your-face kind of guy. No doubt. I always have been. I seek the *bottom-line*. I want to cut through all the other associated garbage and firmly grasp the real message, the bottom-line. Why do I so crave the bottom-line? Only one reason: *I know myself*. I know what I do in battle. In a fight, my responses are purely *reflexive*. They are automatic. All to often, there is no thinking involved. When a relational encounter intensifies, when pandemonium rules in my daily interpersonal battles, my simple mind reflexively brings to the surface that which I consider to be the bottom-line. It is from this bottom-line perspective that my responses to a chaotic relational situation are reflexively generated. I don't know if you are like me or not, but when I find myself engaging an ambush, it is *all* reflexes and the bottom-line *rules*.

This is my command: Love each other. (John 15:17, NIV)

This command, by Jesus Christ, to *"Love each other"* is as close to a statement of the bottom-line as is to be found in the Bible. This command is so seemingly obvious that we often thoughtlessly read past it and are quick to gloss over the magnitude of its true intent. But let there be no doubt in our minds—it is the purest, most focused, and most palpable of God's truth. The command above is unequivocal and the words are chosen carefully—even down to the letter. There is no *"s"* on the end of the word "command." This is not a typo and it is not random. It is exactly as Jesus said it and exactly as the Holy Spirit wanted it written. It is written for us exactly this way for a clear and unequivocal purpose. Jesus wanted to drive home the point that worshiping God is all encompassed in obeying this *single* command. Indeed, Jesus, and later Paul, both assure us that all of the other commandments—in fact, the entirety of the Old Testament law—are wrapped up in this one:

> *So in everything, do to others what you would have them do to you, for this sums up the Law and the Prophets. (Matthew 7:12, NIV)*

> *The entire law is summed up in a single command: "Love your neighbor as yourself." (Galatians 5:14, NIV)*

Even the most profound commandment, *"Love the Lord your God with all your heart and with all your soul and with all your mind"* (Matthew 22:37, NIV), is fully embodied in the command to *"Love each other."* No matter what our feelings in this regard, in the eyes of Jesus these two commands—to love God and to love our neighbor—cannot be separated. Jesus personally spells this out for us in easily understandable, graphic, and undeniable terms. When we choose to love and serve people, we love and serve Jesus; when we mistreat them, we mistreat Jesus. *He* is embodied in the individuals that we encounter in our life.

> *For I was hungry and you gave me something to eat, I was thirsty and you gave me something to drink, I was a stranger and you invited me in, I needed clothes and you clothed me, I was sick and you looked after me, I was in prison and you came to visit me.' "Then the righteous will answer him, 'Lord, when did we see you hungry and feed you, or thirsty and give you something to drink? When did we see you a stranger and invite you in, or needing clothes and clothe*

you? When did we see you sick or in prison and go to visit you?' "The King will reply, 'I tell you the truth, whatever you did for one of the least of these brothers of mine, you did for me.' (Matthew 25:35-40, NIV; emphasis added)

To comprehend the true magnitude of this command to love one another, we must acknowledge that every encounter with every person in every minute of every day of our life is by nothing less than the flawless design of God. God is sovereign over every micro-particle and microsecond of His creation. These are not accidents or random chance meetings—not even one of them, not even the seemingly most insignificant of them. Not a single meeting with a single one of my cardiothoracic surgical partners or patients has been by random happenstance. These were meetings ordained, engineered, and implemented by the Creator for His perfect purpose in my life—and in theirs. He has the same plan for your life. These are meetings engineered to bring us into a closer relationship with God by allowing us to love those people with nothing less than the love of Jesus Himself. We are to love them with His love—His perfect love delivered through us. This is what *knowing* Jesus is all about. This is true worship done God's way.

It is my desire that this book's recounting of these interpersonal vignettes that have littered my cardiac surgical career would—by vivid and sometimes-stinging illustration—drive home one further truth: there are no individuals in our lives who fall outside of God's command to love.

"You have heard that it was said, 'Love your neighbor and hate your enemy.' But I tell you:

*Love your enemies and pray for those who
persecute you, that you may be sons of your
Father in heaven. (Matthew 5:43-45a, NIV)*

The word *except* does not follow a single one of the
countless repetitions of the scriptural command to *"Love
each other."* Most critically, those individuals we would
naturally choose to exclude from this command, our
"enemies," are in fact clearly included. The extension of this
command to our enemies surely must be the most
unmistakably stated, and yet simultaneously ignored
command of the Bible:

*"But I tell you who hear me: Love your
enemies, do good to those who hate you, bless
those who curse you, pray for those who
mistreat you. If someone strikes you on one
cheek, turn to him the other also. If someone
takes your cloak, do not stop him from taking
your tunic. Give to everyone who asks you, and
if anyone takes what belongs to you, do not
demand it back. Do to others as you would have
them do to you. (Luke 6:27-31, NIV)*

The bottom-line can't be any more clearly defined.
God wants us to love the people He brings into our lives.
Period. He wants us to love them all, all the time, in every
circumstance—regardless of the nature of their crimes
against us. In regard to the consequences of that love—for
loving those who have harmed us (and still desire to harm us)
surely cannot come without risk—God wants us to trust Him.
We must trust that God will deliver on His promise to protect
us when we do things His way. We are incapable of *truly*
selflessly and unconditionally loving our enemies without
trusting God. Only in that trust can we know that no matter
the circumstances, we need have no fear in love.

There is no fear in love. But perfect love drives out fear, because fear has to do with punishment. The one who fears is not made perfect in love. (1John 4:18, NIV)

God wants us to live as if there is no person who cannot be loved with the full expectation that Almighty God Himself will control the consequences of any faith-based love that we can muster. He wants us to utilize humble surrender as nothing less than the powerful weapon that it is. We have no strength to do this—to surrender—on our own, but we do not have to do it on our own. The strength to carry off this illogical act of love has only one source, the cross of Jesus Christ. In His cross is the promise that Jesus will be there to do the heavy lifting for us. Our faith has muscle because of Him. We can love them by surrendering to them—no matter who they are and how nefarious they may be—because Almighty God is behind us. Always. This is His promise. And in those moments of extreme surrender there will be extreme worship and Jesus will be there.

I hope the events described in this book have adequately demonstrated the extraordinary beauty and awesome power that is found in complete surrender in the interpersonal conflicts that fill our daily lives. God wants us to get out on that relational edge and love the unlovable. He wants us to forgive the unforgivable and have mercy upon those who do not deserve mercy. By turning over the reins of our heart to Jesus in this manner, we become more like Him. God's ever-present love for our neighbor becomes our love for our neighbor.

By God's precise plan, therefore, our daily relational battlefields are venues of extreme worship. The last place in the world that we expect to be worshipping God—the last place that we want to be worshipping God—is precisely the worship venue that He has chosen.

> *When you spread out your hands in prayer, I will hide my eyes from you; even if you offer many prayers, I will not listen. Your hands are full of blood; wash and make yourselves clean. Take your evil deeds out of my sight! Stop doing wrong, learn to do right! Seek justice, encourage the oppressed. Defend the cause of the fatherless, plead the case of the widow. (Isaiah 1:15-17, NIV; emphasis added)*

This is worship His way. It is just that delightfully simple and that infuriatingly complex. Refuse to love all of the people that God brings into our life all of the time and we refuse to love God—plain and simple. Try to love God only on our terms and we fail to love Him on any terms. It is total surrender or it is no surrender—and in no surrender is guaranteed defeat. Compromise—even a little bit—and we lose everything in the fight to do that for which our hearts were designed. Love our enemies halfway, and we don't love them at all. And if we cannot love *them*, then we really do not love God. Victory in this battle is found only in surrender, and only in complete surrender of "self" is found the true love of God that will fill our eternity.

> *Dear friends, since God so loved us, we also ought to love one another. No one has ever seen God; but if we love one another, God lives in us and his love is made complete in us. (1John 4:11-12, NIV; emphasis added)*

We may not like the fact that God has ordained our relational battlefields as His primary worship venues. Nonetheless, our attempt to self-define the setting in which we love and worship God is like choosing to travel an easy road despite the fact that it goes straight to nowhere. The fact that a road is easier to travel is of no value to us if the road does not take us where we want to go. Similarly, our choosing to worship God the easy way is pointless if *really* worshipping God is our true heart's desire—because it simply cannot take us where we want to go. God is in charge, and any step away from His clear direction on this matter— this most critical matter of loving Him—is a step onto a very slippery slope, indeed.

Loving the people that God brings into our lives is not just some casual afterthought. It is not just something we *ought* to do whenever circumstances allow. It is not just some sideshow activity to fill our time while we, like modern day Pharisees, do the real work of God in the bake sales of the neighborhood congregation. It certainly is not an extra credit activity limited only to *super* Christians.

Loving one another is the whole show.

Loving one another is what true belief in the holy and saving Name of Jesus is all about. It is the whole of the battle to follow Jesus. It is the war that we are in. It is, precisely by God's design, the only way we can know, obey, serve, love, and glorify God—because only in loving our neighbor do we resemble His Son Jesus. Only in resembling Jesus can we succeed at precisely that which this life of ours is all about: subserviently and sacrificially loving God.

So, when our loving God directs our life into the Valley of the Shadow of Death and the sound of interpersonal battle echoes from its cavernous walls, we must respond correctly. As the bullets of a relational ambush ricochet off nearby rocks, we must resist all worldly logic and the command of our "self"-preserving instincts. Instead, We must do exactly what our Savior did for us. When the call comes to love the unlovable by nothing less than utter surrender, we must turn our belief into palpable faith. We must follow the lead of the special warfare operators who know that casualties are always higher when the first response is to run for cover. We must move toward the gunfire.

> *"How I long for the months gone by, for the days when God watched over me, when his lamp shone upon my head and by his light I walked through darkness! Oh, for the days when I was in my prime, when God's intimate friendship blessed my house..." (Job 29:2-4, NIV)*

Acknowledgements

I am so blessed to have married the smartest physician I have ever known. If I were to write volumes about her, it would be inadequate to acknowledge all that she has done for me through these last three decades together. Not only did she go through my cardiac surgical training with me, she weathered the storms of the decades of cardiac surgery and she did it as perfectly as it could be done. God could not have provided a more perfect foil against which to change my warrior heart. As the Medical Director of the Cardiothoracic Surgical ICU, she was right there by my side in the middle of the fight. She accompanied me nearly every day as I journeyed into the Valley of the Shadow of Death. She was also there at home when I took those transplant calls and dealt with all that goes along with a career in the Valley. And, most critically, she somehow helped me shield our four little warriors from the darkness of the Valley.

Many current and past authors have profoundly influenced my life and my writing. Most notably, to A.W. Tozer, C.S. Lewis, Andy Stanley, and Tim Keller I give my heartfelt thanks. If I have gotten too close to quoting your work without acknowledging it, I truly am sorry. I gladly give you all the credit.